Shadows of the Gunmen:
Violence and Culture in Modern Ireland

Shadows of the Gunmen:
Violence and Culture
in Modern Ireland

Edited by
Danine Farquharson and Sean Farrell

CORK UNIVERSITY PRESS

First published in 2008 by
Cork University Press
Youngline Industrial Estate
Pouladuff Road, Togher
Cork, Ireland

British Library Cataloguing in Publication Data.
A CIP catalogue record for this book is available from the British Library

ISBN-13: 978-185918-424-0

Support from the Publications Subvention Program of Memorial University of
Newfoundland towards the publication of this book is gratefully acknowledged.

Typeset by Tower Books, Ballincollig, Co. Cork
Printed by ColourBooks Ltd, Baldoyle, Co. Dublin

www.corkuniversitypress.com

Contents

vi   *Contents*

Acknowledgements

The editors would like to thank the Dean of Arts offices at both St Jerome's University (in the University of Waterloo) and Memorial University of Newfoundland for seed grant funding to allow us to hire research and project assistants. Those energetic assistants deserve our gratitude: Kevin Magri, Rebecca Clyburn and Amanda Tiller. Support from the Publications Subvention Program of Memorial University of Newfoundland towards the production of this book is gratefully acknowledged.

We would also like to thank those who provided us with advice, insight and commentary on this project. At Northern Illinois University, conversations with Rachel Hope Cleves, James Schmidt and Andrea Smalley sharpened the manuscript immensely, helping to place Irish violence in a broader context. Within Irish Studies, James MacKillop and Tom Dunne played essential roles in moving this project from concept to publication. Michael Collins and Sophie Watson spearheaded the effort at Cork University Press, making what is often a difficult process quite smooth.

Above all, we would like to thank the contributors for lending their talents and patience to the project. Nearly three years in the making, this collection provides a rich survey of the vitality of work on violence and the Irish experience. In short, it's been worth the wait. An earlier version of Brian McIllroy's 'Symbolic and Hyperreal Violence in the Irish "Troubles" Movie' appeared in his *Shooting to Kill: Filmmaking and the 'Troubles' in Northern Ireland* (Steveston Press, 2001), and a modified version of Richard Kearney's 'Memory, History, Story: Between Poetics and Ethics' has appeared in his *Navigations: Collected Irish Essays, 1976–2006* (Lilliput Press, 2006).

Introduction

DANINE FARQUHARSON
and SEAN FARRELL

On 28 November 1920, volunteers of the Irish Republican Army's West Cork Brigade ambushed a patrol of Auxiliaries near the village of Kilmichael, just south of Macroom. In IRA terms the ambush was costly but remarkably successful; three volunteers and seventeen policemen were killed. By any measure, the ambush was an important event. As Peter Hart relates in *The I.R.A. and its Enemies*, Kilmichael 'delivered a profound shock to the British system', showing British officials that they were facing an effective and well-organized guerilla force.[1] On a less tangible level the Kilmichael Ambush serves as an excellent example of the complexity of violence and the often contradictory places that such episodes occupy within the modern Irish experience. For the twenty people who died in West Cork, of course, the matter was anything but complex. The violence had the ultimate tangible effect – they were dead. But violence is never that simple – in terms of meaning and interpretation, the ambush was anything but a closed matter.

The struggle over Kilmichael's meaning started in the immediate aftermath of the affray. For many British officials, the ambush provided further evidence of Irish treachery and barbarity. Rather predictably, British officials accused their opponents of 'breaking the rules of war', and constructed narratives that centred on allegations of massacre and mutilation. Conversely, Irish republicans quickly trumpeted the episode as one of the most successful operations of the conflict. Aided greatly in the long-run by the popularity of Tom Barry's paradigm-setting *Guerrilla Days in Ireland* (first published in 1949), the triumphalist interpretation was indeed the story that dominated much of the twentieth century. For men and women across Ireland and its vast diaspora, Kilmichael became lodged in the national imagination as a watchword for Irish tenacity, courage and above all, determination to be free of British rule.[2]

1

The controversy triggered by a recent effort to revisit the Kilmichael Ambush speaks powerfully of the important places violence occupies within national mythologies.[3]

Featuring essays by some of the leading scholars in Irish Studies, *Shadows of the Gunmen: Violence and Culture in Modern Ireland* examines how we can, in fact, speak about that which is deemed to be silent, or that which lingers in shadow. This book offers new and critical investigations into violence and the modern Irish experience (modern is defined here as roughly 1850 to the present). While we do not claim any uniformity of approach or of conclusion, special attention is paid to the cultural construction of violence, for, as the Kilmichael Ambush makes clear, violence is a complex and ever-shifting phenomenon, in which different players attempt to write narratives of violence that support their own agendas and purposes. To put it more succinctly, even a brief summary shows how the Kilmichael Ambush has become part of the language of violence in Ireland.

In his 1989 essay, 'The Language of Sade and Masoch', philosopher and critic Gilles Deleuze writes that 'in principle, violence is something that does not speak'. Here Deleuze brings to our attention the vital connections between language and violence, for if violence does not speak, in a technical sense, it does generate multiple histories, as men and women seek to make sense of, or construct and control the meaning of, violent acts. This is an especially important insight, particularly in an Irish context where violence is too often treated as a flat fact and deemed to be excessively examined.[4] Before situating this work in its Irish context, however, we need to examine the broad theoretical terrain on which the study of violence has been constructed.

Theorizing violence

'The matter is too big for any mortal man who thinks he can judge it.' So wrote the Greek tragedian Aeschylus in the final play of his *Oresteia* trilogy, *The Eumenides*.[5] The 'matter' is a violence so powerful as to destroy the balance of the cosmos and require the intervention of the gods to not only restore order but also to establish a new system of laws and political structure. The great chain of bloodletting and retribution that begins with the murder of Agamemnon (or perhaps with the sacrifice of Iphigenia) unleashes the chthonic power of the Furies, who represent the ravished primordial scream of horror at the violent opening. Aeschylus may have been the earliest but he is not the last writer to consider violence as an open wound or radical rending of the universe. When Deleuze wrote that 'violence is something that does not speak' he deemed violence to be unfathomable in its openness and as such, silent.[6] In 1969 Hannah Arendt wrote that 'no one concerned with history and politics can remain unaware of the enormous role violence has always played in human affairs; and it is at first glance rather surprising that violence is so seldom singled out for special consideration ... no one questions or examines what is obvious to all'.[7] Responding to the Vietnam War and the tangible reality of nuclear destruction, Arendt keenly hits upon a lacuna in the discourses surrounding violence: she believes that no one has attempted to fully and analytically understand what violence is, from whence it comes, and its effects. Such an assertion may sound naïve, even ridiculous, but it was largely correct in 1969. There is a large and diverse literature on war and warfare from von Clausewitz to Marx and Engels to John Keegan (in the last two centuries alone), but, as Arendt notes, such discussions deal with the implements of violence not with violence as such.[8] Even Arendt, for all her provocative beginnings, is more concerned with reconceptualizing power in a nuclear age than with violence per se. Her most useful observation about violence for this collection of essays is its unpredictability: 'all violence harbours within itself an element of arbitrariness.' If violence is an opening and it possesses an element of the arbitrary, then we must briefly consider the question: what is violence?

In his introduction to 'The Violence of Identity,' Glenn Bowman succinctly outlines the etymological origins of the word violence and in so doing he hits upon the key definition. All uses of the word violence – to break, to ravish, to desecrate, to corrupt, to treat roughly, to break in upon – contain 'the concept of an integral space broken into and, through that breaking, desecrated'.[9] Violence is a tearing, a rending open into the absolute. Violence is a radical space of openness that destroys the sacred and creates an imbalance. The ripping of the sacred into an open space is what Arendt sees as the element of arbitrariness: we cannot predict what will happen once the violation has occurred. Because violence is an opening and is also unpredictable, the vast majority of thinkers who seek to understand violence must deal with the tangible results of violence because those results can be, to some degree, measured, assessed and analysed.

Approaches to understanding violence can therefore be categorized into three groups. The first approach is the philosophical, which attempts to comprehend and explain the phenomenology of violence. Several questions emerge from such an approach: does violence have meaning? What is the manifestation of violence? What is the unique structure of the existence of violence? The philosophical approach illuminates the concept of violence but does not necessarily address its materiality. Hannah Arendt is obviously a crucial thinker in this arena, but more recent contributions also exist. Beatrice Hanssen's *Critique of Violence: Between Poststructuralism and Critical Theory* weaves philosophy with political theory and comparative literature to see how these discourses can address the idea of violence and the language of violence.[10] Significantly, hers is a cross-disciplinary approach. Hanssen is one among many contemporary thinkers who recognize that no single discursive mode will adequately answer any of the questions relating to violence.

The second approach is the ethical or judicial. This discourse is concerned with questions of the legitimacy and necessity of violence: under what circumstances is violence acceptable? What are the legal and social consequences of unacceptable violence? The modern library on the legitimacy of violence arguably begins with Walter Benjamin's 1921 'Critique of Violence' and his questioning of whether violence is a just or unjust means to an end.[11] Other contributions to this discussion include Michel Foucault's study of power and the modern prison in *Discipline and Punish* and legal theorist Cass Sunstein's analysis of the political ramifications of violence in relation to freedom of speech.[12] Such engagements are concerned with the state and with authority: how bodies of law and order structure a community that must deal with violence in relation to the good. The essential problem for thinkers such as Benjamin and Sunstein is not so much violence as justice: what mechanisms can be used to protect the community from the amplification of bloodshed? The ethical/judicial approach to understanding violence acknowledges that any concept of justice or communal good must address violence in individuals, groups and nations.

The third and final category encompasses the vast array of works that examine social or cultural aspects of violence. The ethical/legal approach can be interpreted as broadly sociological, but underpinning that approach is a philosophical concern for the good and the just. Scholars interested in the social/cultural dynamics of violence tend to engage the ways in which violence relates to other concerns, such as gender, class, race, nation.[13] By far the most diverse and widely used category of analysis, this social/cultural approach tends to narrow into particular places, times and/or events in order to tease out the various ramifications of violence for individuals and communities. In this regard, René Girard, in his analysis of religion and violence and the role of the sacrifice and scapegoat, is a principal twentieth-century theorist.[14] The social/cultural approach can also be comparative, as in Göran Aijmer and Jon Abbink's *Meanings of Violence: A Cross-Cultural Perspective.*[15] Aijmer and Abbink share with this collection the belief that while 'each discipline has its own distinct contribution to make to the study of violence – the challenge, however, is to integrate some of them into a larger whole and to reshape our perception of the nature and causes or relevant factors of violent behaviour'.[16]

What connects all three approaches is their discursive nature: these are all ways of talking about and writing about violence. All these approaches exist in the realm of the representational. To return to *The Eumenides*, Aeschylus brings the difficulties of theorizing and performing violence to bear on the House of Atreus. When the goddess Athene is called upon to 'render final judgment' in the blood for blood catastrophe of Atreus, she not only casts a vote in support of Orestes – thereby facing the wrath of the Furies, now euphemistically renamed the Eumenidies – but she also establishes the tribunal and system of justice whereby future decisions can be made:[17] That a god must come down into the realm of human beings in order to re-establish order makes clear Aeschylus' belief that the violence of the human world will never be abolished by human deeds. Only the absolute (as personified by the gods) can address the absolute (the opening up that is violence). Before the farewell to Athene, the final words of the chorus are 'Much wrong in the world is thereby healed.'[18] 'Much' but by no means all of the wrong is healed. So it is that even in the earliest (and arguably the greatest) Western literary representation of familial, communal and national violence, the language of violence remains open, ambivalent and unfinished. Are we back to the lacuna so deftly articulated by Arendt? Is Deleuze correct in writing that violence does not speak? Because the essays collected in this volume refuse to ignore the violent and refuse to turn away from the difficulties of writing about violence, we believe that the answer is no, we are not back to the blank space of theorizing violence. We offer nine deliberations on and workings through the phenomena of violence so that some of the 'wrong' may be spoken.

Violence in modern Ireland

Few would challenge the assertion that violence has played a number of crucial roles in the making of modern Ireland. From the tradition of revolutionary violence that remains at the heart of Irish nationalist mythology to the shootings and bombings that marred the Northern Irish landscape between 1966 and 1998, violence has often been seen as nearly synonymous with the modern Irish experience. It certainly has been central to modern Irish artistic production; from Sean O'Casey's Dublin trilogy to the films and documentaries of filmmakers such as Neil Jordan and Desmond Bell, violence has been a dominant theme in Irish literature and film. Studies of history, media, literature and philosophy have circled around the hegemonic idea that violence is particularly important for understanding Irish society and culture. Of course, the study of violence has long been one of the most fruitful areas of research in Irish Studies, producing some of the most innovative and important work in the field.[19]

For all this, recent years have seen dramatic changes in violence studies – both thematically and methodologically. Scholars working across a number of disciplines have extended the study of violence into heretofore marginalized subjects. By exploring the intersections of violence and race, gender, nation, the law and patriotism, scholars such as Veena Das, Manfred B. Steger and Nancy C. Lind have transformed our understanding of the complexity and range of violence.[20] These broader trends have certainly made an impact on Irish Studies, where recent work on previously ignored subjects has sharpened our understanding of the modern Irish experience. To cite one example, feminist examinations of domestic violence have opened up entire new vistas for future scholars, with Margot Backus's *Gothic Family Romance* and Angela Bourke's *The Burning of Bridget Cleary* being particularly important.[21] Moreover, scholars have provided increasingly nuanced critiques of long-held assumptions about the place of violence in nationalist and unionist mythologies. For example, a number of historians, most notably Charles Townshend, have challenged the centrality of the Easter Rising of 1916 to the Irish Revolution, instead advancing the idea that 1918 saw the truly transformative events occur. Such challenges also extend into the literary realm as Sebastian Barry's recent novel, *A Long Long Way*, certainly undermines received narratives of Easter 1916 and situates key moments in his protagonist's life inside the trenches of the Western Front.[22]

But the new dynamism in the study and writing of violence reflects much more than an extension of the boundaries of inquiry or a renewed determination to challenge long-held assumptions. Scholars have also shown an increasing sensitivity to what we might term the cultural construction of violence, to the complex interplay between acts of violence and their representation. This concern with the constantly shifting and negotiated ideological meanings of violence has marked some of the best recent work in the field – most notably Kevin Kenny's award-winning *Making Sense of the Molly Maguires* and Angela Bourke's aforementioned *The Burning of Bridget Cleary*.[23] The emphasis on reconstructing the cultural meanings of violence has led scholars to adopt innovative and increasingly interdisciplinary methodological approaches to their subjects. *Shadows of the Gunmen* is designed to bring the best of this new work together with two overriding purposes in mind: 1) to bring this work to a broader multidisciplinary audience and 2) to raise new questions and inspire new research into this dynamic and exciting field.

Recent scholarship has shown how complex legacies of violence are inextricably embedded within evolving conceptions of Irish national identity. Of course, there is nothing unique about Ireland in this regard. As Jill Lepore's eloquent statement about the links between violence and discourse in her acclaimed study of King Philip's War in late seventeenth-century North America indicates, violence is often central to the making and breaking of community and nation:

> To say that war cultivates language is not to ignore what else war does: war kills. . . . Wounds and words – the injuries and their interpretation – cannot be separated, that acts of war generate acts of narration, and that both types of acts are often joined in a common purpose: defining the geographical, political, cultural, and sometimes racial and national boundaries between peoples.[24]

Recent studies of nationalism in Argentina, Britain, South Africa and India/Pakistan reinforce this crucial point, illustrating the central role that competing narratives of violence play in the formation of national identity.[25]

If Ireland fits into this general pattern, however, the particular relationships between acts of violence and the narratives that are forged to give meaning to them are unique to modern Ireland. Our first five essays explore the island's own violent palimpsests, revisiting some of the most storied national narratives in light of more contemporary concerns. As the current controversy over the Kilmichael Ambush indicates, the questions raised by the violence of the Irish Revolution are hardly settled. The relationship between republican violence and Irish independence has been the subject of countless texts – both scholarly and popular. While many of these have detailed the corrosive legacies of IRA, British, and loyalist violence across the British Isles, few have questioned the necessity of violence in creating an independent Ireland. Peter Hart opens the collection by doing just that in his provocative thought-piece 'On the Necessity of Violence in the Irish Revolution'. Relentlessly detailing available alternatives to armed struggle between 1912 and 1923, Hart explodes many easy assumptions about the period, arguing that the republican (as well as unionist and British) violence of the Easter Rising and the Anglo-Irish War was unnecessary and often counter-productive. Using the successes of the Land War and the Anti-Conscription campaign as models, Hart vigorously argues that a strategy of unarmed struggle based on mass mobilisation and rooted in broad popular consensus would have allowed Sinn Féin and its allies to achieve the vast majority of their goals more quickly and without casualties. In doing so, he brings into question how Irish nationalists have legitimated the ways violence was used in the making of the modern Irish nation. While violence played any number of roles in the formation of the Irish Free State and Northern Ireland, Hart shows that it need not have done so.

Sean O'Casey is arguably the Irish writer most intimately connected to the violence of the Irish Revolution, and his 1923 play, *The Shadow of a Gunman*, gives this book its title. Just as O'Casey exposes and interrogates the use of violence in the making of modern Ireland, so too does Bernice Schrank probe assumptions about Sean O'Casey's representation and use of violence in his art and his life. Indeed, Schrank tackles the hegemonic assessment of Sean O'Casey as a pacifist. Her essay, 'Sean O'Casey and the Dialectics of Violence', opens with a re-assessment of both his autobiographical and theatrical works to argue that O'Casey had no simple opinion or attitude toward the use of revolutionary violence; rather, he took the violent reactions to some of his work (in the form of censorship and repression) and used the resultant controversies to expose the oppressiveness of both Church and State. Focusing then on the clerical rejection of O'Casey's *Within the Gates* and the responses to that controversy in Boston, Schrank's analysis exposes the complicated, and at times conspiratorial, process of censorship and the violent damage done through such oppression.

Danine Farquharson's essay, 'Sexing the Rising: Men, Sex, Violence and Easter 1916', returns to the Easter Rising of 1916, this time to examine how that violent moment is used by two contemporary novelists to comment on current issues in modern Ireland. Focusing on Roddy Doyle's *A Star Called Henry* and Jamie O'Neill's *At Swim Two Boys*, Farquharson analyzes their representation of the Easter Rising through the lens of gender and sexual oppression. While it may be a cliché that going to war makes a man of a boy, both of these novels pose the question: who makes the man? In *A Star Called Henry* the young boy Henry Smart reaches adulthood amid the burning of the GPO, but he has a lot of help from the sexual expertise of Miss O'Shea. *At Swim, Two Boys* is also set during the period leading up to and including the Easter Rising, but in this novel the sexual awakening that parallels the birth of a nation is homo-erotic. O'Neill's text challenges the equation of Ireland to woman with rebel fighter as her lover, by depicting a love that 'dare not speak its name' but that also helps construct the nation and the men. Both Doyle and O'Neill represent violence and its connection to gender and sexuality in unexpected ways: ways that demand investigation in light of nationalism and stereotypes of Irish identity.

Of course, Irish national identity was shaped by forces far beyond the shores of the British Isles, as recent work on the multifaceted links between Ireland and the British Empire makes quite clear. One of the most interesting areas of inquiry has concerned the ways in which broader European colonial racial ideologies shaped the evolution of Irish nationalist identity.[26] In "Dash and Daring': Imperial Violence and Irish Ambiguity', Timothy G. McMahon takes up some of these issues by examining Irish nationalist attitudes toward two imperial conflicts: the Mahdi Wars of the early 1880s in Egypt and the Sudan and the Boxer Rebellion of 1900 in China. Looking closely at a wide variety of newspaper accounts, McMahon finds that Irish nationalists employed narratives of British imperial violence for a kind of double purpose. First, nationalist opinion shapers used accounts to critique British policy, a critique that resonated deeply with trauma-centred Irish nationalist historical narratives. It was not all negative, however. Irish nationalists also shared a number of racial assumptions with their British neighbours and used these racial hierarchies to justify their own political aspirations. In short, McMahon finds that Irish nationalist opinion shapers tried to carve out a distinct, if rather ambiguous and complex, middle ground on British imperial violence, constructing themselves as advanced westerners worthy of self-government yet concerned about the rights of non-western peoples.

Of course, nationalists were not the only Irish men and women to construct narratives of violence for their own purposes. In 'Writing an Orange Dolly's Brae', Sean Farrell examines the relationship between sectarian violence, its representation and the shifting evolution of communal identities. Taking the famous clash at Dolly's Brae in 1849 as his point of departure, Farrell shows how Orange elites and their allies constructed narratives of the riot to harden communal lines of division in

Victorian Ulster. In particular, he looks at how Orange testimonies featured gendered images of the clash that were designed to reinforce and articulate political Protestantism's Manichean communal categories. While these narratives were not taken up outside of the influential but limited spheres of the Loyal Orange Order in the 1850s, they played an important role in keeping the language of sectarian division alive for later use. When the Home Rule Crisis occurred in the early twentieth century, these narratives had a wider appeal to broader communities of Irish and British unionists, a fact attested to by the proliferation of Orange histories and songs that gave prominent place to this Orange writing of Dolly's Brae. Clearly, Irish nationalists were not the only party to sex up their violence.

It has been suggested that in relation to its size, Northern Ireland has been the most heavily researched place on earth. Much of this writing has naturally examined the violence that disfigured the Northern Irish landscape from 1966 to 1998. From the seemingly inexhaustible volume of scholarly investigation to the proliferation of filmic and literary representations of contemporary Northern Ireland, the so-called Troubles have not suffered from a shortage of text. Given the surfeit of material devoted to contemporary Northern Ireland, one might expect a type of 'Troubles fatigue', a reluctance to take up such well-trodden ground. Our next three essays offer a powerful challenge to this idea. Brian McIlroy, Keith Hopper and Elmer Kennedy-Andrews all examine artists engaging in the representation of violence and the violence of representation in order to showcase moments of defiance of stereotypes and ways of rejecting tired rhetorical paradigms. The ways in which Ireland's Protestant communities have been represented on film is the broad subject of Brian McIlroy's 'Symbolic and Hyperreal Violence in the Irish "Troubles" Movie'. Looking at several films that have attempted to tell the stories of the Northern Ireland 'Troubles', McIlroy argues that many filmic narratives strive for the status of thoughtful symbolic violence but often fall short of such goals. Because the violent representations under his analysis take on inevitable political notes, there are few examples that defy the perception of the unionist and loyalist communities as backward-looking or reliant on supremacist thinking. However, McIlroy's discussion of Thaddeus O'Sullivan's *December Bride*[27] and David Caffrey's *Divorcing Jack*[28] – both adapted to the screen from novels – showcases the emergence of a different type of character living in violent times – the 'unmarked secular Protestant'. In the absence of thoughtful symbolic violence, representations of characters such as Sarah Gomartin and

Dan Starkey offer examples of breaking away from and challenging stereotypes of Northern Irish Protestants.

Moving beyond the obvious and the stereotypical is a necessary step in any analysis of violence and is of vital importance in the context of Northern Ireland. Keith Hopper in 'Undoing the Fanaticism of Meaning: Neil Jordan's *Angel*' invigorates the critical debates about Neil Jordan's first full-length feature film; a film that elicited violent responses and sparked controversy over its funding and its subject matter. Hopper teases out a couple of central issues at work in the reception of *Angel* (1982) that are not solely applicable to this particular film. Firstly, Hopper notes a 'sense of unease' among critical commentators about the relationship between Jordan's style (surreal *film noir*) and his substance (violent killings and revenge). Questions concerning adequate or ethical treatments of violence in film, or any representative media, are complicated and fraught with partisan or sectarian tensions. Hopper's essay goes a long way towards answering these questions in not only defining some of these tensions but also in posing a reading of the film that goes beyond the obvious political interpretation. Hopper argues (against seminal texts such as John Hill's 'Images of Violence') that *Angel* vividly imagines an atavistic violence that taps into 'people's fears in a culture overwhelmed by physical violence'. What is perhaps most original and incisive in Hopper's analysis is his treatment of the 'Nobodaddy' or 'Black Man' presence in the film and its textual allusions. The 'nightmarish projection of a culture enveloped by violence' leads to fascinating conclusions about the haunting nature of violence and the resultant traumatized memories.

If Neil Jordan's film is ghostly and surreal, then Ciaran Carson's poetry brings readers into the concrete urban landscape of contemporary Belfast. In 'Ciaran Carson: The New Urban Poetics' Elmer Kennedy-Andrews argues that Carson's poetry not only constitutes a view of society 'in the throes of violent breakdown' (not unlike Jordan's film) but also showcases the necessity to grapple with incompleteness, fragmentation and indeterminancy. Kennedy-Andrews argues that there is a connection between history and art, and in the specific instance of Carson's poetry the connection is between civil violence and textual disturbance. The 'civil' space upon which Kennedy-Andrews and Carson both work is modern-day Belfast. The connections between history and art, text and society, all result in questions about identity (personal, communal, national), sex, violence and memory. What Kennedy-Andrews articulates via Carson's poetry – and what unites all the authors in *Shadows of the Gunmen* – is the notion that the violent ground is exactly the place upon which to re-evaulate pre-conceived ideas and truths about the self, politics, personal agency and ethics. Even if the urban world of Belfast is one of 'alienation, confusion and violence' Kennedy-Andrews still finds an affirmative voice in Carson's poetry that does not shy away from difficult situations or elide complex historical realities. Kennedy-Andrews also points out that even though the specifics of Carson's poetry are embedded in a Northern Irish urban landscape, the poetics of violence reach to many places and different times (such as World War II and the Dresden bombings, the Crimean War, the Indian Mutiny and the Russian Revolution). Artists who represent violence never do so in a temporal or spatial vacuum.

The necessity of violence, the violence of oppression, history and violence, sex and violence, symbolic violence, the violence of fragmentation – studying violence clearly allows scholars to examine and work through a wide array of important issues. The first eight essays in *Shadows of the Gunmen* all use the sociological approach to violence and many also incorporate the judicial and the ethical. It is really only with our final essay that a step into the phenomenological approach to violence is taken; however, this 'coda' to the volume is also about alternatives to violence and possible ways of moving beyond a violent past. Richard Kearney's 'Memory, History, Story: Between Poetics and Ethics' picks up the themes of trauma and memory and offers a philosophical answer to violence in the form of ethical remembering. Working from an analysis of Brian Tolle's 2001 Irish Hunger Memorial in Battery Park, New York City, Kearney presents an ethics of 'hospitality, flexibility, plurality, transfiguration and pardon'. Kearney writes that 'issues of discourse, ethics, memory, aesthetics and politics all intertwine in any commemorative project' and his analysis of the famine memorial as a response to historical violence and trauma connects all of the analyses in this book. If, as Kearney writes, 'the exchange of memories of suffering demands more than sympathy and duty (though these are essential for any kind of justice), and this something "extra" involves pardon in so far as pardon means "shattering the debt"', then all the essays in this collection are an exchange of memories.

The nine essays in *Shadows of the Gunmen* range widely over a variety of subjects and across more than a century. Clearly, violence here is not to be understood in unchanging or monolithic terms; both the factors that motivate men and women to commit acts of violence and the ways that narratives of violence are written and articulated are ever-shifting and contingent. Given that diversity, this collection argues that we need to be more sensitive to the ways in which violence is continually reworked in Irish society. The links between language and violence are especially crucial here. Even if Gilles Deleuze is correct in stressing the importance of these ties, we reject the notion that 'violence does not speak'. The meaning and interpretation of violence may be an open question but it need not be consigned to the realm of the absolutely unfathomable. As noted earlier, *Shadows of the Gunmen* is designed to initiate and enrich a wide-ranging conversation on violence and the Irish experience. It is our hope that students and scholars alike will take up the challenge contained in these essays: that we must engage and confront the intricate and often contradictory sites of violence in modern Irish culture and society. If there is very little silence in the study of violence today, the essays that follow demonstrate the promise held out by continuing this important conversation.

On the Necessity of Violence
in the Irish Revolution

PETER HART

Irish republicans (pro- and anti-Treaty) have often argued that the
Easter Rising was needed to raise national self-awareness, and that it
was necessary for the IRA to go to war in 1919–21 to achieve Irish sovereignty. Defenders of the Treaty and the Free State go on to say that a
second war was required to protect that newly won independence, as
well as democracy itself, in 1922–23. Most anti-Treaty republicans have
contrarily claimed the right to resist a British-imposed settlement.
Across the border, Ulster Unionists assert that only the threat of armed
resistance saved them from a Dublin government in 1912–14, and that
Northern Ireland had to fight for its survival in 1920–22. For the British
government's part, those gunmen deemed to be 'rebels' or 'terrorists'
(i.e. nationalists) have always properly been met with the righteous
application of 'law and order'. Violence has always been justified on all
sides on the grounds of necessity, not choice.

How well founded are these claims? Can we test them? Not without
re-running history, which we can do only in a speculative, counterfactual fashion. Nothing can be determined conclusively this way, of
course, but there are still good reasons to pursue the exercise (aside
from the inherent fun of it). For one thing, it allows us to examine a lot
of half-buried assumptions that should be exposed to open argument.
Such concepts often drive historical narratives, so it is important to see
how well they stand up. It is also useful to look for comparable situations within modern Irish history, to see what role violence played then
in forcing or preventing change.

What follows, then, is a speculative essay based as much as possible
on fact and logic. My various propositions are not presented as firm
conclusions but are intended, rather, to stimulate thought and debate.
Rational disagreement is as valid and valuable as agreement, so if this
essay provokes either it will have achieved its purpose.

We can think a counterfactual argument through in any number of different ways, but let us define a few terms at the outset. First of all, when I refer to 'sovereignty', I mean something more than the devolution offered in the four Home Rule bills of 1886, 1893, 1912 and 1920. Under these arrangements the United Kingdom parliament would have remained legislatively supreme as well as economically and militarily dominant. Ireland would have had no separate status as a nation (except perhaps in sports).

It is sometimes suggested that this form of provincial self-government was functionally similar to dominion Home Rule, the basic constitutional status offered in the Anglo-Irish Treaty of 1921, or that the former would naturally have evolved into the latter, and that therefore republican violence was unnecessary. The first argument is obviously false. We need only compare Canada (the model used in the Treaty) with Northern Ireland circa 1925 to see the two outcomes were constitutionally and practically very different. Thus, for the purposes of this essay, full dominion status will act as a benchmark for basic independence.

This distinction also helps refute the evolutionary argument. While the British parliament could always have increased the power of a Home Rule government, it could also have just as easily decreased or removed it – as happened to Stormont in 1972. Given the electoral dominance of the British Conservative Party in the twentieth century, nationalists would have had to wait a long time for a sympathetic ear in the corridors of power. It is far easier to imagine a fractious relationship between the provincial and central governments – especially over money, economic policy and war. Crises would have occurred; nationalist leaders and voters would have been outraged and radicalized, and some sort of confrontation over sovereignty would have been bound to occur. Thus we return to the essential question: would the British government have ever accepted an independent Ireland without an armed confrontation? Not to mention the enormously complicating question of Ulster and northern unionist self-determination.

Finally, what kinds and levels of violence are we talking about? What was the alternative? I do not think we have to posit two poles: one being total non-violence as practised by Gandhi or King, the other armed struggle as practised by paramilitaries. Many non-violent techniques – such as hunger or labour strikes – were used in Ireland, but no one advocated or practised non-violence as a moral and political principle in itself, not even the major churches. Nevertheless, there are forms of direct action other than killing and there is a world of difference between the manual, reactive and usually incidental violence of rallies, blockades, strikes, prison protests, sabotage and boycotts, and the far deadlier world of battles, ambushes, bombings, assassinations and executions. It is the latter forms of deadly force that I mean when I speak here of violence.

What I am suggesting as an alternative to what happened in 1912–23 is not the fantasy of no violence at all, but rather unarmed, as opposed to armed, struggle. This might include or lead to low-level violence but based on civil disobedience – 'people power' – without resorting to military or paramilitary means. There is nothing physically weak, meekly pacifist, unpatriotic or unmanly about such methods, although such are the usual sneering rebuttals. It is possible to fight and uphold political principles without killing, and in this case thousands of lives were at stake.

We must also distinguish between necessity and inevitability. Asking 'was violence inevitable' calls for an analysis of causation and probabilities rather than choices and possibilities. In this essay, I am interested in exploring whether the goals of armed organizations, and of the various governments involved, could possibly or reasonably have been achieved without open war, but I will return to the question of inevitability later.

Finally, while this essay is largely devoted to exploring options open to nationalists, this should not be taken as suggesting republicans were solely or even primarily responsible for armed violence in this period. Republican volunteers were the one constant in all aspects of armed conflict from 1916 to 1923, and the IRA was the single most violent organization in Ireland.[1] However, causation was not so simple and responsibility was far from unipolar. All armies and police forces joined in the fighting and government inaction could be as escalatory as paramilitary action.

Precedent

One of the things that made the Irish revolution revolutionary was its violence: nothing like the guerrilla and ethnic warfare of 1916–23 had occurred since 1798. Thus, asking why (so much) violence occurred is one of the central questions for historians of the period to answer. The key comparison is with the actions of previous generations. Revolutionary republicans believed that the only way to get what they wanted was to force the government to concede it. As Michael Collins put it in one of his favourite lines when giving speeches: 'nothing would be got from England unless you approach them with the head of a Landlord in one hand and the tail of a Bullock in the other'.[2]

Collins was presumably referring to the land wars of 1879–90 and subsequent decades, and equating these struggles with armed revolution. These campaigns for land reform, and the related fights for Home Rule and political democratization, were accompanied by mass mobilisation, radicalization, coercion and conspiracy, without terrible bloodshed. People were killed in land disputes, in the Phoenix Park assassinations and in dynamite attacks in London, but these were few and atypical. For the most part these struggles were no worse than contemporary industrial disputes – or Irish elections.

The main weapons in the land wars were non-violent or at least non-fatal. Rents were withheld. Evictions were obstructed, legally or physically. Evictees were supported, morally and financially. Enemies of the Land and National Leagues were boycotted. If the leagues came under attack, their money was hidden, their newspapers were printed offshore, new leagues were started up. If members were imprisoned, they resisted in various ways and protests were mounted outside. At bottom such campaigns worked on the basis of class and communal solidarity; at the top was a superb publicity and fund-raising machine, and a parliamentary party. Great things were achieved using these methods, but it must also be noted that permanent gains were made through alliances, negotiations and legislation, and that these never gave nationalist campaigners everything they wanted all at once.

Charles Stewart Parnell, the political mastermind of the 1880s, would have agreed with Collins that the only way to achieve things was to make demands by right rather than seek favours. Government should be confronted directly – in parliament or on the ground in Ireland – and forced to respond. But this did not have to mean guns and war, and it did not mean making absolute and non-negotiable demands. Parnell was very aware of the disastrous political consequences of murder and urged peaceful boycotts as a superior alternative. He often cited Daniel O'Connell's fights for Catholic rights in the 1820s and 1830s as a model for political action; an example later derided by republicans as a dishonourable blot on national honour, given O'Connell's refusal of physical force.

So Michael Collins was wrong in equating the land wars with armed struggle. And the history of Irish legislation between 1829 and 1914 suggests that other nationalist-positive reforms did not require rebellion to enact either. Education, land, agriculture, western poverty, local government, the civil service, the revival of the Irish language: all saw progress through self-help and pressure-group politics, not uprisings. Self-government looked to follow in their wake thanks to John Redmond's successful bargaining with the Liberal government in 1910 and 1911 – until the Home Rule crisis and the Great War intervened. Were politics in 1912–23 so different that only the threat or reality of open war could achieve adequate change?

The Easter Rising

Let us begin at Ground and Year Zero. It is often asserted that the Easter Rising was a necessary political catalyst: that massive, sacrificial violence was needed to inspire/awaken/radicalize nationalist Ireland. Such, of course, is the aim ascribed to Patrick Pearse and his co-conspirators, and their apparent success accounts for their posthumous glorification. The 1916 Rising has always troubled historians as a sort of island in history: a pivotal event seemingly explainable only in the actors' own terms. Where were the structural causes? The institutional or class interests? Can a few people just decide to change history by taking up the gun?

The problem here is not that the Rising had to have had deeper roots. It did not. Instead, we should revisit the aim of the event and its importance. What were its leaders really trying to achieve and did they really make that much of a difference? The men who planned the rebel lion were a minority faction within the Volunteers as a whole, artificially empowered by the backroom connivance of the IRB. The organization's official policy was to defend itself and Ireland's national rights, and to deter any repression or military conscription.[3] A straightforward call to arms in the name of the republic would not have found a very enthusiastic response, and was decried by many as suicidal and counter-productive, so the rebels' first aim was to frame their planned uprising to make it popular with the organization – and perhaps with the nationalist public – as a whole. Thus was concocted the phoney 'Castle Document', to suggest that Dublin Castle was unjustly about to attack them. This aim also gave the smuggling in of German rifles and ammunition a political purpose. These would provide the means for self-defence and trigger the Volunteers' prime directive: to acquire and keep military arms. The resulting mobilization and confrontation would achieve the conspirators' second goal: to make the Volunteers an explicitly revolutionary movement, which it otherwise was not.

But, of course, it all fell apart. The German guns ended up at the bottom of Cork Harbour. Chief of Staff Eoin MacNeill, who was not in on the conspiracy, realized he was being lied to and countermanded the original mobilization orders. Only about a thousand people turned out in Dublin, a group easily portrayed as lunatics or fanatics. That they are not remembered that way is due to their martial discipline and heroism, and to the execution of many leaders, which excited considerable sympathy and anger. This was hardly as miraculous as Pearse and his posthumous spin doctors would have it. Prison had granted a heroic halo at least since Daniel O'Connell, while rebellion and execution had made IRB martyrs in the 1860s. Such suffering had also generated large sums of money, as well as political capital, time and time again, but these things in themselves did not lead to much political progress. That required organization and opportunity.

The most important direct outcome of the Rising was within the Volunteers. It destroyed the power of the defence- and deterrence-minded MacNeillites and, when the organization was revived in 1917, its executive and headquarters were firmly under IRB control. The old struggle for power was far from over (many members would drop out rather than follow the militants' lead) but the Rising probably did lay the basis for the emergence of the IRA in 1920. This counts as an achievement right enough but it only stands as a necessary step towards sovereignty if the IRA was itself a necessity.

Nor was radicalization entirely a product of rebellion. The whole Volunteer movement had become progressively more militant since its break with the Irish Party in September 1914 – more stridently anti-British and more explicitly separatist. MacNeill himself was one of the authors of its increasingly confrontational rhetoric and policies, so this was not the work of the militant wing alone. We can safely assume the Volunteers would have continued to move towards confrontation even if Easter 1916 had not taken place.

Leaving aside the dubious claim of national awakening, what we do know is that returning rebels formed a leadership core in rebuilding Sinn Féin and the Volunteers, backed by a new cadre of young men and women who were personally inspired by their example. So was the Rising necessary to produce this new generation of leaders? Would the genius of Eamon de Valera and Michael Collins have emerged otherwise?

The revolution's deep talent pool was there before the Rising. It drew on the Gaelic League, the Gaelic Athletic Association, Sinn Féin, the Volunteers, the IRB and their assorted projects and newspapers. These Gaels made up a political counter-culture and were very aware of their status as an alternative nationalist leadership. All they needed was an opportunity – a political, not a military one.

For Collins and company to rise to the top, old leaders had first to be killed or pushed aside. Among the former was the really rather extraordinary partnership of James Connolly and Patrick Pearse, the loveable Joe Plunkett and the talented Sean MacDermott. Among the latter, the Rising ruined or cramped the careers of such pioneers as Eoin MacNeill and Bulmer Hobson. Many were lost who might have done as well as or better than their successors: Michael Collins's cousin and mentor, Jack Hurley, for example. In any case there was nothing to stop talented people like de Valera from playing a major role in a new movement even without Easter 1916. Moreover, the downside of the automatic authority granted to Rising veterans was that it promoted people beyond their abilities and allowed incompetents to assume responsible positions – Cathal Brugha being a case in point. Without the rebellion, a more meritocratic leadership might have emerged.

Elections

As an actual electoral issue, the Rising was closely linked to the disastrous collapse of the post-rebellion Home Rule negotiations run by Lloyd George, which left John Redmond with a divided and demoralised Irish Party and made the issue of partition a nationalist litmus test. This failure was the culmination of several years of popular alienation from Redmondism, that peculiar pro-imperial and pro-war form of Irish nationalism. His followers were willing to accept his close alliance with the pre-war Liberal government, but only up to the point where Prime Minister Asquith demanded nationalist concessions instead of facing down unionist belligerence in 1914. When Redmond caved in then, and again when he traded nationalist army recruits for a token Home Rule bill, he departed altogether from Parnellist tradition.

There probably would not have been any negotiations in 1916 without the Rising, but some equivalent attempt to satisfy nationalists was on its way eventually, driven by the need to placate American and Imperial opinion and offered as a carrot to match the stick of military conscription. If we look at other Party problems, Redmond would still have died in 1918 without a younger successor, and the Party would still have atrophied from lack of activity and without its life-sustaining infusions of Irish-American money. Irishmen would still be dying in France, the war would still have been unpopular, and there would still have been rising prices, unionization and strikes, as well as the miniland war of 1917–18. The party's fall was likely near at hand regardless of rebellion. Sinn Féin – or some equivalent or coalition – was the obvious beneficiary if nationalist voters were angry at the party or the government and wanted more aggressive representatives to fight for their interests.

Why Sinn Féin? Its name and its separatist stance were well known and it had many talented activists and publicists. This had not boosted the group's fortunes much before April 1916 though. In fact it had declined alongside the Irish Party as apathy struck them both, until it was widely blamed for the 'Sinn Féin rebellion'. This involuntary rebranding redounded to its credit when the rebels gained retroactive popularity and Sinn Féin clubs began spontaneously popping up all over the country in 1917.

Does this mean that Arthur Griffith and company would have gone nowhere without an injection of insurrectionary fuel?[4] The Sinn Féin of 1917 and 1918 rode a wave of public sympathy and admiration, but what changed the party itself was its alliance with the Volunteers and the IRB, and its absorption of other groups, including Party dissidents and trade unionists (all of whom existed – or were growing – before the Rising). It was this coalition – New Sinn Féin – that triumphed, not old-style Griffithism.

It was the Volunteers who benefited most from rising anti-war feeling in 1915 and early 1916, and they were headed for further growth with or without the Rising. Griffith was a supporter (and a member) but they considered themselves a purely military force, above politics. They shared Sinn Féin's abstentionism, however, and there was nothing to stop members voting, campaigning, or even running for election so long as they did not do so as Volunteers, or take their seats in parliament. Eoin MacNeill for one was keenly aware of the importance of public support to the Volunteers' fate, so the idea of running protest candidates, for example, might have occurred to him and others.

On the other hand, the emergence of a powerful republican faction after the Rising almost scuppered the first condition for separatist victory – unity. Late 1916 and early 1917 saw the emergence of a number of potential parties and leaders jockeying for political space.[5] The IRB even launched its own surrogate party, the Liberty League, and later nearly abandoned the merger talks with what was still Griffith's Sinn Féin. If Griffith had not been smartly conciliatory or if Eamon de Valera had not been available to act as a consensus leader, separatist politics might well have been a competition rather than a movement, ensuring the survival of the Irish Party and the All For

Ireland League, and the early appearance of a strong Labour Party. The Rising might well have led to a balkanized, rather than a radicalised, nationalism.

The first two by-election victories of 1917 – in North Roscommon and South Longford – were not Sinn Féin victories in any case. They were won with ad hoc campaigns and were at least as much the products of local circumstances as of a change in national consciousness or the emergence of a dynamic new party.[6] Long-time local dissidents Father O'Flanagan and Laurence Ginnell were the key players in Roscommon, not last minute blow-ins such as Michael Collins. Presumably Count Plunkett would not have been the candidate if there had been no Rising but another might have performed just as well – and definitely would have worked harder.

The Longford result was much closer. The abstentionist candidate nearly lost and might well have done without the timely intervention of Archbishop Walsh. Even if an anti-Party candidate would not have won without the events of 1916, he or she would almost certainly have registered a strong protest vote, a victory in itself and a harbinger of things to come.

Nor was there anything unprecedented in the scale of Sinn Féin's victory in the 1918 general election. Their biggest advantage was the same one the Irish Party had had: the first past-the-post electoral system. If proportional representation had been in use, the Party would not have been wiped out and southern unionism could probably have scraped a few seats together. Republicans also had the backing of the Labour Party. If it had run candidates, some would have been elected. These factors had little or nothing to do with the Rising.[7]

It must also be kept in mind that Sinn Féin never used – and never needed – violence to achieve its successes of 1917–18, up to and including the general election. Some constituencies, such as Waterford City, could be rough, but this did not alter the outcome of any contests. Dublin Castle was wont to harass party workers and arrested much of the party leadership in 1918, but this may have provided a net political gain as it stimulated public sympathy and support without disrupting the functioning of the organization too much. If the Volunteers had used deadly force in retaliation, the republican image of victimhood and nobility would likely have been badly tarnished. Republican party bosses were smart to stick to a non-violent strategy. Party-building and electoral conquest did not require goons or guns at all.

Defeating conscription

It was the introduction of conscription in 1918, not insurrection in 1916, which catalyzed nationalist public opinion and guaranteed Sinn Féin's great electoral victory. It destroyed the legitimacy of Dublin Castle rule and the remaining authority of the Irish Party, and made good the republican movement's claim to be saviours of the nation. We may question the government's intention to actually enforce the law and we may doubt whether conscripted nationalists would have been forced into combat before the war was over. But conscription was a genuine threat to personal and collective rights – and it was defeated without violence.

The victors were perhaps the most impressive nationalist coalition ever assembled. Sinn Féin, the Volunteers and the Irish Party were joined by the Catholic Church and the newly powerful labour movement, not to mention the nationalist press. Dublin Castle and its police forces were helpless in the face of potential mass resistance, boycotts and strikes. Only massive military force could have done the job, in which case the mostly unarmed Volunteers could not have stopped it.

In a sense the conscription crisis proved the efficacy of the pre-1916 MacNeillite strategy of maintaining a defensive posture. The Volunteers probably were not even needed for this, as the prospect of facing Land League-style crowds, a paralysed economy and transportation system, and international disapproval would quite possibly have stopped the government anyway. Using armed force could have been grossly counter-productive even if the government had tried to enforce its decision. Volunteer units would have had strong justification for defending their communities, but Cathal Brugha's infamous plan to shoot British cabinet ministers in the House of Commons was a different matter. Allied opinion would have been outraged and the great British public – and its politicians – might have insisted on crushing Irish republicanism as an Al-Qaeda-like threat. The biggest beneficiaries would have been Irish unionists.

The Republic

Parliamentary abstention and the creation of a parallel assembly and government had been Sinn Féin ideas long before 1916. It was never conceived of as a military plan, nor did violence prove necessary to carry it out. Dáil Éireann was set up in January 1919, and departments and policies followed in due course, run by revolutionary civil servants and local activists rather than guerrillas (although these were sometimes the same people). The all-important Dáil Loans were based on largely voluntary donations. The much-publicized Dáil court system also worked by consent rather than force. The fact that the republican police were widely felt to be incompetent only shows how useless coercion was under the circumstances.

Government harassment and the eventual outlawing of the republic and its institutions in autumn 1919 did not stop the revolutionary state-building process. It took the Restoration of Order in Ireland Act and the Black and Tans to do that in the following year. These measures were taken in response to the IRA's 1920 offensive, just as the banning of Sinn Féin and the Dáil were responses to the killing of policemen (especially by the Dublin 'Squad') in 1919. Without these deadly provocations, repression might well have come later, with much less severity, or not at all.

As in 1917–18 Sinn Féin was able to win many of the vital 1920 local elections without force and despite legal restrictions. The lack of any serious nationalist challenge to republicanism in the rural south does suggest a degree of intimidation but there is no evidence of systematic violence being used. And where competition was present in urban areas, Sinn Féin was willing to accept defeat, coalition and compromise. Local governments could thus declare allegiance to the republic and carry out the Dáil's policies in a democratic and mostly peaceful manner.

Sinn Féin candidates were also free to stand for election in the 1921 elections for the southern and northern parliaments – and once again did not need violence to achieve a near-complete sweep of the former. The fact that no one was willing to run against them in the south (outside Trinity College anyway) no doubt reflects the universal expectation that any non-republican candidate would be risking his or her life. But it was primarily a result of voluntary withdrawal by the Labour Party and other groups in favour of Sinn Féin, and of the near-unanimous opposition to the government's brutal mishandling of the insurgency. Sinn Féin would probably have retained its hold on the electorate in the midst of a national struggle even without the IRA.

Making Ireland ungovernable

If the object of guerrilla war was a military victory – to impose one's will on the enemy – it not only failed, it had no hope of success. But if the aim was to make Ireland ungovernable – to paralyse the Irish administration – it succeeded. The question is, would other methods have been just as effective?

Other methods worked in the 1880s. The Land War and the Plan of Campaign both demonstrated that the 'unwritten law' of popular nationalism could be enforced without a paramilitary army. Normal law and order broke down, the police needed military assistance and emergency laws were required. Arresting and holding hundreds of people for political activity eroded government legitimacy and bolstered public support for the Land and National Leaguers – in Britain as well as in Ireland. Fighting the Plan exhausted the Conservative government of 1886–91 and contributed to its defeat in the following election. The struggle also ensured massive financial support for the Leaguers from the United States.

The rise of Sinn Féin and the Volunteers in 1917–18 was accompanied by many of the same developments. Once the legal and penal systems became a battlefield in early 1917, the separatist movement was able to decisively outmanoeuvre the police and the government. Witnesses, juries and magistrates all refused to cooperate in court, a trend that was evident as early as 1915. Arrest and conviction rates fell even as political 'crime' rose.[8] If resident magistrates or military courts were used to ensure convictions, the prisons could not hold those convicted, thanks to prisoner protests and public pressure. Hunger strikes gave the rebels a winning weapon. Again and again Sinn Féiners and Volunteers had to be released early, to the dismay of the undermanned, underpaid and unpopular police, whose morale and effectiveness were correspondingly affected. All without firing a shot.

There is no reason why the same sort of campaign could not have been maintained in 1919–21. Indeed, civil disobedience was successful when used, and could have been more so. Strike action by railway workers directed against the British army disrupted troop movements in 1920,[9] and might have been even more effective if the republican movement had backed it with more effort and money; such at least was Michael Collins's opinion. The bulk of the Dublin Metropolitan Police refused to bear arms and essentially took themselves out of the struggle. The Royal Irish Constabulary was fiercely boycotted in much of Munster and Connaught, and Irish recruits to the undermanned force dwindled while resignations rose. Some of this can be attributed to the rise in violence, but Sinn Féin and the Dáil also missed a huge opportunity to encourage and reward defectors. Although the idea was endorsed in principle, there was no proper campaign to bring about police resignations, and even when a bureau and a fund were set up to help such people, they were too small to make any difference. Here again Collins – who was in close touch with disgruntled policemen – felt they had missed a trick. Without a spendthrift Department of Defence, money would have been plentiful. Without a war, policemen might have been more willing to listen.

What of the argument that the IRA served to defend the Dáil, and that without it, the underground government could not have got off the ground – or survived? In Dublin, Collins and his Intelligence Department have gotten the credit for this by eliminating hostile detectives and secret agents, as well as their informers and spies. Would the revolutionary cabinet and its employees have been rounded up without their guardians?

It seems fair to say that Collins's counter-intelligence efforts did make a difference and that the police and British intelligence would have done better if so many of them had not been bumped off. The IRA's key police agents were in place before the assassinations began, however, so Collins's tip-offs about raids and agents would still have been forthcoming. Spies could have been exposed and shamed, rather than killed – a tactic that worked well when tried. British agencies would still have been prevented from achieving their main objective: penetrating the movement.

Secondly, Collins and many others managed to evade capture for many months before the assassinations, and were still being hunted afterwards. The Dáil ministries and IRA headquarters were forced underground, subject to raids and arrests at any time, and still managed to carry on. Those who were arrested could always be replaced, one of the strengths of the movement. Its passive defences – anonymity, concealment and evasion – were more important than the active policy of killing the pursuers. At best, the 'Squad' killings won the Dáil administration only a temporary respite in 1919–20.

Republicans outside Dublin never had 'the Squad' or numerous police informers to protect them, and also managed to keep going. The flow of information to the RIC had dried up by 1918, and when the British army temporarily took over in Munster in early 1920, its successes were reversed by a mass hunger strike, not a military counter-offensive. The subsequent appearance of Dáil courts and republican police owed something to the RIC's strategic withdrawal from isolated rural barracks, but it was at least partly owing to a softening of government counter-insurgency policy in the spring and summer of 1920. In no sense could the IRA ever physically prevent Crown forces from acting.

Nor is there much evidence to support the frequent IRA claims of defending targeted communities from reprisal attacks following ambushes (not to mention the fact that one would not have happened without the other). Similar claims were made in Belfast, where Catholic neighbourhoods came under ferocious assault from Protestant arsonists and killers. IRA snipers and bombers certainly attacked Protestants and policemen in return, but this only provoked further escalation, as loyalist vigilantes took it as confirmation that any Catholic presence was a threat.[10] The republican army could do almost nothing to protect Catholic homes and businesses.

If all the energy and money devoted to war making had been devoted to other forms of resistance, what other ideas might have been tried? A tax strike? A boycott of British goods? A boycott of selected government employees? Force Dublin Castle to shut down local councils and run local government itself? Blockade police stations and other government offices – perhaps the Castle itself? Picket the homes of senior civil servants or policemen: put them under siege? Shut down ports as well as the rail system? None would have been decisive but then neither was guerrilla war. The cumulative effect on the government might well have been comparable in terms of bad publicity, political pressure and untenable logistics. It would still have killed Dublin Castle as a workable system and demonstrated Sinn Féin's enduring support. And if the Government of Ireland Act had been brought in just as it was in 1920, the new parliament of Southern Ireland could have been boycotted just as easily as Westminster. If it was necessary for the Dáil members to sit as such legally for the purposes of achieving compromise – well, that is just what happened anyway in 1922.

Forcing the British government to negotiate

Lloyd George's coalition government of 1918–22 was dominated by the Conservative Party but the Prime Minister was far from being a mere captive of his partners. Liberal leaders had long negotiated with Irish nationalists: Lloyd George had done so before the war and during it. Neither he nor Tory leader Austen Chamberlain would ever have openly recognized the Dáil as the legitimate authority in Ireland but they were far likelier to talk to a purely political group than to people considered terrorists. Republicans were seen as radicals but, without the Easter Rising, they would not have been scorned as traitors backed by German gold.

Of course the British cabinet would not have chosen to negotiate as their first option. We can assume they would have tried to impose their own preferred settlement first. Something like the Government of Ireland Act would have been cobbled together no matter what happened, and the Dáil would have utterly rejected it as even being a starting point for negotiations. This fourth Home Rule bill was widely seen as unworkable (at least in the south) long before it was finally passed. Thanks to war and conscription, by the 1918 election all nationalist parties had upped their demands to at least dominion Home Rule. The government would have had to come up with a better offer, violence or no. Assuming Sinn Féin's continued resistance and political success, Home Rule would therefore still have failed in the 1921 elections, leaving a near-empty parliament.

Thus, Home Rule was politically dead after 1918 except, ironically, in unionist Ulster. Faced with the options of trying to resume contested direct rule via Dublin Castle or of declaring Ireland a crown colony, the government might well have offered a truce and an improved offer to bring the rebels to the table – or to split the moderates from the militants if they refused – much as happened anyway in the summer of 1921.

Lloyd George might have acted even earlier than this. Anglo-Irish peace talks nearly worked in late 1920 before the government demanded IRA decommissioning as a precondition. If there had been no IRA, there would have been no such obstacle and – shades of the Kilmainham Treaty of 1882 – secret negotiations might well have produced freedom of assembly for the Dáil and a formula for talks acceptable to both sides.

What was needed for the revolutionaries to get to this point was a sustained and politically expensive crisis, with the government facing mass nationalist opposition and no prospect of beating Sinn Féin, regaining public legitimacy or re-establishing order. Peace, stability and a long-term solution to the Irish question required a nationalist negotiating partner who could make a deal stick. That was what happened in 1880–85 and again in 1919–22. As I have suggested, the same leverage could have been applied without a war so long as Sinn Féin remained united and popular.

Dominion status

Even if the British government had agreed to talks with the Dáil, would it have been willing to concede independence? It has often been asserted that, while Home Rule within the United Kingdom may have been achievable by constitutional means, nationalist Ireland had to use force to win true self-determination. Was the political distance between devolution and dominion status that great? What prompted the British cabinet's shift from one to the other in 1920–21?

In fact Irish policy began to change well before 1920. The rise of the Labour Party, the fall of the Liberal Party, and the Conservative success at the 1918 polls all made Ireland a far less important issue in British politics. Once most Liberals accepted the necessity of partition to satisfy northern unionism, and many Conservatives accepted the principle of Home Rule, Irish self-government no longer defined the party divide. Thus, the Government of Ireland bill was driven as much as anything by a desire to remove Ireland from British politics – and by the legal requirement to deal with the legacy of the 1914 Home Rule bill.

Partition removed the greatest obstacle to a deal in British political terms, as it removed Ulster unionists from the equation. After Northern Ireland was established in 1921, there was no serious Irish-based opposition to Home Rule of any kind. Nationalists certainly objected to the new border but, as Redmond, de Valera and Collins all proved, the north was ultimately judged as being secondary to a Dublin parliament. Partition was not a deal-breaker if it could be traded for independence.

So what was needed to move the government to accept the idea of an independent Ireland was the same as that which would force it to negotiate – a united, mobilized and recalcitrant nationalist population. A non-insurrectionary revolution might also have assuaged the two chief worries of British policy makers: that an Irish dominion would secede from the Empire altogether, and that it would threaten national security. The existence of the IRA only increased these fears.

What republican violence failed to achieve

It is worth reminding ourselves that physical force did not, in fact, achieve a republic. This was only achieved by successive Irish governments, using democratic, legal and peaceful means. The Treaty granted southern Ireland the same status as Canada – within the Empire/Commonwealth, and with considerable military and diplomatic reservations. This was not what Patrick Pearse had stood or died for, nor any of the other martyrs. Would they have been willing to lose their lives if they had known the actual results?

Militant republicans were undoubtedly correct to believe that they could only attain immediate and full independence through massive or sustained violence. The problem was, they were never going to be capable of exerting enough force to impose their will, as the IRA's 1920–21 and 1922–23 campaigns proved. The IRA was far from defeated in 1921, and no matter what happened, it could have survived for a long time to come. It was under great pressure, however, and Britain's war effort could have been increased far beyond anything the republican movement could match – just as happened in the Civil War. This was not something British leaders wanted, but they would have been willing to do it to prevent a perceived threat to their national security. Once the offer of open negotiations and dominion status was made, most nationalists would not have tolerated continued fighting to uphold republican principles. Without such support further guerrilla war would have failed, just as it did in the Civil War.

Nor did the IRA win an all-Ireland state. One of Sinn Féin's chief criticisms of the Irish Party was its willingness to consider partition and its inability to stop it. And one of the great rationales and motivators for violence the world over is the defence of a nation's territorial integrity. Yet, in the end, neither the IRA nor Michael Collins's Provisional Government could do anything to halt the establishment of a separate Northern Ireland or alter its boundaries, either directly or by giving negotiators the leverage necessary to keep Ireland united.

If anything, northern nationalists were in an even worse position after the IRA's exertions. The Redmondite approach might have kept majority-Catholic Fermanagh and Tyrone under a Dublin government but the revolution helped to ensure that they stayed in Northern Ireland. The Anglo-Irish Treaty did not give people the option to vote for their own future, as had been mooted in 1914. Paramilitary arms had done nothing to protect the minority in Belfast but they had given loyalist mobs and death squads political cover for their ethnic violence. Without the IRA there might have been no UVF revival and definitely no Special Constabulary.

Sinn Féin's political resistance to the unionist state was no more effective, mind you. Abstention from the Northern Irish parliament achieved nothing, and the Fermanagh and Tyrone county councils' non-recognition of the new government's authority simply got them dissolved. On the other hand, unionist measures such as the abolition of proportional representation might not have passed British scrutiny if there had been no security threat. London (especially Winston Churchill) allowed the Belfast regime a lot more leeway in 1922 because it was under attack. And, in the end, non-violent measures were as ineffective as violent ones because the northern government was supported by a large majority of its population, and Sinn Féin did not even have the full support of the Catholic minority. Governments do not usually lose under such circumstances.

What republican violence did achieve

First and foremost, what republican violence created was a new republicanism, based on the timeless verities of the Rising, the Dáil and the Civil War. 1916 created a new militant tendency within the IRB and the Volunteers, who were able in turn to rewrite the Sinn Féin constitution. This vanguard was still only one faction within the revolutionary coalition, but it was able to launch a guerrilla war and – thanks to the British response – bring much of the movement along with them. Militarization meant further radicalization and the marginalization of Sinn Féin while the IRA grew in power. This growing militant strength was reflected in the second Dáil elected in 1921, which nearly defeated the Treaty in the January 1922 vote. Indeed, this was just what Michael Collins and his brothers in the IRB had planned and striven for, and was a key rationale for ongoing violence: to push for a full revolutionary settlement and ward off any compromise. His opponents' dedication and strength in resisting the Treaty was an ironic tribute to his success as a strategist and organizer. The use of physical force was not just a matter of honour or military necessity: it was part of a political agenda of a particular group manoeuvring to create and control the revolution. It did not just happen: it was prepared for, planned and deliberately chosen.

But political violence and war always have unforeseen consequences. The most obvious unexpected result of the rise of the IRA and its armed struggle in 1918–21 was the Civil War of 1922–23. Any Treaty-like compromise would have split the movement and defined the new Irish party system, but without the existence of a radicalized and battle-hardened paramilitary force, this would merely have meant a hotly contested election in 1922, not a second war. Any accounting of the War of Independence must include its sequel.

As for the anti-Treaty republicans who fought against the Free State, how did fighting a second war possibly serve their interests? The answer, in part, is that they had no desire to wage civil war, did not plan it and did not start it. Why resist, then? Many did not and paid no penalty, but enough did to keep up their end of the war for a few months. It certainly did not help them in electoral terms, as Sinn Féin leaders like de Valera knew only too well.

The answer lies, in part, in the ideological makeup of the Volunteers/IRA. Even before 1916, the existence of an armed national militia was its own justification – proof and guarantor of nationhood. Hence the anti-Treaty IRA's emphasis in 1922 on maintaining autonomy and a republican identity. Disbanding was unthinkable for people with these genuine – if convenient – convictions. In a sense, then, the very existence of the force made some such confrontation at least possible, if not probable.

Another unintended effect of political violence in the south was the flight of Protestants and other 'enemies' of the Republic out of Ireland. Tens of thousands of people were lost who might have stayed. The resulting population loss was not so extensive it crippled the Free State or its economy, but it certainly did not help.

Nor can we ignore the other civil war in Northern Ireland, where the terrible suffering in 1920–22, especially in Belfast, at times recalled the brutality of the 1790s. Partition would probably have happened no matter what form self-government took, and no doubt there would have been sectarian riots and expulsions to accompany it. Without rival paramilitaries, and against the backdrop of guerrilla warfare, they would not have been been nearly so sustained or so bloody, however. It would be wrong to blame the IRA or Sinn Féin for this, given Unionist/Protestant aggression and paranoia, but escalation took place on both sides, and republican violence helped their enemies legitimize their actions.

British violence

Needless to say, republicans were not the only practitioners of violence. Can the same points about less harmful alternatives be made about the British government's use of force? For example, would trying to negotiate with Sinn Féin and the Dáil in 1919 rather than waiting until 1921 have produced better results – or the same result at less cost? It is possible that a British offer of talks would have been seen as a kind of surrender, and republicans would have refused any mere offer of dominion Home Rule with partition. If so, and if a war had broken out anyway, such an offer of sovereignty might well have reduced nationalist support for the IRA and raised British public backing. The government would have been on much firmer ground morally and politically – and therefore militarily. It might well have been a win-win proposition, except perhaps for Lloyd George with his Conservative partners.

The IRB and militant Volunteers would probably have still insisted on taking their chances with the gun in such circumstances but with much less justification. The end result? Perhaps another rebellion but with limited public backing as in Easter 1916 and ending in a similar defeat. After that, maybe a split in the movement and a political deal with the more amenable wing of Sinn Féin. In other words, something like the Treaty, but earlier and with fewer casualties.

Given the IRA campaign that did take place, can we argue that the violence of 1919–21 was needed to wear down republican intransigence at least as much as the government's? Eamon de Valera, Michael Collins, and the IRA's GHQ had to be convinced they could not win by continuing the guerrilla war before they would agree to a truce and negotiations. Republicans argued that war was needed to bring Britain to the table, but, ironically, the same may have been true of themselves. Would there have been a republican compromise or a Treaty without the Tans, and the threat of worse to come?

What the police and army could not do was defeat republicanism as a political force, or crush the IRA so long as it had that popular backing. This was the great mistake Lloyd George and his cabinet made in December 1920, when they tried to push the Dáil into a disadvantageous ceasefire. Collins and Griffith were willing to talk without such preconditions, as were such future hard-liners as Cathal Brugha and Austin Stack, but the opportunity was lost because the British government thought victory was imminent. Once these first tentative peace moves had fallen through, it seems fair to say that further IRA efforts were required before the government saw the error of its ways.[11]

The Free State at war

It was the Treaty-based Provisional Government that actually started the Civil War and was the more violent of the two 'sides' in that struggle. Its defenders have always asserted that this was required in defence of democracy and independence. In this case, it might be argued, Michael Collins and his colleagues were forced to choose between two wars, with the IRA or with Britain. The anti-Treaty forces were not even united, and at least one faction might have been planning an assault on British troops or Northern Ireland. Pre-empting such an attack was thus the lesser of two evils, as British blockade and/or re-conquest would have been far worse than the alternative.

On the other hand, one reason why the attack on the Four Courts was launched on 28 June, and why the campaign was pursued aggres-sively, was that Arthur Griffith and others in the Irish cabinet wanted to use force to eliminate the IRA instead of attempting reconciliation or compromise. The timing may also be explained by the fact that the Dáil was soon to reconvene, with an agreed coalition cabinet to be formed from the warring factions in Sinn Féin. Why not wait? And why refuse to heed Labour Party appeals for a ceasefire, or other groups' attempts to broker a peace? Presumably because this would have interfered with the creation of a stable state with an apolitical and subordinate army and police. Judged by these goals, Free State violence as used was prob-ably necessary, but it was not necessarily in the best interests of Irish democracy, nor was it the only rational option available.

Ulster unionist violence

What made Ulster unionist threats of armed resistance in 1913–14 so successful was the fact they never had to be carried out. Liberal and nationalist opponents of Edward Carson and James Craig frequently accused them of bluffing: if push came to shove, they would back down rather than launch a paramilitary rebellion. In fact, the UVF probably would have taken the field even if some of its leaders got cold feet.[12] Their threats were a bluff in the larger sense, however. To act would have been to lose: morally, politically, and probably militarily once the army was involved. All the Ulster-is-right propaganda would have gone for naught in British eyes if soldiers had been killed. At that point, only civil disobedience would have had a chance of political victory.

If the Great War had not broken out, and northern unionism had taken armed action to defend itself from Dublin, we might be looking back at the terrible legacy of unionist rebellion and martyrdom, con-trasted with the emergence of an Irish nationalist state in accordance with its cherished and long-standing principles of peaceful struggle and liberal democracy.

The Ulster Protestant uprising that did finally take place in 1920 bears witness to just how bad a 1914 eruption might have been. The war on the Catholic minority in 1920–22 was certainly effective in forcing Catholic families back into ethnic enclaves, and workers out of many workplaces. The Special Constabulary was also successful in combating the IRA, especially in border areas. In neither case was there actually much of a threat, however. Belfast was not becoming more Catholic, nor was its workforce, despite loyalist fears. The city's nationalists were badly divided, Sinn Féin was not strong, and the IRA was painfully weak.

The same was true throughout most of Northern Ireland. Nowhere was there a major insurgency or invasion that had any prospect of toppling the new mini-state. It may be that the heavy police presence in Fermanagh and Tyrone helped reduce the possibility of these majority-nationalist counties being shifted to Free State control in 1922 or after, but the boundary was set by the Government of Ireland Act long before then and any chance of changing it was pretty much gone once the Treaty was signed in December 1921.

Nor did Protestant and Unionist behaviour improve their standing in the British political arena, where their fate was ultimately decided. Many Conservative backers of Ulster – including in the cabinet and the press – were dismayed and repelled by anti-Catholic murder and arson. The alienation of the nationalist population by loyalist violence and the state's failure to deal with it (not to mention its own palpable anti-Catholicism) also damaged Northern Ireland's long-term stability and viability.

There was a political purpose to it all, though, however vicious and counter-productive. The threat of violence in 1913–14, and its reality in 1920–22, did help the Unionist Party gain its great objective of keeping Protestant voters unified under its banner. Ultraloyalist competition was squeezed out by the party's hard line and by the creation of the Specials. Left-wing political threats were dealt with by playing up the rebel threat and by bullying socialists and trade unionists into silence or exile. Rather than violence allowing a hearing for moderation, as William O'Brien famously suggested, it promoted extremism on all sides.

Inevitability

The alternatives I have suggested are possibilities. By no means were they at all likely once the Home Rule crisis got underway in 1913. I would argue that significant armed violence became very likely once the Ulster Volunteer Force was formed and armed in 1913–4, and the Liberal government did nothing to stop it. It was this that prompted a nationalist paramilitary response – the Irish Volunteers – and raised the prospect of armed conflict.

Incidentally, this raises the question of whether preventative action by the government might have worked to suppress the UVF and ensure a democratic and constitutional outcome to the Irish crisis. In other words, is this a case where force was indeed called for? It depends on how the government might have acted. If the army had been moved in as planned in 1914, to forestall any seizure of power, and if concessions had been made to regional autonomy under Home Rule, it would have placed unionist leaders in a very awkward position. For the UVF to take the offensive would have been politically disastrous, as discussed above, making passive resistance the best choice available until the Conservatives returned to power in London. If militants had acted on their own, their efforts would probably have been localized and easily crushed. Sustained violence might not have been necessary if the unionist bluff had been turned against them in this way.

The eruption of the Great War added a complicating factor as the Irish Party backed the government, which put off implementing Home Rule. The Volunteers split, the radicals inherited most of the organizational apparatus, and the government again preferred to tolerate a dissident militia rather than confront it. The stage was thus set for the 1916 Rising and the eventual merger of the IRB and Volunteers that would become the IRA. Whatever happened after this, armed republicanism would probably have had to be suppressed by one government or another. And this, in turn, made a popular Protestant backlash almost certain.

In the end violence only succeeded where it had the will of a majority behind its objectives – and opposed to its targets. Unionist resistance could prevent Ulster (or some part thereof) from being ruled by Dublin but it could not halt Home Rule altogether in the teeth of the well-established nationalist demand. Republican violence could be sustained in 1919–21 because nationalists had rejected British rule outright and loathed the Tans. It was doomed in 1922–23 because their great goal had been achieved, at least for the twenty-six county Free State. And it was practically a non-starter in the six-county North, where only a third of the population was Catholic, only a minority of whom supported the republican movement in the first place. Finally, Britain's 'police war' in 1920–21 failed not only because it was waged in the teeth of a hostile population, but also because British public opinion itself condemned it and did not much care what form Ireland's government took. If Irish negotiators had insisted on a thirty-two county republic in 1921, however, and war had resumed, the republicans might well have been deserted by supporters and sympathisers all round, and suffered the same fate the anti-Treatyites did the following year.

If a majoritarian mandate was the deciding factor in these matters, does that mean these various populations preferred the use of violence? There is no evidence that this was so, except under certain specific and limited conditions. The great majority of Ulster Protestants probably did not want the UVF to fight the police or army, or nationalists elsewhere in Ireland. Only a defence against perceived nationalist attack or oppression was thoroughly endorsed.

The Easter Rising certainly received no popular endorsement until well after the fact. Nor did most nationalist voters want Sinn Féin to launch a second insurrection when they voted for them in 1918 – even if the party did scrupulously leave the option open in its constitution and manifesto. Guerrillas would be backed against a brutal British gendarmerie or military occupation, but that was again a matter of self-defence and of choosing one's own people against outsiders. The IRA was also aided by Britain's failure to offer a palatable political option. So long as the Government of Ireland Act was on the table, the IRA could be seen as the champions of self-determination. As soon as the offer was upped to dominion status, that majority backing – or tolerance anyway – for insurgency was withdrawn.

Which leads me to suggest the following point: if a non-violent Sinn Féin had evolved, revolutionary in its aims but akin to the Land League in its militancy and methods, it might well have got just as many votes, been just as successful and made the IRA unnecessary. A great many Sinn Féiners, from Arthur Griffith on down, looked askance at pro-war republicans, and deplored the kind of war they fought. They lacked an explicit non-violent ideology or tradition, however; that belonged to their discredited opponents in the Irish Party. The pressure for a separatist united front overrode any internal debate on the subject, so long as the government chose repression over negotiation. The IRA did not need or want anyone's permission to act but in these circumstances it could count on their acquiescence, at least for the most part.

It took unionist initiative, and British vacillation or support, to create Irish paramilitarism. Only when this was seen to work, when the Asquith cabinet began to waver in late 1913, did a countervailing nationalist response take shape. Later British misjudgement and intransigence was as culpable as republican zealotry in whipping up a full-blown war in 1920, and in keeping it going in 1921. Nor was the republican leadership's tolerance of violence any worse than that of their Ulster Unionist counterparts. All parties to the struggle had choices and all, at one time or another, chose to use violence to achieve their ends. It need not have been so.

Sean O'Casey and the Dialectics of Violence

BERNICE SCHRANK

O'Casey's dynamic view of violence

Violence inhabits every corner of Sean O'Casey's life and art. He was engaged both by the violence in the world around him and by the challenges posed by representing it. Whether in the world or on the stage and page, that violence has many faces: verbal attack, artistic censorship, natural disaster, debilitating disease, physical assault, economic deprivation, clerical fascism, revolutionary upheaval, political repression, world war. Indeed, O'Casey's autobiographies and plays take up most of the epic struggles of the twentieth century from the Irish war for independence and its disillusioning aftermath, to the Russian Revolution, the Great War, the rise of fascism, the Spanish Civil War, the Second World War and the emergence of the Cold War. That he dealt with the violence of the world is obvious. How he understood and presented that violence, however, is complex and multifaceted.

O'Casey's engagements with violence stem from his recognition that violence is an essential component of life. It is no accident that *I Knock at the Door*, the first of O'Casey's six-volume autobiography, begins with his mother's birth pain, struggling to bring Sean into a world in which her two previous sons died because the family was too poor to pay for the necessary medical attention. So it was that

> [i]n Dublin, sometime in the early 'eighties, on the last day of the month of March, a mother in child-pain clenched her teeth, dug her knees home into the bed, sweated and panted and grunted, became a tense living mass of agony and effort, groaned and pressed and groaned and pressed, and pressed a little boy out of her womb . . .[1]

What this passage misses in autobiographical accuracy (O'Casey could not have witnessed his mother's labour), it more than makes up for in the striking power of the image of new life being wrenched from old. It is significant that, except for the mention of Dublin and the March date, the passage lacks particularising detail. O'Casey's mother is, in this moment of agony, 'a mother', and is, in fact, any mother. O'Casey thus made his own painful birth a metaphor for the universal birthing process. The passage also illustrates how deeply O'Casey embedded violence in the most fundamental experience of life, and how compatible he made it with creativity.

O'Casey was, moreover, as much interested in the constructed violence of man as he was in the intrinsic violence of nature. His expertise on this subject was gained first hand. In his autobiographical writing, O'Casey characterized the world he was born into as cold, damp, dark and fallen; a place in which poverty was endemic, disease was rampant and suffering was constant. Writing about *I Knock at the Door* in *'Tis*, Frank McCourt notes that:

> there is no happily ever after in Sean O'Casey . . . . He's the first Irish writer I ever read who writes about rags, dirt, hunger, babies dying. The other writers go on about farms and fairies and the mist that do be on the bog and it's a relief to discover one with bad eyes and a suffering mother.[2]

Violence is not, however, the only truth of O'Casey's world. As O'Casey's politics became more radical and Marxist over the course of his life, his vision of life became increasingly dialectical. The autobiography, like so many of O'Casey's plays, contrasts the brutality of an uncaring nature with manifestations of intense natural beauty.[3] That same dialectic controls O'Casey's portrayal of man-made violence. Although the indifference, if not outright malignancy, of social and religious institutions and their representatives dominated O'Casey's world, he appreciated the immanence of joy and goodness. The portrait of O'Casey's mother, whose ceaseless devotion to O'Casey persisted until her death, provides a striking example of the self-sacrificing beneficence of humanity. There are other such portraits including the larger than life one of Jim Larkin, whose heroic role in the General Strike and Lock-out of 1913 enabled O'Casey to present him as a secular saint of labour.[4] O'Casey did not, however, believe that institutional evil was adequately answered by individual demonstrations of decency and self-sacrifice. The task, as O'Casey understood it, was to work to create social change to moderate the pain and suffering that violence inevitably inflicts in unequal portions on the poor, the innocent and the vulnerable, and thereby to allow the goodness and love that exists within the human collectivity to be realized.[5]

He opposed much of the man-made violence he wrote about, such watershed moments as the Easter Rising (*The Plough and the Stars*) or the Great War (*The Silver Tassie*) – because that violence was, from his Marxist perspective, antagonistic to the interests of the working class with whom he identified all of his mature life. He was never, as Ronald Ayling has recently reminded us, 'a pacifist, though many commentators have presented him in this light'.[6] Good Marxist that he was, O'Casey went beyond the mere recognition of violence as a fundamental aspect of life to a belief that it was possible to use violence in a revolutionary way to end poverty, exploitation, and other forms of political and economic oppression. In other words, for O'Casey, violence might become a precursor to, and accompaniment of, progressive social change. Indeed, in the late autobiographical volumes and in such plays as *The Star Turns Red, Purple Dust, Cock-a-Doodle Dandy* and *Red Roses for Me* O'Casey celebrated the potential of revolutionary violence.[7]

O'Casey's support for the Spanish Republican cause even after the fall of the Republic in 1939 illustrates the degree to which O'Casey endorsed the use of violence to defend humane values and to create a just society. From the outbreak of the insurrection in Spain until his death, O'Casey, too old to fight himself, supported those volunteers who fought for the Republic. In *Purple Dust* (1943) he has the play's hero O'Killigain, the man who has come to redeem the wasteland that is rural Ireland, recall that he 'was fightin' in Spain that you might go on singin' in safety an' peace.'[8] What is interesting about O'Killigain's comment is that neither he nor O'Casey sees the need to specify on what side O'Killigain was fighting. For O'Casey and for O'Killigain support for the Republic was the only possible side.

O'Casey's interest in Spain was not limited to the activities of the Irish volunteers like O'Killigain. He was engaged by the anti-fascist efforts of all foreign volunteers who fought in Spain on behalf of the Republic, amongst them the Americans of the Abraham Lincoln Brigade. In 1950, for example, responding to a request for support and assistance from Dr Edward Barsky, an American physician who, in 1937, went to the aid of the Spanish Republic as leader of a fully-equipped American hospital unit, and, after the defeat of the Republic, continued to offer medical assistance to anti-fascist Spanish refugees, O'Casey wrote of the necessity to oppose the fascist spirit wherever it is found.[9] In 1960, in another uncollected letter published for the first time in *The Canadian Journal of Irish Studies*, O'Casey wrote to the Veterans of the Abraham Lincoln Brigade denouncing Franco for the ongoing imprisonment of Spanish and other anti-fascist veterans.[10] O'Casey's continued interest in the Spanish Republican cause provides strong evidence that O'Casey believed unequivocally that violence on behalf of, and as was the case in Spain, in defence of progressive social change was fully justified. For O'Casey the problem in Spain was not that there was violence, but that the wrong side won.

How audiences[11] respond to O'Casey's radical engagement with violence is, like O'Casey's response, complex and multifaceted. O'Casey wrote for audiences disinclined, often passionately, to accept his critique of Irish nationalism, his insistence on the iniquities of capitalist exploitation and his attacks on clerical and other forms of fascism. This is not to say that O'Casey portrays all clerics as fascists. Certainly Father Ned in *Drums of Father Ned* represents liberation theology at its best; nevertheless, he is one of O'Casey's exceptions. It is not surprising, therefore, that O'Casey's challenges to hegemonic social, economic and religious assumptions were frequently met with anger and the more damaging social forms that anger often takes, covert and overt censorship and marginalization. With the exception of the disturbances at the early performances of *The Plough and the Stars,* the violence directed against O'Casey and his work was not physical. Nevertheless, the various forms of censorship imposed on his work and the persistent refusal in his lifetime and after to grant him the status and respect to which his talent and achievement entitled him were, in effect (if not always in intention), efforts at killing the spirit of a non-conforming writer by limiting the availability of his work, by circumscribing his ability to earn a living by his writing and by inflicting emotional and psychological wounds often as painful as any that might come from direct physical assault. In short, O'Casey's representations of violence often produced violent responses, a tit for tat of offence and counter-offence. These included riots during the early performances of *The Plough and the Stars*; paper wars over the Abbey's rejection of *The Silver Tassie*; the official banning of *Within the Gates* in Boston; the kind of ostracism implicit in the assertions that, in plays such as *Cock-a-Doodle Dandy*, O'Casey simply had lived too long abroad and no longer understood Ireland; and the theatrical neglect of many of the late plays, which are rarely performed in Ireland or elsewhere.

Far from silencing O'Casey, many of these counter-offensives offered him (and in the case of *Within the Gates*, his supporters) the opportunity to extend the shelf life of his concerns. Fashioning for himself the persona of the Green Crow and the Flying Wasp, a cross between the gadfly and the provocateur, he used the criticism of his work and life as a platform for articulating and advancing his political and artistic agenda in wider public forums.[12] Responding to his critics through letters to the editor, articles in newspapers and essays, O'Casey generated controversy. He was thus able to move from what Ronald Ayling has called O'Casey's 'theatre of war' to an equally volatile theatre of the real in which his views continued to be heard, even after his plays had closed (or failed to open).

In the 1960s, American academic critics, responding more judiciously to O'Casey's treatment of violence than the early audiences at the Abbey, confused O'Casey's revulsion at the pain and suffering caused by violence with a commitment to non-violence, a misreading that privileges his early plays which are then re-read as embodiments of humanistic values. One of the consequences of this approach is that it justifies the neglect of his later, more overtly political and Marxist writing. Unfortunately, by the time this particular critical 'line' fully matured, O'Casey was dead, and could make no response.

The rest of this paper takes up in greater detail the complex interrelationships between O'Casey's representations of violence and the hostility those representations so often provoked. 'Anatomizing nationalist violence' deals with O'Casey's presentation of violence in *The Plough and the Stars* and the immediate violence that play prompted. 'Performing religious conservatism' takes up the controversy surrounding the attempted opening of *Within the Gates* in Boston and the official violence in the form of banning and censoring that followed. Although censorship is a less direct form of violence than is a mob attack, its aims are the same: suppression of unpopular artistic (or other) expression. The final section, 'Neglecting the later plays' explores the oblique violence of erasure that became the fate of many of O'Casey's late plays. Affecting O'Casey's reputation, income and influence, neglect is a subtle but damaging form of suppression. Despite substantial differences of detail, these three narratives reveal a dynamic pattern, dialectical in nature, in which O'Casey's challenges to the status quo stimulated violent opposition, and that opposition, at least in the cases of *The Plough* and *Within the Gates*, enabled a counter-response that exposed O'Casey's underlying political concerns to a wider audience than might be found in a theatre.

Anatomizing nationalist violence: *The Plough and the Stars*

Any discussion of O'Casey's presentation of violence in *The Plough and the Stars* needs to begin with O'Casey's attitude toward the Easter Rising; but, for O'Casey, that event is inseparably linked to the Dublin General Strike and Lockout of 1913, the formative event of O'Casey's early manhood. Before the strike O'Casey was a fervent nationalist; during the strike he was secretary of the Irish Citizen Army, the paramilitary branch of the Irish Transport and General Workers Union, formed to protect workers from police brutality during the strike; after the strike, he was a deeply committed socialist. The strike lasted nearly a year, and for O'Casey it produced a profound awakening to the importance of class solidarity. As the strike dragged on, O'Casey came to believe that, as a member of the working class, his primary antagonist was the Irish employer who daily exploited him and all other Irish working people, not the British 'colonialists' *per se.*

It was not that O'Casey accepted the colonial condition as just; it was that he understood his subjugation as primarily class based, and the employers who had kept him on the street without wages for nearly a year were Irish not British. So in 1916 O'Casey chose not to support the Easter Rising, arguing that a successful Rising in nationalist terms would empower the Irish middle class, precisely those people who had opposed the workers in 1913. In O'Casey's view, it was absurd to rely for liberation on a class whose position was dependent on the exploitation of Irish workers. These sentiments, loudly voiced, made O'Casey equally unpopular amongst Irish nationalists and Irish socialists, who, in the period between 1913 and 1916, were working together for independence from Britain.[13]

The logic of O'Casey's position was to deny the nationalist version of Irish identity, but likewise to reject its monolithic and demonic construction of British identity.[14] Nevertheless, in *The Plough and the Stars*, O'Casey's dramatization of the Easter Rising from the perspective of the Dublin slums, O'Casey recognized that there are moments of historical crisis when Marxist analysis failed to conform to the contours of reality. If, in *The Plough*, the Irish republicans and Irish socialists such as Jack Clitheroe are presented as accepting too readily the illusory solutions offered by strong, simplistic identity claims on behalf of nations, the Covey, the play's radical socialist, is shown to accept too easily the notion of an internationalism based on class alone, a collective identity that, in his formulation, does not require any further political commitment from him besides the recitation of several Marxist clichés. The Easter Rising is that moment of illumination when the claims of both nationalist and Marxist discourses are tested.

O'Casey's overall strategy was to demythologize the Rising and the nationalist discourse that created it. In the famous second act, O'Casey provocatively overlaps the speeches at a nationalist street meeting, words that were instantly recognizable to his Abbey audience as those of Padraic Pearse, one of the martyred leaders of the Easter Rising, with the drunken brawling in the pub. The nationalist speaker sanctifies violence by exploiting nationalist demonology. His speech is characterized by an explicit dichotomy of 'us' (Irish) and 'them' (British):

> *Voice of the Man.* Our foes are strong, but strong as they are, they cannot undo the miracles of God, who ripens in the heart of young men the seeds sown by the young men of a former generation. They think they have pacified Ireland; think they have foreseen everything; think they have provided against everything; but the fools, the fools, the fools! – they have left us our Fenian dead, and while Ireland holds these graves, Ireland, unfree, shall never be at peace![15]

The nationalist speaker's call for violent resistance is juxtaposed with a series of verbal and physical assaults in the pub. O'Casey's point is surely to deflate the speaker's 'God-with-us' sanctimony by underlining the quality of intoxication that links the violence of speaker and drinkers.

The Covey, the spokesperson in the play for radical socialist values, contests all nationalist appeals. In the first act, as nationalist forces are mobilizing, the Covey attacks the nationalist construction of identities by positing a scientifically grounded materialist essentialism that dissolves all national identities into a single, all encompassing generalization, 'humanity':

> Look here, comrade, there's no such thing as an Irishman, or an Englishman, or a German or a Turk; we're all only human bein's. Scientifically speakin', it's all a question of the accidental gatherin' together of mollycewels an' atoms.[16]

This view gains no adherents, if only because the Covey's anti-nationalist politics are embedded in a show-off rhetoric that alienates the tenement audience and commits him to no other action but further 'mouthing off'. When Fluther objects to the Covey's definition on grounds of obscurity, dialogue becomes altercation:

> *Fluther.* Mollycewels an' atoms! D'ye think I'm goin' to listen to you thryin' to juggle Fluther's mind with complicated conundhrums of mollycewels an' atoms?
>
> *The Covey [rather loudly].* There's nothin' complicated in it. There's no fear o' th' Church tellin' you that mollycewels is a stickin' together of millions of atoms o' sodium, carbon, potassium o' iodide, etcetera, that, accordin' to th' way they're mixed, make a flower, a fish, a star that you see shinin' in th' sky, or a man with a big brain like me, or a man with a little brain like you!
>
> *Fluther [more loudly still].* There's no necessity to be raisin' your voice: shoutin's no manifestin' forth of a growin' mind.[17]

In the bar room setting of the second act, the Covey takes up directly the missing component of class in Irish nationalist discourse:

> *The Covey.* What's th' use o' freedom, if it's not economic freedom? ... There's only one freedom for th' workin' man: conthrol o' th' means o' production, rates of exchange, an' th' means of disthribution.[18]

But if the fighting in the pub ironizes nationalist calls for violence by dramatizing the kind of boozy aggressiveness to which the characters are prone, then the characters' propensity for turning all verbal interactions into noisy squabbles deflates the Covey's Marxist pronouncements about the unity of the working class.

Nevertheless, his perception that class not nationality is the crucial determinant of identity finds support in the way O'Casey constructed the play. In the third act, as word reaches the tenement that an Irish republic has been declared and the General Post Office turned into its headquarters, some of the characters are mildly sympathetic, but the majority are hostile to the rebellion on differing grounds. Nora, for example, is afraid that her husband, who has gone out with other members of the Irish Citizen Army, will be killed and her dream of domestic bliss shattered. Bessie is a British loyalist. Whatever their political views, the tenement dwellers do not rally to the republican cause. Except for Nora, who goes into central Dublin to try and find her husband, and Fluther who follows to protect her, the tenement dwellers remain passive until word reaches them that the shops are being looted. Then they go off to loot with the rest. For them, the nationalist construction of an English oppressor is too abstract and remote from their daily struggle for them to be prepared to join the insurrection. They are not cowards; they will face bullets, but the liberation for which they are prepared to take such risks has nothing to do with British oppression or Irish independence, and everything to do with attempting to alleviate their poverty and deprivation by direct action.

The play thus lends itself to Marxist analysis even as it works to discredit the Covey's naïve interventions. Having said his piece about the means of production, the Covey offers to lend Rosie, the local prostitute, a copy of a Marxist tract, Jenersky's *Thesis on the Origin, Development and Consolidation of the Evolutionary Idea of the Proletariat.*[19] To say that Rosie's interest in such works is minimal is to exaggerate. As Ireland hovers on the verge of full-scale rebellion, the Covey's attempts at initiating the local prostitute into the mysteries of Marxism can hardly be taken as an effective political strategy.

But even a cleverer political strategist than the Covey would be unable to puncture the nationalist appeal with calls to an essentialist humanity. O'Casey is at pains to show how, for better and for worse, nationalism becomes the energizing and dominant force. Even though the insurrection is not widely supported in the tenement, when the British respond by sending in a gunboat and shelling the city, an act represented on stage in the third act by terrifying background noise, feelings about the insurrection change. Overnight, this British over-reaction galvanizes popular support for the rebels, creating Irish martyrs and heroes where only nationalist blunderers had existed before, an accurate reflection of what took place in Ireland after the British executed the leaders of the Rising.

In the first half of the play, when the only palpable British presence is found in references to 'them' in nationalist discourse, O'Casey problematizes the nationalist discourse on the grounds that the violence it advocates does not advance the interests of the tenement dwellers, who are victims less of British domination than of Irish exploitation. In the final act, when the play dramatizes the British presence as an on-the-scene muscle-flexing colonial power, bringing death and destruction to the tenements with wanton disregard of civilian life, the nationalist construction of 'us' and 'them' is more compelling, even if the nationalists are in many ways responsible for this polarized construction.

At the end of the play, Dublin is in flames, Mollser, Bessie, Jack Clitheroe and the Clitheroe baby are dead, Nora is mad, the remaining male occupants of the tenement are on the verge of being arrested and the tenement is soon to be occupied by British soldiers. Two British soldiers appear in person to remove the corpse of Mollser. They inquire about the cause of her death, and in the process they test the Covey's claim that all identity is class based.

> *Corporal Stoddart.* Was she plugged?
>
> *The Covey.* Ah, no; died o' consumption.
>
> *Corporal Stoddart.* Ow, is that all? Thought she moight 'ave been plugged.
>
> *The Covey.* Is that all? Isn't it enough? D'ye know, comrade, that more die o' consumption than are killed in th' wars? An' it's all because of th' system we're livin' undher?
>
> *Corporal Stoddart.* Ow, I know. I'm a Sowcialist moiself, but I 'as to do my dooty.
>
> *The Covey [ironically].* Dooty! Th' only dooty of a Socialist is th' emancipation of th' workers.
>
> *Corporal Stoddart.* Ow, a man's a man, an 'e 'as to foight for 'is country, 'asn't 'e?[20]

Working-class Corporal Stoddart is an international socialist in Britain; in Ireland, in response to the Rising, he accepts the essentialist identity of British colonizer. In conflating masculinity ('a man's a man'), aggression (men have to fight) and nationality (men have to fight for their countries), he provides the mirror image for the nationalist discourse of the Irish Speaker in the second act, for whom manhood, shedding of blood and Ireland were intimately connected. Given the seductiveness of these identity claims, it is not surprising that Corporal Stoddart sees the Rising as an unwarranted attack on Britain rather than as the opening skirmish of a justifiable anti-colonial struggle. In this way Corporal Stoddart makes acceptable to himself the ferocious British retaliation of which he is a part.

Despite the validity O'Casey attaches to a Marxist perspective, he shows how, at moments of historical crisis and polarization, transnational appeals like the Covey's Marxist internationalism may be superseded by mutually reinforcing yet antagonistic constructions of national allegiance. So, in *The Plough*, the consolidation of Irish nationalism takes place in the context of British counter-revolutionary terrorism. Similarly, Corporal Stoddart's abandonment of his socialist identity and his creation of a narrower nationalist self-definition occurs in the context of Irish insurrectionary activity. At this time and in this place, Marxist discourse is marginalized; but the relativity of all positions in *The Plough* strongly suggests that there will be other times when its ability to contest the narrow and destructive discourses of nationalism may prove more effective.

The subtleties of this interpretation were unavailable to early Abbey audiences, who, as might have been expected, understood O'Casey's point to be the deflation of the heroes of the Rising. When the play opened in February 1926, the first few performances were tranquil, but on the fourth night there was an organized disturbance by nationalists led by Hanna Sheehy-Skeffington, widow of one of the martyrs of the Easter Rising. Members of the audience mounted the stage to prevent the play from continuing. Barry Fitzgerald, who played Fluther Good, was reported to have knocked at least one rioter off the stage. The curtain came down for some ten minutes while police were called to restore order. W. B. Yeats made a splendid speech in defence of O'Casey, but was not heard. Anticipating the problem, he distributed a written copy of it to the newspapers. When order was eventually restored, the play resumed.[21]

Although there were no further disturbances in the theatre, the newspapers were flooded with letters to the editor, by and large sympathetic to the rioters, the most passionate of which were written by Hanna Sheehy-Skeffington, who attempted to justify her interventions on the Abbey stage by advocating 'the free censorship of popular opinion', in other words, mob violence. Clearly those offended by O'Casey's treatment of Irish nationalism thought they could deal with their irritation by shouting down the play. O'Casey, however, was not intimidated. Dismissing the letters of others as beneath notice, O'Casey defended himself against the attacks of Sheehy-Skeffington in letters to the *Irish Times* and the *Irish Independent* using arguments that made no conciliatory gestures.[22] O'Casey insisted that there were no cowards in the play as Sheehy-Skeffington had asserted, and he defended his assessment of the Covey's judgement that the Speaker's words (those snippets from Padraic Pearse) were 'dope', rubbing more salt in the wound by pointing out that 'James Connolly [labour leader, socialist and one of the martyrs of the Easter Rising] said almost the same thing as the Covey'.[23]

About a week after these letters were exchanged, a public debate between O'Casey and Sheehy-Skeffington took place in which the differences of opinion regarding the play were vented in a public forum and reported in the newspapers.[24] In this way the violence surrounding the reception of *The Plough and the Stars* became as much a theatrical event as the play itself. Moreover, the publicity surrounding the riots gave a boost to the box-office. Ticket sales for *The Plough* continued strong, and, perhaps because of the violent outburst of the nationalist protestors, O'Casey's dramatization of his counter-hegemonic views of the Rising retained their theatrical platform.[25] Clearly, the mob violence that attended the opening of *The Plough* was limited in scope and soon contained. Such was not the case with the official violence directed against *Within the Gates* when the play came to Boston.

Performing religious conservatism: *Within the Gates*

Within the Gates (1934), O'Casey's fifth play, is Depression based, full of the edginess and incipient violence of a world in deep crisis. Abandoned by her natural parents, Jannice, a young prostitute, is befriended by an allegorical character, the Dreamer, and the two attempt to fashion a life of joy and creativity in a world of sordid motives, physical illness (Jannice suffers from tuberculosis) and social disintegration. The play takes place within the gates of a park reminiscent of Hyde Park in London. Each of the four acts has a symbolic seasonal setting, beginning with the promise of spring and ending with the death implied by winter. Characters like the Atheist, the Gardener and the Policeman drift across the stage offering explanations, giving advice, sounding warnings, making minatory noises, all of which are insufficient to save Jannice from expiring on stage in the final moments of the play, the victim of poverty, rejection and a general social indifference.

Significantly, in the background on the stage throughout the play is a War Memorial which serves not only as a reminder of the Great War but also as an indicator of the ongoing class war and as a warning about the possibilities of another European war. In the foreground are the legions of the unemployed, the lumpen masses, represented by the Down-and-Outs, who march on and off stage, a chorus of the misguided and miserable, adding substantially to the sense of dislocation and anxiety produced by the symbolic War Memorial. The world O'Casey depicts in *Within the Gates* is in economic collapse, lacks social purpose, evinces a persistent hostility toward artists and other non-conformists, severely circumscribes the possibilities for individual fulfillment and happiness and is ideologically dominated by religious repressiveness. The setting may evoke Hyde Park, but its subject matter evokes Ireland as well as England in the 1930s. It is a world ready in O'Casey's view either to implode or explode.

O'Casey uses this sense of crisis to examine and reaffirm Marx's perception that religion is the opiate of the people. The play is populated with generic religious figures from Evangelists and Salvation Army Officers to an Anglican bishop, all of them insensitive to the suffering around them. Their attitudes toward Jannice are censorious. Not one of them appreciates that she has made the best of inadequate circumstances, and if there is blame, then it attaches to a society that forces her to choose between starvation and street walking. Indeed, whatever their doctrinal differences, these religious professionals direct attention away from the causes of social dislocation and toward what O'Casey regarded as the fiction of a redemptive hereafter. O'Casey uses their inattentiveness to the here-and-now to demonstrate that religion functions as a handmaiden to the oppressive status quo. In place of faith, the play valorizes 'the good fight', the often violent struggle to find purpose despite the seductions of false otherworldly hope. That this inflammatory treatment of religion would produce outrage was predictable, particularly when it was allied with experimental dramatic techniques.[26]

Within the Gates premiered in London on 7 February 1934 to mixed reviews. While some were wildly enthusiastic, others judged the play a pretentious disaster.[27] Given such a lukewarm response, it is not surprising that the play did not survive long in the West End. Despite the difficulties in London, there was a New York production eight months later. In an effort to drum up business, O'Casey came to New York a month before the show opened.[28] He gave several interviews to well-placed drama critics[29] and, on the night before the play opened, O'Casey wrote an article for the *New York Times* in which he explained his intentions and provided a key to the symbolic meaning of the characters.[30]

The first night reviews in New York were, unfortunately, as mixed as the reviews in London had been. Nevertheless, several of the most influential New York critics were ecstatic. Brooks Atkinson, writing in the *New York Times*, showered verbal confetti over both the play and the production. George Jean Nathan proclaimed the play 'one of the finest plays of our time; it is one of the most successful amalgams of true literature and true drama that our modern stage has known'. Robert Garland found the play an enriching theatrical experience, 'a passionate affirmation of faith in life', while Edith Isaacs praised the play as poetry's gift to the theatre.[31] There were nay-sayers as well. Arthur Ruhl of the *New York Herald Tribune*, for example, thought the production was 'spotty', occasionally impressive, but more often confusing.[32] John Mason Brown slammed the performance as a tiresome jumble of muddy symbolism.[33] Not every reviewer who disliked the play found the drama muddleheaded. Left-wing critic Stark Young and Leon Alexander, drama critic for the Communist *Daily Worker,* had no trouble understanding the play; they simply thought what it had to say was banal and platitudinous. Part of Alexander's irritation with the play may be attributable to the play's poetic style.[34] In this period the Communist Party sought to make drama function as a weapon of the class struggle, and the lyricism of *Within The Gates*, despite its neo-Marxist critique of religion, appeared inconsistent with that goal. Ideological opposition to the play came not only from the left but also from the Catholic right. In her article in the *Catholic World*, Euphemia van Renssalaer Wyatt attacked the play as a 'combination of clean earth and strong fertilizer'. The perceived offensiveness of the play's content also impressed Elizabeth Jordan, writing for *America*, another journal of conservative Catholic opinion. In attacking the apparent immorality and unwholesomeness of the play's content, both Wyatt and Jordan prefigure one aspect of the Boston controversy.[35]

Having done what he could to boost box-office sales, O'Casey left for home in December in anticipation of the birth of his second child in early 1935.[36] *Within the Gates* closed on Broadway on 12 January 1935 after 101 performances.[37] It was the intention of the producers to take the play on tour with the same cast to Philadelphia, Boston and Toronto, with one-night stands in Providence, Rhode Island, and Springfield, Massachusetts, and split-week engagements in Hartford and New Haven. Such, anyway, was the plan. According to an article in the *New York Herald Tribune*, advance sales in Boston already insured 'a prosperous run'.[38] Little did the author of that news report know that Boston was to become the reality test for and confirmation of O'Casey's hypothesis in *Within the Gates* that organized religion was inimical to the creative life.

The move from New York to Boston involved more than just a geographical shift. Ethnically and racially mixed, culturally diverse, polyglot, with strong left-wing political parties, New York had a considerable history of hospitality toward artistic experimentation. Boston was different. It had, by the 1930s, become a predominantly Irish-American Catholic stronghold, with strong ties to the mother country. Irish immigration to Boston over the previous fifty years had marginalized old-stock Boston Brahmins, and the anxiety and resentment associated with these shifting demographics (and the rearrangements of power, patronage and sentimental affiliation that accompanies them) were responsible in part for the explosive confrontation over O'Casey's *Within the Gates*. For those old-stock Boston Brahmins, the muscle flexing manoeuvres of Irish-American Catholic Jesuits associated with the banning of O'Casey's play must have, at some nearly conscious level appeared as confirmation that the newer immigrants wished not only to run the city but also to make Boston a satellite of either or both the Irish Republic and the Vatican.

Before the play had a chance to open in Boston and pressured by Jesuits, the mayor of Boston 'requested' that the play not be staged.[39] The use of the term 'request' was purely technical. The mayor could not unilaterally ban the play. That action could only be taken officially by the three-person Board of Censorship, and then only after the Board had seen a performance of the play. De facto, however, the mayor's 'request' amounted to a ban, as he was in a position to exert considerable influence on the Board of which he and his chief of police constituted two-thirds of the voting members. What followed from this 'request' was a lengthy and highly publicized controversy in which the forces of Catholic reaction sought to criminalize not only the performing of the play but also the selling of the text of the play and the reciting of lines from the play in venues other than a licensed theatre. As efforts by Catholics to suppress the play became more strident, they provided ample evidence that O'Casey's negative depiction of religion was correct. That stridency in turn created an opposition that took full advantage of the absurdities of the censors and made them out to be not only louts, but also clowns. The agitation itself became living theatre as efforts were made to thwart the censors by performing the play in public spaces other than the theatre, among which were, ironically, church halls.

Early on, two Jesuits closely associated themselves with the ban: Fr Terence Connolly and Fr Russell Sullivan, professors of literature and philosophy respectively at Boston College, a small Jesuit institution.[40] Fr Sullivan was also head of the Boston Legion of Decency. It strains credibility to believe that these two priests, both with Irish backgrounds, in a city with a large Irish population closely tied to Ireland, were responding to O'Casey's play in separation from any of the hostility surrounding the man and his work in the Ireland of De Valera. It seems far more plausible to see their determination to deny O'Casey access to an audience as an outgrowth of the hostility toward O'Casey cultivated on the other side of the Atlantic. They argued, as had Wyatt and Jordan before, that the play was irreligious and immoral. The first salvo on behalf of the ban was fired by Fr Connolly, who provided the *Boston Traveler* with a lengthy analysis of the play's moral offensiveness that undoubtedly did much to increase the interest of Boston playgoers.[41] In the days that followed, Fr. Connolly and Fr. Sullivan continued their attack, insisting, rightly, I think, that the play condemned religion and viewed it as futile in the modern world.[42]

At the same time as Fr. Connolly and Fr. Sullivan expounded their views, Boston theatre aficionados who did not wish to be protected from O'Casey's play by the Jesuits were beginning to express theirs. As had happened in Dublin after *The Plough* riot, the Boston newspapers swelled with articles about the growing controversy.[43] The Harvard Dramatic Club committed itself to an oppositional and interventionist role. On 16 January 1935 the Club began gathering signatures on a petition protesting the ban and circulating it at Harvard, Radcliffe, Wellesley, Tufts, the Katherine Gibbs School and the New England Conservatory of Music.[44] Several days later a citizens' committee began organizing further opposition to the ban.[45] Newspapers were bombarded with letters to the editor, the majority of which opposed the ban.[46] The National Council on Freedom from Censorship, a section of the American Civil Liberties Union, forwarded a telegram to the Board of Censors signed by various playwrights urging that the mayor's ban be lifted.[47]

The producers appealed the mayor's ban to no avail. Having prevented the play's performance in Boston, the mayor took steps to ban the sale of the text of the play.[48] The banning of the book in Boston was followed, a day later, by its banning in Cambridge, an adjoining city that houses Harvard University.[49] It appears that Bostonians, trying to find out for themselves what the fuss was all about, flocked to the bookstores of Cambridge. There, greatly increased sales of the text of the play attracted the attention of the police chief, who having read fifty pages of it, determined that it was 'immoral and indecent,' and ordered it banned. For the book to be officially banned, however, the police had first to find and buy a copy, and then charge the bookseller. Curiously, no copies could be found in Boston or in Cambridge.[50]

While the police went shopping for books, Rev. Emerson S. Schwenk, pastor of the Church of Redemption, Universalist, announced that he intended to read a condensed version of the play from the pulpit of his church on Sunday, 20 January 1935.[51] As a result of Rev. Schwenk's advance notice, his sermon was attended by a police stenographer, a number of plainclothes police, representatives of the press and about forty others. Rev. Schwenk defended the play and the right of O'Casey to be heard. Despite the interest of the police, no charges were laid against Rev. Schwenk.

Rev. Schwenk's performance demonstrated that there was a loophole in the censorship law wide enough to allow amateur dramatic groups to perform the banned play in churches and other unlicensed halls. Taking advantage of the loophole, Henry Wadsworth Longfellow Dana, an adjunct professor of drama at Harvard and grandson of both the poet Henry Wadsworth Longfellow and the novelist Charles Dana, announced that he would be reading the play on 21 January 1935, the day *Within the Gates* was supposed to open in Boston.[52] He secured the hall of a local church, but on the evening of the reading, officials at the mayor's office notified the trustees of the church that they would lose their licence to run a public hall if Professor Dana read the banned play. Under pressure, the trustees withdrew their permission, but not before a large crowd had gathered in front of the church hall. Professor Dana's lecture was moved to a near-by private home, and there he gave a one-man performance of *Within the Gates* to an enthusiastic crowd.[53]

On 23 January 1935, in response to the ban on Professor Dana's reading in the hall of the Community Church, the opponents of the ban announced that Dr Clarence R. Skinner, Dean of Tufts School of Religion and a leader of the Community Church, would take the banning of the play as the subject of his sermon on the following Sunday.[54] The sermon would be delivered at Symphony Hall. City officials understood these plans as another challenge to their prohibition on reading the play in a public hall. The venue for the sermon was, however, well chosen. A suspension or revocation of the licence of Symphony Hall would leave the famed Boston Symphony homeless, thereby infuriating an even larger segment of the Boston populace than had been angered by the banning of O'Casey's play. The sermon proceeded in Symphony Hall only after Dr Skinner provided the Mayor with assurances that he would not read the banned play.

About 1,000 people attended. Dr Skinner discussed the banning of the play. In his view, although the play was banned because it was allegedly immoral, the real reason was that 'there are special religious groups who do not want the public to see any exhibition which upholds religion as futile.'[55] According to Dr Skinner, Irish Catholics were the largest and most important group behind the ban. While Dr Skinner expressed sympathy for the hurt O'Casey's criticism of religion might give to Catholics, he nevertheless insisted that others had a right to see the play. Dr Skinner may not have read from the play, but he delivered a very public reiteration of O'Casey's critique of the role of religion. As well, his sermon made explicit the degree to which opposition to O'Casey's play was rooted in the Irish Catholic community.

Dr Skinner also recommended changes in the censorship law and in the regulation and licencing of halls and theatres. Ten days later the mayor announced revisions to the city's censorship policies. The practice of the Board of Censorship of providing opinions in advance of theatrical production would be discontinued. In future, plays would have to be produced first and judged later. While this reform abolished the policy of prior restraint, it did not eliminate censorship. Nevertheless, it was no small victory to have the mayor's ability to act unilaterally curtailed.[56]

When the play was banned in Boston, the road trip to twenty-two cities collapsed. The producers decided to capitalize on the free publicity created by the banning and bring the show back to the National Theatre in New York. It reopened in New York on 22 January 1935, and had a successful revival, largely because of the efforts to suppress it.[57] The New York revival, moreover, provided Bostonians still interested in seeing the play with their opportunity. The producers made arrangements to provide rail transportation, the O'Casey Special, on Saturday 2 February 1935 at a cost of $16.50 for those in Boston who wished to come to New York to see the show.[58]

For several weeks in early 1935 the ban on *Within the Gates* and the ensuing controversy took on a life of its own. As the mayor and his clerical allies encroached further and further on fundamental rights of free speech, they mobilized an inventive and energetic opposition that finally forced on the mayor's office important limitations on the right to ban. Officialdom prevented the play from being performed in Boston, but their attacks created a public platform in which O'Casey's critique of the reactionary role of religion was made available to far more people than would have come to the Boston performances of *Within the Gates*. In the end, moreover, the banning brought into being what it had tried so hard to prevent, the successful staging of the play, which reopened in New York for a second successful run. Nevertheless, despite the seeming resilience of the play, as late as 1996 the play had only one revival. In 1974 it had a modestly successful run in Belfast at the Lyric Theatre.[59] It has never been performed in the Irish Republic.

Neglecting the later plays

The efforts to suppress and punish O'Casey's work by direct assault (*The Plough* riots) and by legal authority (the banning of *Within the Gates*) were in some ways counter-productive. Censorship of either kind calls attention to itself and makes the work it seeks to erase more visible than it would have been had there been no attempts to suppress it. Neglect, however, is a seemingly benign cultural practice that appears to flow naturally from the perceived outdatedness, irrelevance or inferior quality of the work being marginalized. It would, however, be a mistake to view neglect as uninflected by politics. It may be that the plays O'Casey wrote after *The Silver Tassie* were less satisfactory than the plays written before, but such aesthetic judgements are not value neutral. The shunting aside of so much of O'Casey's opus is, in my opinion, rooted less in the intrinsic deficiencies of the work, and more in their radical Marxist critique of contemporary Irish society and their efforts at political change through cultural intervention. In other words, neglect is a form of censorship, less visible than the overt violence of the mob and the more subtle violence of official bans, but more pernicious and enduring.

Many of O'Casey's later plays[60] have had a bad press. To start with, a substantial number of theatre reviewers disliked them. Then, from the early sixties on, many literary critics made disparagement the dominant critical response.[61] Typical are the attenuated assessments of Robert Brustein and David Daiches, two highly regarded critics of the early 1960s. Brustein writes confidently and briefly that O'Casey 'has always struck [him] as an extremely overrated writer with two or three competent Naturalist plays [by which he means presumably the three early Dublin plays] to his credit followed by a lot of ideological bloat and embarrassing bombast'. With similar brevity and assurance, although with greater politeness, Daiches advances a judgement of equivalent dismissiveness:

> In his later plays O'Casey's own passions and prejudices tend to come between him and the dramatic work he is trying to create, and when in addition he turns to expressionist techniques suggested by German dramatists and the American Eugene O'Neill the result is generally unsuccessful.

Global in scope, mandarin in tone, devastating in effect, these pronouncements brook no opposition.[62]

Neither critic believes that O'Casey's later plays merit any attention, or that their political preoccupations (which Brustein captures in the phrase 'ideological bloat' and Daiches in the kinder, gentler, but no less denigrating words, 'passions and prejudices', both being 1960s' code for Marxism) warrant any explication. In fact, they seem to be saying, at least in part, that because O'Casey's later plays have ideological content they deserve to be neglected. Perhaps even worse, in their opinion, is O'Casey's way of giving dramatic expression to those political beliefs, which Brustein faults as 'embarrassing bombast' and Daiches criticizes as bad imitation Expressionism. Using the language of apparently value-neutral aesthetic judgement, Brustein and Daiches advance an ideology of art as autonomous that is at odds with O'Casey's commitment to drama as a vehicle for social change, and they judge him on their terms.

It is possible, of course, that O'Casey's later plays deserve their bad press, but I for one would like to come by this position via cogent argument rather than cavalier assertion. This section of the paper is an inquiry into the reasons for that glib negativity. I contend that if O'Casey's post-*Within the Gates* plays are understood in relation (1) to each other (2) to the political views the plays express (3) to the political realities of Ireland in the 1940s and 1950s, which is their subject (4) to the political attitudes and concerns of the American critics of the early 1960s who made O'Casey into a respectable academic subject, then the reasons for this negativity become apparent. Certainly there may be deficiencies in the plays, but, whatever they are, they are not explained by their bad press. In my opinion, the negativity of reviewers and critics alike is rooted in the plays' radical critique of the policies of Eamon De Valera, their attempts to subvert the status quo and their efforts at radical political transformation and change through cultural intervention.

This attitude is most apparent in the responses of Irish theatre reviewers to the Dublin premieres of the later plays, in particular to *The Bishop's Bonfire* and *The Drums of Father Ned*, reactions which then lend weight and credibility to the dismissive manoeuvres of academic critics like Brustein. In general, while paying lip service to production values, the Irish theatre reviewers were fairly explicit and vociferous in rejecting O'Casey's later plays because of their strident assault on the repressive domestic policies of Eamon De Valera, who held power in Ireland almost continuously from the 1930s to the end of the 1950s.[63] These reviewers denied that O'Casey's catalogue of De Valerean social failure was accurate. It is, to be sure, a sweeping catalogue. According to O'Casey, by the end of De Valera's tenure in office, this failure ran the gamut from clerical domination, with its attendant sectarianism, censorship and sexual repression, to economic backwardness and emigration.

Beginning in the middle 1980s, Irish historians (such as Terence Brown) produced studies that support O'Casey's view of the increasing stagnation of post-revolutionary Ireland.[64] They agreed with O'Casey that De Valera pursued ultra-conservative policies that were parochial, repressive, anti-modernist, male chauvinist and biased in favour of the Roman Catholic clergy, farmers and small business interests. O'Casey was a premature opponent of De Valera, launching his immoderate attacks before the demise of De Valera as a political force made those positions broadly acceptable. In such circumstances it is not surprising that O'Casey's pre-revisionist Irish contemporaries distanced themselves from his later work.

At least as damaging to his chances of acceptance as his hostility toward the government of Eamon De Valera was O'Casey's advocacy of revolutionary social change. It was American literary critics who were to make O'Casey a respectable subject for academic scrutiny. Unfortunately, by the time O'Casey was discovered by American literary critics in the late 1950s and early 1960s, the United States was experiencing the effects (and then the after-effects) of its most recent red scare.[65] University professors were fired for being Communists, or for being associated with Communist causes. The signing of loyalty oaths remained a requirement of employment at major post-secondary institutions like the University of California.[66] Academic criticism, like everything else, is deeply embedded in the circumstances of its creation. The anti-violence reading of O'Casey is an offspring of American O'Casey criticism of the late 1950s and early 1960s, a particularly repressive moment in modern American history. In this period, in an American university, to deal with Marxism as a respectable philosophical tradition, even if it were in relation to a prickly and iconoclastic Irish dramatist like O'Casey, was a risky business.[67]

McCarthyism inevitably influenced the assessment of O'Casey's plays by American critics. It is not surprising that critics making their way in academia during the period of McCarthyism found O'Casey's politics deeply troubling. For these and later critics strategies like periodicity were a godsend. Periodicity, or chronological compartmentalization, allows critics to separate early plays such as *Juno and the Paycock*, which lend themselves to interpretations that focus on transcendent human values, from later ones such as *The Star Turns Red* and *Purple Dust*, which are inescapably and unapologetically Marxist. At least in part a result of the segmenting and then privileging of O'Casey's 'early period', the critical attention devoted to any one of the three early Dublin plays easily exceeds the attention devoted to all the late plays combined.[68] Taking into account the reactions of the Irish reviewers and the lacunae in the American academic criticism, the narrative of O'Casey's neglect illustrates the degree to which socially created cultural artifacts create responses which are likewise socially created.

To better appreciate what O'Casey, the reviewers and the critics are up to, it is helpful to examine the reception of O'Casey's last full-length plays, *The Bishop's Bonfire* and *Drums of Father Ned.* These companion pieces, taken together, depict a dialectic of oppression and resistance. *Bonfire* portrays the Roman Catholic Church in Ireland of the 1950s as creating and enforcing political, economic and social practices best described as clerical fascism; *Drums* dramatizes the other half of that dialectic, the desire for liberation in sexual relations and revolution in political and economic arrangements, desires which are, in O'Casey's view, the inevitable and intensified consequences of repression.

It will not come as much of a surprise that these views were unwelcome in 1950s' Ireland. The premiere of *Bonfire* in Dublin in 1955, directed by Tyrone Guthrie and produced by Cyril Cusack, was a popular success despite (or perhaps because of) intermittent disturbances during the opening night's performance.[69] The disruptions within the theatre were nothing compared to the hysteria in the Irish press. Quite simply, Irish reviewers declared war on O'Casey. Some were quietly disdainful.[70] Others were openly vituperative. *The Standard,* a conservative Catholic weekly, was the worst of all, and led a lengthy campaign to discredit the play and the playwright.[71] O'Casey, however, found most provocative and off-base those commentaries[72] which claimed that O'Casey's long Devon exile rendered him incompetent to comment on the contemporary realities of Ireland, a view O'Casey disputed forcefully.[73] Subsequent productions in London (1961, Mermaid) and Boston (1988, Lyric) generated none of the buzz associated with the Dublin performances, and the play receded into theatrical obscurity where it now resides.

Given the reception of *Bonfire* in Dublin in 1955, it is curious that in 1957, the Dublin Tóstal (Festival) Council, in preparation for a theatre festival in the spring of the following year, invited a submission from O'Casey. Despite the hostility that *Bonfire* generated only two years before, it would appear that there was a recognition, possibly quite begrudging, that a Dublin theatre festival could not be launched without including Ireland's best-known living playwright. O'Casey offered the Council a new work, *Drums,* which dramatized the liberation of an Irish country town from clerical domination through celebratory preparations for a festival. Although O'Casey's new play mirrored the activities of the Tóstal, its contents were more provocative than placatory.

O'Casey's play was to be produced along with a dramatization of James Joyce's *Ulysses* entitled *Bloomsday* and three mime plays by Samuel Beckett. By early 1958, plans for the theatre festival began to unravel. *Bloomsday* was dropped from the programme. The Tóstal Council raised

various objections to O'Casey's *Drums*. These objections (like the drop-
ping of *Bloomsday*) were fueled by the refusal of the Roman Catholic
archbishop of Dublin to open the festival with a Votive Mass if either
Drums or *Bloomsday* were to be performed. Under increasing pressure to
make changes with which he did not approve, O'Casey withdrew his
play. Reading between the lines, it appears that the Tostál Council was
reluctant to reject O'Casey's play outright and be seen to be censoring
his work, so they demanded revisions they knew O'Casey would find
unacceptable in order to force him to withdraw the play and assume the
onus of cantankerousness.

In this way, like *Bonfire* two years earlier, O'Casey's newest work
became the centre of an Irish controversy. In the by now usual manner
of O'Casey controversies, articles were written, letters to the editor were
sent and answered, rumours and accusations abounded. Perhaps the
most dramatic moment of this particular imbroglio came when O'Casey,
in a tit-for-tat response to the de facto censorship of his work, banned
the production of his plays by any professional theatre in Ireland and
refused permission to Radio Éireann to broadcast *Juno and the Paycock*.
(O'Casey did not lift the ban until shortly before his death in 1964.)

In the midst of the growing furor, as a gesture of solidarity with
O'Casey and a rejection of clerical censorship in whatever guise,
Beckett withdrew his plays. Without any of the plays originally sched-
uled for production now available, and without sufficient time to make
alternative arrangements, the Tostál Council was forced to cancel the
Theatre Festival.[74]

Drums had an inauspicious world premiere in 1959 at the Little
Theater, Lafayette, Indiana, directed by Jeanne Orr and Robert
Hogan, who was then completing his doctoral thesis on O'Casey's
experimental dramatic techniques. Even though Hogan enters the
story as a director, his engagement with O'Casey is primarily text
based, and illustrates the transformation of O'Casey within his own
lifetime from living dramatist to academic subject, a transformation in
which he participated, as his letters responding to inquiries primarily
from American academics attest.[75]

In 1966, two years after O'Casey's death, Thomas MacAnna tried
to breathe new life into *Drums*, directing a production at the Olympia
(Dublin). Some twenty years later, MacAnna tried again. As artistic
director of the Abbey, he embarked on a revival of O'Casey's works,
including *Drums*. The Dublin reviewers were underwhelmed. In a
typical commentary, Michael Sheridan of the *Dublin Evening Press* found
nothing of interest in the MacAnna effort. '*The Drums of Father Ned*',

Sheridan writes, 'is a classic example of how even the great may fail, and Thomas MacAnna's overplayed and pompous production cannot rescue the diaphanous material.'[76] Like *Bonfire*, *Drums* receded into theatrical obscurity. For most of these critics, the plays were dated. By the time of their revival De Valera was long gone and Ireland had changed dramatically. Later developments such as Ireland's entry into the European Union have created an economic miracle, and with it, a much more cosmopolitan outlook. So when O'Casey's critique had immediate relevance, it was deemed politically unacceptable; when it became politically acceptable, it was perceived as irrelevant.

Although academic interest in these plays has not been great, it is certainly true that scholarship has been more attentive to *Bonfire* and *Drums* than the theatre has been. The survey form of many of the book-length studies of O'Casey's drama invite treatment of all his plays.[77] Particularly in contrast to the visceral hostility of the Irish reviews, these studies are tolerant and intelligent. Nevertheless, in dealing with the late plays, there is a well-intentioned tendency to translate O'Casey's feisty Marxism into a refined communitarianism, a tendency which effectively displaces the immediacy and topicality of O'Casey's critique of the domestic policies of the De Valera government into generalizations about the affirmation of life. It is not that these readings are in themselves obtuse or inadequate – far from it. It is just that, in de-emphasizing their social connections, the abstractions which the plays undoubtedly embody appear remote, bloodless and apolitical. The attention given to these plays in book-length studies is unmatched by an equivalent attention in articles in the scholarly journals.[78] As a result, unless they have reason to consult these books, those in the academic and literary community who do not specialize in O'Casey studies are rarely reminded that the late plays exist. So the violence being done to O'Casey's artistic achievement perpetuates itself.

The combined effect of these critical responses to O'Casey's later plays, whether on the stage or the page, has been to establish a durable paradigm of diminished expectations, making subsequent re-readings appear defensive efforts of nostalgic rehabilitation. Even so, the narrative of O'Casey's neglect tells us as much about the beliefs of reviewers and critics (and the social realities from which those beliefs emerge) as it does about the merits of O'Casey's plays. O'Casey's work withstood mob violence and official censorship. It remains to be seen whether his later efforts can survive the better disguised violence of neglect. Whatever the social progress of Ireland, the rest of the world provides ample examples of economic distress, social inequality, sexual repression, clerical fascism, book burnings and official censorship, particularly in relation to religious issues. It seems odd in these circumstances that a creative director or an adventurous producer could not find ways to make O'Casey's later plays resonate. Those directors and producers are yet to be heard from.

Some conclusions

O'Casey was a politically engaged artist. His views were heterodox. He lacked the ability to trim his ideological sails to the prevailing winds. He deeply offended many of his countrymen and country-women. He did not, according to Murray, have that smooth personal style that might have overcome some of the hostility he generated. Worse, he appeared to encourage violence and acrimony, and he seemed to thrive on dispute and controversy. He wrote about many facets of violence and he generated violent reactions to what he wrote. Some of those reactions were immediate and explosive expressions of outrage bent on silencing him and his work. Other reactions were more deliberate manipulations of custom and law that likewise were intended to mute his words. Neither of these two responses worked exactly as intended. O'Casey would not tone down. He used every opportunity afforded by his attackers to advance his own positions. After O'Casey's death, his work was academicized, but instead of an O'Casey 'industry' developing in the manner of the Yeats, Joyce and Beckett 'industries', in which the full range of each writer's work is given respectful academic attention, O'Casey's work was segmented into the early 'good stuff', that is, *The Shadow of a Gunman, Juno and the Paycock* and *The Plough and the Stars*, and the later 'not so good stuff'. It may be that the climate of growing intolerance in the world will have the positive side-effect of encouraging the full range of O'Casey's dramatic legacy to be retrieved from the undeserved obscurity into which at least the later material has fallen.

Sexing the Rising:
Men, Sex, Violence and Easter 1916

DANINE FARQUHARSON

Liam O'Flaherty's 1950 novel, *Insurrection*, makes obvious and grotesque the connection between violence and sexual pleasure amidst the 1916 Easter Rising. Protagonist Brently Madden is lost, confused and angry at his various misfortunes, as he is absorbed into the chaos and violence in Dublin. Madden is attracted to the rebels he accidentally encounters; more specifically, he is 'infected' and 'enchanted' with the 'great beauty' of Pearse's proclamation of the Irish Republic.[1] Pulled into the fighting, Madden is given a rifle imbued with such erotic connotations as to make clear O'Flaherty's awareness of the inextricable link between shooting a gun and sex:

> Like a lover in the first flush of a newborn passion, he was utterly indifferent to the presence of the creatures that dodged from his path. . . . His mind was bereft of thought; but his whole being was intensely conscious of the weapon that he carried. Its touch gave him a marvelous sense of power and dignity. . . . Such an astounding and glorious fact was beyond the realm of thought. It could only be felt through the blood, like the sensual possession of a beloved one. It was more intoxicating than the strongest liquor.[2]

Here, as in several other passages in *Insurrection*, manliness, power, virility, glory, violence and sexuality are all knotted together in an anti-romantic narrative about the birth of the modern Irish nation. O'Flaherty's criticism of revolutionary romance is obvious in Madden's lack of 'thought' and his continuing 'intoxication' by both the words of the rebel leaders and the act of firing his gun. For all the awkwardness of O'Flaherty's prose, the novel remains unambiguous in describing a circular, emotional momentum that defines the man in battle: sexual arousal changes to rage, then to joy, then to satisfaction and then back to rage.

> Like a man bedded with an insatiable wanton, he became entan-
> gled with these yellow creatures he could not master. . . . Yet
> when they charged again and he began to fire his rifle at them,
> his rage changed into a mysterious and satisfying feeling of unity
> with these men, on whom he spent his passion. . . . As he took
> careful aim and waited for the man to move forward again, a
> new and ugly passion took possession of him. It came from the
> depths of his soul, which were now being scoured for reserves of
> strength to sustain the terrible strain of battle. It was a brute
> hatred of the man that lay hidden behind the tree; no longer his
> partner in a dance of death, but another animal for whose blood
> he lusted. His barbaric joy did not last long.[3]

Madden's love affair is with his enemy (a 'dance of death'), and the tool
of his erotic and barbarous passion is his rifle. There is nothing complicated in O'Flaherty's depiction of killing a man (bloodlust) as akin to
orgasm: 'he spent his passion'. *Insurrection* is not concerned with questioning the valences of sex and violence; rather, the connection between
the two is the *sine qua non* of the story. What *Insurrection* does interrogate,
however, are the romantic visions that inspire revolutionary violence in
Ireland in 1916, as well as the consequence of fanatic following that
characterizes Brently Madden's involvement. The end result of such
romantic and violent endeavour is death and any sense of heroic,
glorious purpose in the novel is inevitably doomed. *Insurrection* concludes with Madden taking a suicidal rush at the enemy. The final
image of the book is Madden's dead body, 'each outstretched hand
gripping a pistol', being stared at with incomprehension by passers by.[4]
There is no rational reason offered for his action, there is no redeeming
moment that gives the reader any sense that all the violence had any
effect. Madden simply ejaculates all his passion in one final climax. The
sexual death drive is complete.

   As embittered as O'Flaherty's narrative can be about the leaders of
1916 and the Madden-like men who followed, the novel nonetheless
establishes a fascinating matrix of sex, violence, nation-building and
masculinity that plays itself out in different ways in more contemporary
Irish fiction set during the Easter Rising. In the following discussion
that matrix will be analysed in two such novels that sexualize the
Rising: Roddy Doyle's *A Star Called Henry* and Jamie O'Neill's *At Swim,
Two Boys*. Both novels represent the violence of Easter 1916 in relation
to sex, and not obliquely. Both have scenes of sexual intercourse right in
the middle of or during the violence of the rising, and that sexualized
violence (and in the case of Henry Smart and Miss O'Shea, the violent

sex) offers two occasions upon which to interrogate the rise of the Irish nation. What Doyle and O'Neill share with O'Flaherty's novel is a criticism of the way in which the Easter Rising has been mythologized and valorized. However, Roddy Doyle and Jamie O'Neill also use the setting of the Rising as a narrative vehicle through which to comment on contemporary Ireland. The violent sexual matrix is used by both novelists to cross-examine, albeit differently, notions of Irish heroism, identity and history. Additionally, *A Star Called Henry* engages in a postmodern critique of historical realism and *At Swim, Two Boys* must also be read as a contemporary commentary on gay rights in an increasingly globalised and Euro-centric Ireland.

'I'd spurted everything': Henry Smart becomes a man

Traditional, or official, versions of Irish history in the twentieth century begin with the Easter Rising in April of 1916: the failed attempts of Patrick Pearse and Jim Connolly to take possession of landmarks of British colonial control in Ireland, such as the General Post Office, and to overthrow British power in Ireland. The story most often told of 1916 is one of heroic martyrdom and blood sacrifice. Pearse and Connolly failed, they were executed, and their deaths ignited the dream of independence in the hearts of Irish people and spurred them on toward revolutionary war and eventual independence. I might be exaggerating the rhetoric of national romance, but not by much.

Artists such as Roddy Doyle, and contemporaries such as Neil Jordan, grew up and were educated in an Ireland where these stories were sacred, unquestioned, institutionalized. In an interview with Seamus McSwiney, Neil Jordan says:

> We were taught a version of history that stopped at 1916, basically that said that these great heroic men, Padraig Pearse, Thomas McDonagh and all went out in this glorious revolution and died for Ireland and that was it, and they were wonderful and they were pious and they were holy and they were saints. We were taught nothing about the War of Independence, the Civil War, the brutality of that period, nor the complexity of the politics or the issues.[5]

Thus, one representation of the Easter Rising has been entrenched in the Irish educational system in a particular way. Not only was the revolution 'glorious', but also the men who led the revolt and died for it were 'great, heroic men' worthy of sainthood. Jordan's 1996 film *Michael Collins* is an attempt to get beyond the myths of the Rising and present individuals caught in a messy ethical world where taking sides is a very dangerous act.[6] And yet the overall effect of the film, and one that I believe Doyle rejects in his novel, is a version of the Great Man of History. Jordan's narrative of the revolutionary period is told through the life of Collins and his death is presented in that film as the death of political negotiation and mediation. Jordan's characterization of Michael Collins borders on the hagiographic. The cinematic Collins is saucy, brutally strong and courageous; while no saint, he is nonetheless a speaker capable of rousing crowds into action, he is a powerful commander of men and a very effective wooer of women. *A Star Called Henry* stands in contrast to Jordan's depiction of Irish heroism and Irish history. Jordan's film and Doyle's novel both work against hegemonic representations of this period of Irish history, but the texts move in different directions. Jordan is recuperating one image of Collins, while Doyle roars into and demolishes many images of Irish heroism. If Doyle's novel disrupts conventional representations of heroism, he is also questioning the authority and centrality of any/all representations.[7]

Roddy Doyle's *A Star Called Henry* is about a young man, Henry Smart, who is first caught up in the revolutionary violence of 1916 and is then sucked back into the subversive guerilla war with England in 1919. Through this story Doyle tackles the behemoth of Irish nationalism, and he – unlike Jordan – does not hold back. The prevailing critical opinion about Roddy Doyle's representation of historical events in *A Star Called Henry* is that he subverts the 'official' history and popular mythologies, and by doing so he challenges the 'hegemonic nationalist version of the birth of the modern nation' of Ireland.[8] Jose Lanters is one such critic who writes that the novel 'presents events through a late twentieth-century lens that highlights politically correct issues such as class, gender, and ethnicity'.[9]

Dermot McCarthy has written that *A Star Called Henry* is a novel that should be read in a broader context that takes into consideration three recent movements: 1) the new cultural nationalism that emerged in Ireland during the mid to late 1990s; 2) the ongoing debate over historical revisionism; 3) the more recent discursive-ideological controversy over the application of postcolonial theory to Irish politics, society and culture.[10] McCarthy goes on to argue that *A Star Called Henry* is knee deep in what David Lloyd calls the 'struggle over representation of the past'[11] – a struggle between the state and its ideologues, and those with other ideological outlooks. 'Doyle has written a historical fiction that enters into a negative dialectic with both official history and elite nationalist historiography'.[12] McCarthy claims that Doyle does all this to seamlessly construct a textual fabric of history and fiction, invention and research that challenges both the history of 1916 and the genre of the historic novel itself. I agree that Doyle exposes the official histories and myths of the Irish nation to be fragile and inadequate. However, McCarthy argues that the 'most important revisionist feature of the novel is its construction of a *social* and *economic* rather than nationalist-political context for the 1916 Rising'.[13] The social/economic context is undeniably vital in *A Star Called Henry*, but the following analysis proves that a sexual context in relation to the violence of the Rising cannot be avoided, dismissed or reduced to secondary status.

If we take the Easter Rising of 1916 to be the event that marks the 'birth' of modern Ireland, then that birth had to start with sex. Doyle seems completely aware and wonderfully, subversively, interested in the connections between violence and sex and, indeed, masculinity. In the second part of the novel, which is Doyle's re-writing of Easter 1916, there is a significant scene wherein our protagonist Henry Smart believes he has been made a man. Henry is not 'made a man' by surviving the dire, abject poverty of the Dublin slums. He is not made a man by his father's abandonment of the family. He is not made a man by joining Jim Connolly's Transport Workers' Union. He is not made a man – as Brently Madden is – by becoming a soldier, by firing a gun, by killing a man. Henry Smart is made a man by one Miss O'Shea, in the basement of the General Post Office, arse stuck to a pile of stamps, at the exact moment when the glass is melting off the windows from the heat of artillery shells bombarding the rebels inside the building. The scene is worth quoting at length:

> Henry Smart, the freedom fighter, had gone down to the basement with conquest on his mind. There were new territories to explore, uncharted rivers behind little ears. I was coming off the bottom step when she saw me. She looked around, saw a clear coast and pulled me by the bandolier into the storeroom.
>
> And now she was shoving my shoulders down into the stamp sheets and lifting and dropping and there were slaps now banging out a beat and gumming my arse to the stamps. She'd break the rhythm now, again, dip herself to my face, to remind me that she was there, the inventor, and torturer if she wanted to be.
>
> Her mouth was on my ear.

– What if they come in now, Henry?

– *Who?* I said. – The other women?

She grunted.

– Pearse and Plunkett?

She licked my ear.

– The *British?*

– Oh God.

– The Dublin Fusiliers?

– Oh *God.*

– The Royal Norfolks?

–Yes.

– The Royal Irish Rifles?

– Ye*ssss.*

I was running out of soldiers. She pulled my ear with her teeth. She growled.

– The Scottish – oh fuck – the Scottish Border*ers?*

– *Maithú*, Henry!

–The Sherwood Fah-fah-foresters?

– *Maithúúúúú* – oh – *maithú*

– The Bengal fuckin' Lancers!

And we came together – although I didn't know it – in a froth that cemented the pair of us to the stamps and nearly frightened the shite out of me because nothing like this had ever happened to a woman before and I didn't know if she was dying or laughing on top of me. She hammered me into the gum. She pounded my chest, She cut my neck. She gave me a hiding I never recovered from. She growled and hummed while I guffed and heaved, my teeth were chattering, I'd spurted everything and she dumped herself beside me. We were freezing, gasping and soaked in sweat, spunk and post office glue.

– God, she said. – The mess.[14]

Obviously, there is a lot going on in this passage. McCarthy views this scene as an 'adolescent fantasy realized in the midst of adult horror'[15] and one which sets the 'erotic act of fiction midst the solemn pigeons of nationalist history'.[16] Again, I agree with McCarthy but I also believe that there is much more at work.

The first sentences set Henry up as a romantic, indeed colonial, 'freedom fighter' – off to the basement with conquest on his mind and

'territories to explore'. Even in those few sentences, Doyle unearths
baser motives than nationalism and independence behind so-called
freedom fighters. But there are other ironies at work here: earlier in the
novel Henry makes it quite clear that his motives for joining the Rising
have nothing to do with politics, colonial history or romantic dreams of
self-determination. He says:

> Why had I told the King of Great Britain and Ireland to fuck
> off? Was I a tiny Fenian? A Sinn Feiner? Not at all. I didn't even
> know I was Irish. . . . Ireland was something in songs that
> drunken old men wept about as they held on to the railings at
> three in the morning and we homed in to rob them; that was
> all.[17]

Henry's childhood is one of horrific poverty and shocking suffering
(and Doyle's descriptions of that childhood owe much to Sean
O'Casey). Henry's younger brother Victor dies of starvation and
disease in a Dublin gutter. Henry becomes involved in Jim Connolly's
Transport Workers' Union because he believes a socialist Ireland might
prevent other Victors from dying. When Easter 1916 comes along,
Henry is barely out of childhood. He tells us:

> I was fourteen. None of the others knew, or would have believed
> it. I was six foot, two inches tall and had the shoulders of a boy
> built to carry the weight of the world. I was probably the best
> looking man in the GPO but there was nothing beautiful about
> me. My eyes were astonishing, blue daggers that warned the
> world to keep its distance. I was one of the few real soldiers
> there; I had nothing to fear and nothing to go home to.[18]

Thus, Henry is no freedom fighter at all; he is barely an adolescent.
His youth and naïveté are proven in the claim he makes in the first
passage that 'nothing like this had ever happened to a woman before'.
Such is the fourteen-year old's fantasy. But Henry also sets himself
apart from the others fighting in the GPO – he is the only real soldier
there because he has nothing to lose, so he is alone in his deprivation,
in his absence of big reasons to fight. Further, his hunt for conquest is
purely sexual as he is looking for Miss O'Shea during the bombardment
of the GPO. Doyle wonderfully subverts the notion that the men who
died in the Easter Rising were not only dedicated to an ideal of an
independent Irish Republic but also that they were men at all. As Jose
Lanters has described the scene, 'for Henry, sex is a positive negation:

an affirmation of life and a way of saying "uck off" or "uck you" to the likes of Pearse'.[19]

The scene with Miss O'Shea in the basement could be read as an allegory for nation building: the young lad has rambunctious, hard-hitting, violent, sexual intercourse just as the young men of the nation need to pass through the violent fire of revolution before they can construct a new order. Sexual initiation is the rising of the nation to arms. But such a reading is too easy. First of all, it is Miss O'Shea who pulls Henry into the storeroom. It is Miss O'Shea who shoves Henry down into the stamp sheets – she controls the rhythm and the beat of the sex. Doyle takes us as far away as possible from the mythic figure of mother Ireland, the ethereal Cathleen Ni Houlihan, but I think it is far more interesting that Miss O'Shea is aroused and finally brought to climax by the mention and threat of the British soldiers. The idea of colonial violence – from regiments such as the Scottish Borderers and the Bengal Lancers (and those names are not randomly chosen) – is enough to sexually stimulate Miss O'Shea.

Further, if one places the scene in suspension for a moment – Henry is on top of the pile of stamps, Miss O'Shea is on top of him, the stamps would have been British in 1916 and so the face on the stamps would have been that of King George V – what one has is Miss O'Shea using Henry to take the gum out of King George V. Henry Smart may be our little man of history, but it is Miss O'Shea who pounds the life out of the face of colonial power in Ireland. 'All this uninhibited, unbridled sex reverses the national myth, according to which every Irish woman is a chaste virgin or an adoring mother, and according to which "excess of love" means dying for your country. Either version, of course, is too extreme to be anything other than a myth.'[20] Could there possibly be a more revisionist image of Irish rebellion? Is not this scene, and the repeated references to 'the mess', exactly the kind of representation that contemporary theorists claim to be a key to reading postcolonial texts? These types of questions are vitally important to the current debates and dialogues in Irish studies, but such questions also lead to my own ambivalence toward the full impact of Doyle's demythologization project.

The desire to seek out new perspectives on identity often retains – or is itself retained and restricted by – a narrow understanding of the subject. Terms of subjectivity are frequently set by political and economic rather than social or cultural history. Irish culture does not arrange itself neatly under the heading 'Irish'. For Irish feminism, questions of nation and identity are particularly vexed because women's bodies are regulated – in terms of birth control, abortion, even divorce laws – differently in the Republic than in Northern Ireland. Contempo-rary Irish women writers, critics, and artists turn again and again to the interrelation between body and land, and the embodied nature of citi-zenship and subjecthood. I mention all this because I believe that Doyle and others are trying to mark out a space between reverence and scepti-cism; to create narrative strategies that do not merely clear away tired clichés, but also examine the power of clichés and stereotypes them-selves. Readings that use postcolonial, or feminist, or cultural theories should locate moments of transience, instability or inauthenticity; and thereby question the frames in which ideas of state and nation and self are articulated. In writing a scene where a woman symbolically and sex-ually violates the colonial power, has not Doyle achieved a significant rejection of Irish myths of masculinity and nationality?

My answer is yes and no. In their post-coital conversation, Miss O'Shea asks Henry if he is surprised at her and Henry replies 'No' and then he thinks to himself 'that's the biggest lie of my entire life. I was still so surprised, I was almost unconscious'.[21] Then Miss O'Shea clari-fies what her motives are for being involved in the Rising: 'I'm here for my freedom. Just like you and the men upstairs. . . . I want my freedom to do what I want. Do you know what I'm talking about Henry?' 'Yeah, I said – you want to behave like a man. But they'll never let you'.[22] Henry is right in the logic of the novel's narrative: Miss O'Shea is not allowed to behave like a man. What is disappointing about these char-acterizations of Miss O'Shea is not her rebelliousness but the fact that Doyle's masculinization of her is rather traditional. There are few fic-tional representations of Irish female rebels. Where they exist they are peculiar, odd and outcast.[23] While I believe that Doyle is satirizing the feminized image of Ireland as a Dark Rosaleen or a victimized Hibernia, I am disappointed that his representation of the female rebel is so close to earlier examples. Miss O'Shea is completely other. Fol-lowing the Easter Rising, the leaders of the IRA view Miss O'Shea with suspicion because she is untrustworthy. Her radical manoeuvres (burning buildings and intimidating the public in the countryside) label her 'a holy terror' and a threat to the IRA's objectives. Her life is in danger at the end of the novel as the organization decides that she must be eliminated. And while Miss O'Shea does not die, she is imprisoned. The de-feminizing of Miss O'Shea is not nearly as radical as Doyle's flawed narrator-cum-freedom fighter, Henry Smart.

The novel is really all about Henry: he is our protagonist; he is the site of Doyle's resistance to nationalist myths. The conclusion of the novel makes Doyle's commentary on contemporary Ireland very clear: the economically successful Ireland of the late twentieth century (and early twenty-first century) is 'the genealogical descendant' of those same gangsters, thugs and criminals that Doyle characterizes as Ivan Cooper and Alfie O'Ganduín.[24] For Roddy Doyle, Ireland's revolution born in 1916 is not only unfinished but also a failure: 'not because of the status of the north, but because of continued class and gender inequities that can be traced directly back to the nation's founding moments'.[25] And while Doyle goes far in questioning the status and representation of Ireland's founding moments, I believe an opportunity has been lost to push the envelope of the image of women in 1916 and the revolutionary years.

So it is that I come to Jamie O'Neill's *At Swim, Two Boys*, a novel that makes homosexual the all too heterosexualized Easter Rising. While the novel is in many ways a traditional romance (coming of age during the birth of the nation), that such love is between two boys is a significant shift in Irish literary production. The novel marks another challenge to the myths and sacred stories of Irish nationalism. If we return to my earlier formulation of 1916 as being the birth of the modern Irish nation, and that birth is necessitated by a sexual act, then what happens when the central sexual moment in the violent narrative of the nation is between two men?

'Come what may': Jim and Doyler's Utopia

At Swim, Two Boys, set in 1915 and 1916 Dublin, traces the maturing relationship between Jim Mack and his boyhood friend Doyler amidst the increasing activities of the Irish Citizen Army and the Irish Volunteers. Reviewers and critics have often noted Jamie O'Neill's stylistic inheritance of both James Joyce and Flann O'Brien (the latter most obviously acknowledged in the title), as well as how Oscar Wilde haunts the novel in the character of MacMurrough – imprisoned for two years hard labour in England for sodomy.[26] Within such an intimidating literary sphere, O'Neill establishes the erotic and romantic love between Jim and Doyler clearly and directly in the context of the love of nation. Writing in *The Guardian*, O'Neill offers the following as the novel's inspiration:

> One evening I stood under the walls where Pearse was executed, and I wondered was the love of Ireland, for which he gave his life, so different from loving an Irishman?

In London, when asked was I Irish, I would often reply, 'No, I'm gay'. For the two identities seemed incompatible In *At Swim, Two Boys* I wanted to ask the same question and answer, most affirmatively, Yes. Two Dublin boys would fall in love, and in their friendship discover their country whose freedom was worth their fight.[27]

O'Neill may be channelling the great Irish writers of the early twentieth century, but he also shares with Roddy Doyle a desire to re-write the narrative of the Irish nation and to re-envision the tropes of Irish heroism and masculinity. As Joseph Valente argues, '"queer nation" represents the master trope of *At Swim, Two Boys*'.[28] In order to queer the Easter Rising, O'Neill turns to non-Irish writers such as Walt Whitman and St Augustine to herald the kind of Irish nation about to be written. Even though critic Michael Cronin emphasizes the novel's failure to articulate any significant political agency for gay men and that 'gay identity can only be imagined in the novel as a personal liberation, without any actual political valence',[29] *At Swim, Two Boys* nonetheless adds another crack to the foundation of Irish nationalist mythologies and it does so with love and sex and Utopia. If, as Cronin argues, 'masculinity, sexuality (and in a particular way, male homosexuality) and revolutionary nationalism constitute faultlines in contemporary Irish culture',[30] then one more faultline needs to be added into the mix: violence.

At Swim, Two Birds opens with an epigraph from Walt Whitman's famous 'Calamus' no. 5 poem, eventually titled 'For You O Democracy'. The epigraph, 'I will make inseparable cities with their arms/about each other's necks;/By the love of comrades' is a cry for a democratic nation held together by – let us say for now – brotherly love. Whitman's Calamus poems are famously held together by 'a sentiment of manly attachment'[31] even if Whitman variously denied their homoeroticism. What is more interesting in the context of this novel and this essay is that O'Neill has removed the next line of the poem: 'By the manly love of comrades'. Removing the reference to manly love in this instance, the first page of the novel, before the manly love of the characters becomes obvious, is coy and teasing. However, any one familiar with Whitman would immediately recognize the homosocial desires at play. The title in combination with this epigraph makes it plain that O'Neill will not only be sexing the history of Ireland in 1915–1916 but will also be queering it as well. The direction of such re-working is toward a possible future not for the novel's characters but for a contemporary Ireland in the middle of change: 'For O'Neill, the only good nationalism, nay the only Irish nationalism, is a queer nationalism.'[32]

The first part of the novel, set up with those Whitmanesque notions of a loving democracy, establishes the love between Jim Mack and Doyler alongside the various movements toward Irish independence. But, as Cronin rightly points out, the homosexual relationship between the two boys is but 'grafted' onto the history of the Rising instead of made integral and connected. 'O'Neill is concerned with registering the historical emergence of male homosexuality as a social identity and as a form of human subjectivity, as distinct from a sinful, criminal, or psychopathic activity' argues Cronin and '*At Swim, Two Boys* again privileges the private sphere of the sexual and affective bonds of identity over the political as a locus of agency'.[33] In Cronin's view, the Easter Rising is really just a convenient moment in time upon which to write Jim Mack's self-actualization as a gay man. I agree that there is no sustained politicization of the boys' love in terms of contemporary Irish politics, but a brief analysis of the consummation scene will prove that not only is the love between two men a political act, but it is also doomed to a violent end in the logic of O'Neill's novel. O'Neill may not have produced a satisfactory critique of contemporary Irish politics, but he does articulate a future possibility.

Even though young Doyler is a Larkinite and a keen member of James Connolly's Citizen Army, it is really the Wildean character of Anthony MacMurrough who connects Irish politics to the rights of gay men. While swimming at the Forty Foot (and swimming is the *leitmotif* of the novel), MacMurrough saves a man from drowning: that man is Edward Carson – the famous prosecutor of Oscar Wilde as well as one of the fomenters of 'Orange trouble in his native sod'.[34] As MacMurrough retells the event to his Aunt Eva (the one who draws MacMurrough unwillingly into the ranks of the Irish Volunteers), he relishes the end of the tale wherein he kisses Carson:

> Yes he had kissed him, clamped his mouth on that awful mug, lips on rubbery lips he pressed, propelling his tongue inside the portals, kissed for all he was worth. And Carson had staggered away, spitting and spluttering as though all the Irish Sea had vomited into his mouth. And MacMurrough had laughed like a schoolboy, and he heard now his aunt was laughing too.[35]

This childish act of revolt, like a 'schoolboy', causes laughter but does nothing to alleviate MacMurrough's fear of being again caught and imprisoned for gay sex. What is more interesting to me is that the act of saving a man from drowning is re-enacted later in the novel after Jim and Doyler make their pledged swim to the Muglins on Easter Sunday 1916.

Jim and Doylers' love for each other has a talismanic centre in their oath to swim together to the Muglins, 'come what may'. All through 1915 and the early months of 1916, while Connolly and Pearse marshal their forces, Jim and Doyler become closer friends, Platonic lovers until the epic swim to the islands where they have sex for the first time. That Jim and Doyler miss the beginning of the Rising is important: there are more vital actions of love to be done than fighting for the nation (although Doyler only shows up for the fateful swim when he hears that the Rising has been called off). The consummation of their relationship occurs far away from the violence of the Rising, and it occurs in what Cronin labels a 'pastoral' environment cut off from the demands of family, society and history. Further, their sexual coming together has profound personal significance for Jim, as it is the moment when he achieves a self-awareness and even a unified idea of himself.

Before Jim and Doyler swim to the Muglins, Jim is haunted by feelings of disassociation. 'He was aware of his detachment, of his being a witness to the moment, witness not participant.'[36] Jim has always suffered from such detachment. Earlier in the novel Jim is uncomfortable with the signifiers of his identity: 'he counted the clues to his identity: school cap, shop name on bike, bills in the pannier. His availability to interpretation intimidated him'.[37] Jim chafes against an all-too easy reading of who he is, and part of what attracts him to Doyler is the latter boy's confidence: 'it awed him that Doyler was not bemeaned by his life as Jim felt bemeaned by his. The lithe and wind-tanned body awed him too, so that he dared only glance at it obliquely'.[38] Jim is established in the early parts of the novel as a watcher and as an unformed identity. His sexual relationship with Doyler will not only solidify his identity but also bring Jim into agency: 'This is my body. See how it fits. Everything fits.'[39] Immediately after this wondrous transformation of self, however, Doyler nearly drowns in the return swim to the shore.

Before the young men have sex on the Muglins they plant Jim's home-made green flag on the island. Doyler may have clear political beliefs, but Jim is simply marking the island and the flag as commensurate with his love for Doyler. Their sexual union is narrated with repeated references to their 'arms' about each other as if they are enacting Whitman's dream of an American nation, but it is also a moment of sexual union that is beyond historical time. Over and over again Doyler says, 'there's all the time'. Utopian bliss is what characterizes this sexual union. I am using Richard Kearney's definition of

Utopia, wherein myth 'opens up a "no-place" (*u-topos*). It emancipates the imagination into a historical future rather than harnessing it to the hallowed past.'[40] Kearney sees utopian myth as 'oppositional' and 'predicated upon an operation of estrangement. It alienates us from the inherited state of affairs and engages in the imagining of an alternative community, other ways of seeing and existing.'[41] Within this definition Jim and Doylers' love and sexual union is a utopian myth – it is enacted away (estranged) from the inherited state of affairs of the Easter Rising in Dublin. What is fascinating about O'Neill's myth of the Rising is that the 'imagining an alternative community' is done by MacMurrough; he is the one whose nationalist dream is not Pearse's or even Doyler's socialist world, but a 'nation of the heart'.[42] Later in the novel Jim makes it clear that his nation is entirely constructed around Doyler: 'He's my country'[43] and MacMurrough is left as an outsider, a watcher. He initially constructs the image of the boys' love and union as utopian, but he is also the one who must save their bodies from an inevitable destruction of that bliss.

As if Jim and Doyler's utopian moment does in fact parallel the Easter Rising, their return swim is darkened by Doyler's near-drowning because he is entangled in Jim's flag. This near-death is anticipated with O'Neill's epigraph to the second part of the novel from St Augustine's *Confessions*, book 4, chapter 4. O'Neill keeps the epigraph in Latin (Rex Warner's English translation is: 'you took him away from this life, when he had scarcely had a year of this friendship with me, a friendship that was sweeter to me than all sweetness that in this life I had ever known'[44]) and as such is another form of estrangement. Readers are perhaps held back from realizing a death will occur, or O'Neill is commenting on the ancient histories of love between men. Whatever the case, the epigraph signals an end to any utopian visions.[45]

Jim and Doyler are both saved from drowning because MacMurrough has rowed out to witness their swim and the consummation of their love. In a deadly rewriting of the kissing Carson scene, he saves the drowning man once more:

> He could make out one head in the water. There was a slick on
> the surface, a spill of something – never oil? The glare was bewil-
> dering. He had to throw water in his eyes. One head, yes. Down
> it ducked. Not oil: that wretched flag. He shouted to the men,
> 'Row, row', as he pulled at his clothes. The head came up. It was
> Jim. A breath, then down again. The flag was sinking, had sunk.
> But Jim was safe. He registered no relief. A kind of training took

over, that his mind and dreaming body these months had rehearsed. . . . He kicked at the current. His eyes still smarted, but the water was clear. He saw the cloth, a dark jelly-fish below. Beneath it, the boy had stopped struggling. In silence, dreamily, MacMurrough unwound the cords that had wrapped themselves round, propelled the imponderable weight to the surface. . . . He dragged the boy to the stern and Jim, inside now, helped pull the body over.[46]

The sex ends with near-death and the need of a dramatic rescue. Doyler almost dies because his body is caught up in the make-shift green flag. However, Doyler will actually die within a few more pages. While Doyler is recovering from the swim, Jim steals his uniform and heads into the fray of the Rising. Doyler and MacMurrough eventually figure this out and follow Jim into the violence. Doyler dies, Jim becomes broken, bitter and vengeful:

> He never looked again for his friend, until one time, though it was years to come, years that split with hurt and death and closed in bitter most bitter defeat, on time when he lay broken and fevered and the Free State troopers were hounding the fields, when he lay the last time in MacMurrough's arms, and MacEmm so tightly held him close: his eyes closed as he drifted away, and that last time he did look for his friend.[47]

And thus the idyllic swim to the Muglins and the sexual bliss encountered there actually set up a critical paradigm for the Easter Rising: *At Swim, Two Boys* criticizes the usurpation of brotherly love in the name of war and nationhood. The logic of the novel is the logic of O'Neill's two epigraphs. There is a dream of a nation and that dream dies when the 'sweetness' of friendship dies; manly love is doomed in the violence of national war. Jim's disaffection with absolutely everything but revenge at the end of the novel is the result of the twisting of love and friendship in the name of war. The end of Jim's life and his new-found sense of self becomes the beginning of the modern Irish nation. The novel may indeed play into contemporary notions of a plural, liberal Irish world, but it does so at a heavy cost. The penalty for the rise of the nation is the death of friendship and love and sex.

While *A Star Called Henry* sexes the Easter Rising in such a way as to interrogate prevailing myths and icons of the rebels in Dublin, *At Swim, Two Birds* lays bare the damage done to possibilities and dreams of a future because of the violence. Both Roddy Doyle's and Jamie O'Neill's novels present the Easter Rising in radically different terms from the 'traditional' story I outlined earlier in this essay. Both writers are also working with what can now be called a tradition of de-mythologization in the Irish novel that arguably began with Liam O'Flaherty. Despite the power of all three radical critiques, sex, violence and masculinity remain contested faultlines in Irish history and the literary representation of Easter 1916.

'Dash and Daring':
Imperial Violence and Irish Ambiguity[1]

TIMOTHY G. McMAHON

Reading violence: China, 1900

'There is no further reason to doubt the reliability of the latest news from China regarding the Legations in Pekin [*sic*] and their occupants', pronounced the shocked leading article in the *Freeman's Journal* of 17 July 1900. 'Both, it is only too certain now, belong to the past.'[2] This sombre conclusion seemed, at the time, beyond question. According to patchy reports cabled from Shanghai by the correspondent for the *Daily Mail*, forces associated with the so-called 'Boxer' movement – whose attacks on missionary stations and businesses had received considerable attention in European newspapers throughout the spring and early summer – had moved with fury against Beijing's diplomatic quarter on the night of 6–7 July. The nearly two thousand Europeans in the city were holed up in the British legation, but their defences – including a small force of Chinese soldiers – were few, and a desperate attempt to break through the Boxer lines, with European men forming a square around their women and children, failed. In turn, the *Freeman* reported, the 'revolutionary horde' 'became like wild beasts' and assaulted them using artillery and light arms. 'When the heavy guns were loaded, they were all fired simultaneously, and the foreigners were swept away like grass that is being cut. The Boxers rushed upon them and hacked and stabbed at those who were dead as well as those whom the guns had not killed.'[3]

Similar, shock-filled tales adorned the pages of newspapers of all political stripes in Ireland. For instance, the *Belfast Newsletter* claimed that only a people 'bereft of humanity' could have perpetrated such acts, while the *Irish Times* mourned the dead and called for punishment to be meted out to their 'murderers'.[4] The assault upon the legations confirmed Western powers in their resolve to act jointly against the Boxer movement, but the siege itself did not result in the massive loss of life apparent from these early reports. Indeed, when relief forces arrived in Beijing in mid-August, they found that only sixty-six foreigners had been killed and another one hundred and fifty wounded.[5] For the purposes of the present study, however, the inaccuracy of these reports is of less interest than is their common depiction of the Boxers' inclination, as Easterners, to employ violence against their European 'victims'.

Irish identity and imperial violence

As scholars have broadened the concept of 'the political' to encompass all aspects of cultural exchange, they have raised the question of how far one might also extend the adage that 'in politics, perception is reality'. If, in fact, one can apply that aphorism to culture, it has profound implications for understanding the construction of identity. One's self-perception, either as an individual or as a member of a collective body, is inherently interconnected with power relations – a contested and ever-shifting terrain, but a terrain that can, I submit, be charted with the right tools.

One possible method of mapping shifts in identity would be to select a period when opinion shapers – such as public officials, the media or members of the wider community – attempted to establish or re-establish the parameters that defined a contested identity. During such periods opinion shapers express assumptions or make claims about a group's characteristics, its past behaviours, its beliefs and expectations, and its position relative to others. On close examination such statements may be shown to be false, but their very presence in the public sphere play a role in shaping perceptions about the group at a given point in time. Whether one's statements were grounded in fact or fiction, to be considered as an opinion shaper, an individual or a group must have a message and a means to disseminate that message beyond a core group of like-minded thinkers.[6]

Two important caveats ought to be made about any attempt to gauge the impact of opinion shapers on questions of identity. First, one should be careful not to read exceptional voices as representative of opinion shapers. In order to avoid this trap, one must look for *patterns* of expression over time and through several incidents rather than merely select provocative statements pertaining only to a single incident or momentous event.[7] Second, one must be aware that opinions can and do change over time. Such shifts must then be explained through careful attention to the political, social and cultural changes that affected opinion shapers and, ultimately, the general populace whom they informed, represented, and/or influenced. It is in studying such dynamics that we can better understand the mutable nature of identity.

In order to test this methodology I want to focus on a period at the end of the nineteenth century when the question of Home Rule for Ireland was becoming a key issue in the United Kingdom. This era was also the highpoint of the age of new imperialism, which was marked for Britons by numerous incidents, including the Afghan wars, the Boer wars, the establishment of a protectorate in Egypt, the Mahdi wars, the Fashoda Crisis and the Boxer Rebellion in China. From the late-1870s, Irish nationalist spokespersons in Parliament and their allies in the press objected vigorously to the most acquisitive acts undertaken by successive Crown governments, seeing them as parallels to past British aggression in Ireland. More recently, however, scholars of Ireland have recognized that Irish men and women played key roles in these very theatres of empire, as missionaries, soldiers, merchants and civil servants. Thus, as Joseph Lennon noted in his important study *Irish Orientalism*, the Irish relationship to the Empire was liminal: the Irish belonged to it and yet they did not.[8]

Indeed, the double attitude of the Irish toward the Empire was perhaps most evident in press accounts of violence on the imperial frontier. Press sources would, of course, serve as only a single example among the many opinion shapers that fashioned Irish identity, but the nineteenth-century newspaper press was highly influential in the United Kingdom. As one authority on the press and Irish identity has pointed out, 'journalists, readers, and politicians regarded the press as an authoritative expression of public opinion. The public in turn used newspapers as a primary source of political information and as a tool to effect desired political change.'[9] In looking at accounts of violent incidents – including incidents perpetrated by imperial forces against native peoples and actions by native peoples aimed at westerners – I want to ask several pertinent questions: did the nationalist and unionist press portray violence perpetrated by Europeans and non-Europeans in different ways? If so, what assumptions lay behind these differences, particularly about whether or not violence is acceptable when perpetrated by one group or in a certain way? And what light might these accounts of imperial violence shed on the shaping of Irish identity in the Home Rule era?

Such an exercise is fraught with methodological pitfalls. For example, the selection of newspapers and frontier clashes is necessarily arbitrary: coverage of other incidents may have provoked very different commentaries from the same newspapers, *and* coverage in different newspapers than those examined below may have created different pictures as well. Thus, I propose to examine incidents that book end the last two decades of the nineteenth century from two separate theatres of empire – Egypt and the Sudan[10] during the 1880s and China at the time of the Boxer rising. In order to ensure relative balance in terms of the editorial stances of the newspapers from which I have collected data, I have looked at two large circulation unionist papers – the *Irish Times* and the *Belfast Newsletter* – and two large circulation nationalist papers – the *Freeman's Journal* and the *Nation*.[11] One should recognize as well that while Irish newspaper editors often wrote their own leading articles (what are called editorials in the United States), their news coverage of events outside of the United Kingdom consisted primarily of redacted stories from British newspapers or wire services. Therefore, since my intention is to focus on opinion shapers, my evidence will come primarily from the commentaries offered in the leading articles of the papers under review. Recognizing, however, that the selection of what news stories to include and the interplay of news stories with editorials are important to creating readers' views of events, I will occasionally point out distinctions between the news stories and editorial coverage of the same events.

During the years under review Irish men and women became quite familiar with various imperial crises through the press, including the United Kingdom's increased role in Egypt and the Sudan after 1880 and the response of the Boxers in China to the rapid expansion of Western spheres of influence in the 1890s. With regard to the former situation, both the British and the French governments throughout the later 1870s and early 1880s had sought to stabilize the financially insolvent Khedivate (government) in Egypt, which – though nominally a province of the Ottoman Empire – had been run as a separate state since the early nineteenth century. Although British and French officials may have helped control the Khedive's financial crisis, they also catalyzed instability in the state on two fronts. On the one hand, they exacerbated growing nationalist sentiment among members of the Egyptian army associated with Colonel Arabi Pasha. On the other, they lent focus to an Islamic separatist movement led by the charismatic Mohammed Ahmed – known as El Mahdi (the 'Chosen One') – in the Sudan, a region that had been incorporated into the Egyptian state only a few decades earlier.[12]

In 1882 when the administration of W.E. Gladstone authorized the bombardment of Alexandria to face down troops loyal to Arabi, it involved the Grand Old Man in what might be called the muddy swamp of state-building. These actions profoundly angered at least four blocs of opinion: indigenous forces in Egypt and the Sudan; French business and government circles, which felt that the British had unfairly used the unrest of 1882 to seize control of Egypt; Irish nationalists – the *Nation* described the initial campaign as 'the Alexandrian Infamy', 'a national crime', and a mark of 'British Hypocrisy';[13] – and British Tories and their Irish allies – the *Irish Times* revelled in the apparent split between elements in the Liberal Cabinet and did not hesitate to point out the ongoing ministerial muddle over Egyptian policy until the Gladstone government fell in 1885.[14] The fate of the government had been virtually assured after Gladstone's decision early in 1884 to send out General Charles George Gordon on an ill-fated mission to relieve Egyptian troops stranded at Khartoum. The Gordon mission backfired on the prime minister when the Mahdi's forces trapped and killed this 'eminent Victorian' adventurer.[15] It would be more than thirteen years before Egyptian and British forces under General Horatio Herbert Kitchener wiped out the Mahdi's forces at Omdurman, finally securing control of the Sudan.[16]

Slightly more than a year later, in China, several thousand members of a militantly xenophobic religious sect known as the I-ho Ch'uan (the Boxers) lashed out against growing Western influences in their homeland.[17] Focusing their actions in the northern provinces of Shantung, Shansi, and Chihli, the I-ho Ch'uan were an entity unto themselves, but by the spring of 1900, they were receiving support from the government led by the Dowager Empress Tzu Hsi. During the summer months they laid siege not only to the diplomatic quarter in Beijing but also to the port of Tientsin. Wherever they went, the I-ho Ch'uan targeted symbols of the economic and cultural encroachments that had marked the expansion of European influence during the preceding decade: merchants, railway engineers, and Christian missionaries. Moreover, they showed a special contempt for those Chinese who had converted to Christianity or who worked for western employers. For much of the summer rumours fed concerns in Europe and the United States that the entire diplomatic community had been slaughtered during July. This phantasmagoria led to a brief spell of Great Power unity, including the dispatch of troops and ships to combat the Boxers and to rein in Tzu Hsi.

What can coverage of such events tell us about efforts to define Irish identity? First, when imperial forces engaged in violent acts in defence of European lives or interests it was generally seen as acceptable in the unionist papers. The nationalist papers, meanwhile, distinguished

between the actions in 1882 and what they saw as the more justifiable
response of soldiers and sailors to the mixed signals they received from
the Gladstone government in 1884 and especially the threat to European religious, economic and strategic interests in China in 1900.[18]
Within these accounts there were different inflections, however. For
instance, the *Irish Times* rejoiced in the joint actions of English, Scots and
Irish sailors and soldiers as a sign that the kingdoms were truly united
as a British state. Thus, after the battle of Tel-al-Kabír in September
1882, at which the army under Sir Garnet Wolseley defeated Arabi's
forces, the leading article dismissed those who had predicted defeat:

> Malicious prophets, whose veiled enmity to their own country's
> flag suffers immediate rebuke, learn that the Irish soldier fights
> as loyally for his Sovereign as any other Briton, and is first in the
> rush and boldest in the stroke. Foot to foot with the gallant High-
> landers, the Royal Irish – meet brothers – marched steadily
> onward in the darkness to the task before them . . .[19]

The nationalist press was, not surprisingly, less comfortable with the
multi-ethnic makeup of the imperial forces in the Sudan. Still, both the
Freeman's Journal and the *Nation* recognized that the dangers and successes of the frontier could be shared by those labelled as Irish fighting
under a British banner. For instance, in its news summary of General
Gerald Graham's encounter with Osman Digna, one of the Mahdi's
most capable lieutenants, at Tamanleb in 1884, the *Nation* pointed out
that the imperial forces had included the Scottish Black Watch regiment
and the Irish Fusiliers under the command of Sir Redvers Buller. At a
key moment in the battle, the report noted, Osman's men had breached
the 'English' square, but Buller's Irish force 'advanced to the assistance
of their wavering companions, and this timely help saved the British
arms from what would probably have been a total defeat'.[20] Meanwhile,
when the *Freeman's Journal* gave its account of Wolseley's ill-fated campaign to relieve Gordon at Khartoum, it described Wolseley (who had
been born at Goldenbridge, Co. Dublin) as 'the Irish general'.[21]

Nevertheless, both nationalist papers expressed concern about
violent excesses perpetrated in the name of civilizing Egypt and the
Sudan, and such actions were consistently labelled as 'English' or
'British'. In 1882, for example, the *Nation* refused to accept that the
destruction of Alexandria had been caused by Arabi Pasha's men,
instead noting that 'brute force, as was fully anticipated, is to be the
arbiter in the East'.[22] Two years later, the *Nation* claimed that even a
supposedly advanced nation could resort to 'uncivilized' excesses

when confronted with a foe 'that still cannot boast the veneer of Western culture, and that has no press to state its case to the rest of the human race'.[23] The French and the Americans, according to the *Nation*'s leader writer in March 1884, had 'sinned' in this way, but 'of all those offenders England is the worst, and of this fact the present "war" in the Sudan furnishes the latest and not the least convincing proof'.[24] Specifically, the paper claimed that 'English' troops had burned entire villages and taken no prisoners in any engagements, instead killing an estimated 16,000 men to date, while Admiral William Hewitt had offered a reward for the assassination of Osman.[25] The *Freeman* recalled such accusations several months later and voiced the hope that the soldiers under Wolseley's command would refrain from such actions, implying that the original reports may have been true. After Wolseley's arrival at Khartoum, the paper then drew an important implied contrast to the earlier English excesses by congratulating 'the Irish' commander for his 'splendid qualities of stern resolution as well as sterling judgment'.[26]

Nevertheless, in their treatment of non-European combatants, nationalist and unionist papers showed remarkable similarities, incorporating Orientalist assumptions about Egyptian and Sudanese propensities toward bloodlust and cunning, as well as racialist assumptions about the superiority of European peoples to non white peoples and the relative 'ranking' of non white peoples.[27] Readers should note in the example from the *Nation* cited in the preceding paragraph that the 'sins' of English, French and American arms resulted from encounters with enemies 'that cannot boast the veneer of Western culture'. The *Irish Times*, meanwhile, recoiled at reports of the destruction of Alexandria's European quarter in 1882. Showing none of the scepticism evident in the *Nation*'s account, the unionist daily argued that Arabi's forces had engaged in 'a murderous orgie [*sic*]'.[28] These actions showed him to be more savage than 'the worst of the tribes that have their lairs in the southern jungle of the African continent'.[29] His defeat two months later, the paper claimed, had 'saved civilization from an Oriental despotism'.[30] The *Nation*, while railing against the destructiveness of the invasion, was not immune to such depictions of Arabi. In a biographical profile of the Egyptian commander picked up from an American newspaper, the paper recorded that 'he is ambitious, restless, contentious'. According to this account, readers of the *Nation* learned that Arabi would 'permit his *ill-balanced zeal* to blind his judgment'.[31]

This editorial emphasis on emotion and bloodlust, rather than intellect, as the primary motive forces for Sudanese and Egyptian forces reoccurred throughout the Mahdi wars. Thus, in February 1884, after Colonel Valentine Baker's men had defeated a force of Osman Digna's at El Teb, the nationalist *Freeman's Journal* noted that Osman had decided not to spend much time regrouping before attacking the imperial troops again: 'Osman has rightly estimated the character of his army, to the cohesion of which nothing is more destructive than inactivity, and upon whose dash and daring more confidence is to be placed than on the equally requisite qualities in soldiers – steadiness and discipline.'[32] 'We are told', the leader continued,

> that these brave Arabs have determined to face the Krupp guns and the rifles of the British with nought [*sic*] but spear and shield . . . Osman's answer to the English proclamation shows that the fanatical zeal of the Sheiks has been inflamed, and that the Arabs will rush upon the British ranks with a heroic devotedness, rivalling [*sic*] if not surpassing, the reckless valour displayed at El Teb. Such a foe cannot be encountered, even under the most favourable circumstances, without great danger and considerable cost.[33]

Similar themes of racially determined fanaticism and depravity reappeared in even starker language during the Boxer rising. The *Freeman's* commentary, for instance, was tinged with condescension in spite of the paper's recognition that the Chinese had a right to object to outsiders partitioning their territory: 'Human nature – even Chinese human nature – could not endure to look on quietly at this process forever.'[34] Once aroused, the *Freeman* claimed, the Chinese 'invariably' showed themselves to be as 'savage' as black Africans: 'They murder, burn, loot, and commit the most awful crimes against Christians and inoffensive strangers. They are naturally a peaceable, industrious, plodding people, but when they declare war against the stranger they are more sanguinary and cruel than Zulus.'[35] The following month, the unionist *Belfast Newsletter* described the Boxers as 'swarming' into Beijing, 'urged on by fanatical frenzy against foreigners'. 'China is in a terrible condition at the present moment . . . The interests of civilisation are gravely imperilled.'[36]

The 'interests of civilization', we have seen, had underlain unionist rhetoric as far back as the Egyptian campaigns, but it was equally pronounced in the nationalist and unionist coverage of the Boxer rising.[37] Much of this common ground was attributable, no doubt, to the Boxers' particular emphasis on attacking Chinese Christians and European missionaries. Thus, both the *Belfast Newsletter* and the *Freeman's Journal* in early July 1900 noted comments by the Archbishop of Can-

terbury to the effect that 'a barbarian temper has put all the missionaries of the Church in that part of the world in the gravest peril'.[38] Fears
that all symbols of Western culture and authority were under assault
seemed to be confirmed two weeks later when reports reached Ireland
that the Boxers had massacred the diplomatic legations at Beijing. The
Freeman considered the news to be ominous:

> This is the greatest blow Western civilization has sustained in
> modern times. How is it to resent it? Apparently the [European]
> Powers are unable to agree amongst themselves, so that as
> matters stand at the moment, Europe and Christianity are
> utterly powerless to assert themselves . . . The fact is that Europe
> stands aghast at this ominous uprising of the Yellow Race [*sic*]
> and its terrible sequel, and what the outcome of it all will be for
> Western civilization and the world no man can tell today.[39]

Indeed, the papers under review considered the outbreak of violence
in 1900 potentially to be a manifestation of a coming clash between the
Eastern world and the West. Such notions had been present in Irish
public discourse since at least the preceding year, when the Anglo-Irish
writer Standish James O'Grady had produced a serialized futuristic
novel (*The Queen of the World*) in the *Kilkenny Moderator* and the *Irish Weekly
Independent* depicting a world dominated by a tyrannical Chinese
empire.[40] Thus, what filled the leader writer of the *Irish Times* with fore-
boding was that the Chinese had adapted to the techniques of modern,
western warfare:

> The Yellow Man has shown himself expert in the use of such
> weapons as are found in the hands of Western European troops.
> More than this, he has manifested a courage with which he was
> not credited, and lashed now to fury by the sights and sounds of
> war, fearful, too, that further encroachments will be made upon
> the sacred soil of the Celestial Empire, he at last has taken the
> initiative, and boldly threatens the borders of Russia.[41]

Meanwhile, in its ongoing discussion of the Boxer movement, the
Freeman's Journal sympathised with the desire of many Chinese not to
have their ancient civilization completely destroyed by Western
encroachment. But its editorials betrayed a dim view of the condition of
China at the turn of the twentieth century:

> There is no race in the world that stands out from the rest with
> such marked peculiarities of shape and make and mind and

> manners and customs. They have a kind of Rip Van Winkle
> civilization, which was in vigorous growth when the other
> Powers of Europe were mere babies. But that premature Chinese
> civilization has grown ugly and decrepit in its old age.[42]

As a result, the *Freeman* claimed, Chinese prejudices against the rest of
the world had grown 'in intensity', which created a dangerous situation
for the rest of the world. 'Under the surface of stolid calm', the leader
continued, 'fury passions lurk, to leap at any moment into destructive
activity. Many things combine to make the race formidable. Their
teeming numbers, their powers of labour and endurance, their stolid
contempt of death for others or for themselves.'[43]

Such depictions of violence – real, supposed, or expected – on the
imperial frontier shed enormous light on the shifting efforts to define
identity in the Home Rule era. In particular, they make clear that an
influential corps of Irish opinion shapers from both the unionist and
nationalist traditions stood in the mainstream of European racialist
thought in the late nineteenth century. But they did so for very different reasons. On the one hand, unionists saw themselves as heirs to
the besieged of Londonderry and the victorious forces on the Boyne.
Faced with the prospect of a Home Rule government, which would be
dominated by men tied to agrarian agitation, attention to the empire
emphasized their place in the larger British community: they celebrated and feared for the empire in the face of preternaturally violent
foes abroad and at home. On the other hand, nationalists had to overcome the hurdle of racialism within the European context, where 'the
Celt' was assumed to possess many of the same inherently violent
traits attributed to non-European peoples. By staking out a position as
a Western, civilized people who opposed Oriental violence, they distinguished Irish agitation – including the ongoing land campaigns –
from that of the 'savage' races.

Such a claim was more clearly made by nationalist opinion shapers
at the time of the Boxer rebellion than it had been during the
Egyptian campaigns of the 1880s, and it served as a crucial riposte to
the specifically racial rhetoric employed by opponents of Home Rule
in 1886 and 1893. Most famously, at the time of the first Home Rule
bill, Lord Salisbury couched his opposition to the measure as a
defence of representative institutions, which could not be trusted to
racial inferiors. In a speech to the National Union of Conservative
Associations in 1886 Salisbury stated that self-government could not
be confided to the Irish any more than it could be granted to the

Hottentots of the Cape Colony.[44] 'When you come to narrow it down', he said,

> you will find that this which is called self-government, but which is really government by the majority, works admirably well when it is confided to people who are of Teutonic race, but that it does not work so well when people of other races are called upon to join in it.[45]

Thus, by increasingly differentiating the 'Irish' from the 'savage' races, nationalist opinion shapers positioned Irish identity uniquely as western yet distinct from either those unionists claiming a British identity or from Britons themselves. Thus, in their attention to violence on the imperial frontier, nationalist opinion shapers laid claim to the ability of the Irish to stand on their own.

Writing an Orange Dolly's Brae

SEAN FARRELL

Come all ye blind-led Papists, wherever that ye be,
Never bow down to priest or Pope, for them they will disown;
Never bow down to images, for God (you must) adore
Come, join our Orange heroes, and cry 'Dolly's Brae no more'.[1]

On 12 July 1849 a large body of Orangemen, military and police clashed with an armed Catholic crowd determined to block a controversial Orange procession at Dolly's Brae, an isolated pass between Rathfriland and Castlewellan in the southern part of County Down. The fight quickly moved from ritualized threats to murderous violence with terrible effect: at least nine men and women died in the clash. After a contentious investigation three prominent County Down magistrates, the Earl of Roden and Francis and William Beers, all influential figures within the Loyal Orange Order, were suspended for their roles in the affray. Moreover, in response to the furor caused by the clash and its aftermath, the Whig government passed the Party Processions Act in 1850, which would be used to make partisan marches expressly illegal for the next twenty years. With the controversy that surrounded the event, it should come as no surprise that Dolly's Brae quickly became a symbol of loyalist martyrdom, Catholic treachery and British betrayal within Orange political culture.[2] Historians, however, have not accorded the fight the same significance. While nearly all modern surveys of the period mention the clash, there is only one scholarly article on Dolly's Brae itself, a short, largely descriptive piece by Christine Kinealy.[3] While Kinealy's essay is clearly written and a welcome addition to the literature on nineteenth-century sectarian violence, it's hardly exhaustive. The one full-length study in recent years, W.J. Martin's *The Battle of Dolly's Brae, 12th July 1849*, was published by the Grand Orange Lodge of Ireland and seems much more concerned with defending the Order's stand on Drumcree than providing an historical

90

analysis of sectarian relations in mid-nineteenth-century Ulster.[4] Given the importance of the fight to evolving communal identities in the north of Ireland, the absence of scholarly work on the affray is unfortunate and more than a bit troubling, symptomatic of a broader problem within Irish historiography. While there has been a great deal of excellent work done on particular aspects of Ulster sectarianism in the late nineteenth century,[5] there has been comparatively little work done on the experience and nature of sectarian violence,[6] particularly when we compare Ulster to other frontier or divided societies around the world. On the plus side there have been two substantial examinations of sectarian violence in the North of Ireland in recent years,[7] but neither work has the theoretical sophistication or creative methodological innovation that characterizes the best recent work in British history and beyond.

Recent trends in the study of violence hold out tantalizing promise for the study of sectarian conflict. In examining how the actual experience of violence is erased from thickly constructed 'national' narratives, historians like Gyan Pandey, Linda Colley, Kathleen Wilson and Jill Lepore have focused our attention on the cultural construction of violence, particularly on the interrelation between violence, its representation and communal formation. Jill Lepore is particularly eloquent when she describes the importance of these linkages:

> To say that war cultivates language is not to ignore what else war does: war kills. . . . Wounds and words – the injuries and their interpretation – cannot be separated, that acts of war generate acts of narration, and that both types of acts are often joined in a common purpose: defining the geographical, political, cultural, and sometimes racial and national boundaries between peoples.[8]

This focus on the relationship between violence, the writing of violence and the construction of communal identities has been tremendously productive, providing rich insight into a wide array of previously marginalized subjects. Within Irish Studies it has perhaps been best employed by Kevin Kenny in his award-winning study of the Molly Maguires.[9] This cultural approach has obvious applicability to the study of sectarian violence in the north of Ireland, not least because of the sheer torrent of words written about Catholic/Protestant violence in nineteenth-century Ulster.

The sectarian riots that increasingly coloured Ulster's and especially Belfast's reputation did not suffer from a shortage of textual description. Between the inquests and investigative reports of a rapidly expanding British state, fairly detailed coverage in the lively reports of the Irish and

British press and a substantial polemical literature sharpened by the increasingly contentious politics of a rapidly politicizing island, a wide array of players created and used representations of nineteenth-century Catholic/Protestant violence for a variety of purposes. Historians long have recognized the value of these reports in documenting the increased tempo of communal violence in modern Ulster. What has not received sufficient notice is that these representations of sectarian clashes are an inextricable part of the violence itself, that they are essentially contests over the control of what violence meant and thus give us a view of how communal identities evolved, how these meanings were fought over by various players and why they remained so powerfully relevant even as northern society changed so radically. After a brief overview of the Dolly's Brae clash itself, the remainder of this essay centres on an analysis of the Orange Order's writing of Dolly's Brae, focusing on two questions: 1) how efforts to militarize representations of the Catholic participants at Dolly's Brae were utilized to clearly articulate the meaning of the conflict; and 2) the ways in which narratives of female participation in the riot were framed to solidify already powerful notions of communal categorization. By looking at how gendered narratives of the Dolly's Brae fight were constructed to assert fundamental communal lines of division in mid- to late-nineteenth-century Ulster, we get a better sense of how the language of violence was employed to reinforce and extend the power of sectarian division.

The Dolly's Brae fight of 1849

Like most large-scale nineteenth-century sectarian riots the Dolly's Brae fight was shaped by the dynamic interaction between national and local politics and had an almost choreographed quality to it. Located two miles outside of Castlewellan, Dolly's Brae itself had been a party flashpoint since 1814, when a young Catholic man had been killed there in a sectarian clash. According to local legend, his mother's dying injunction had been to 'never let the Orangemen pass'.[10] Of course, whether the anecdote was true or not is beside the point; local historical narratives marked this space with a personalized symbolic sensitivity – above all, giving Catholic opponents of Orange power politics an emotive legitimacy to block marches across the pass. Fortunately, this did not prove to be much of a problem, as both parties developed an informal compact during the intervening years – local Orange lodges simply avoided this controversial space during the marching season. Of course, this local compact was aided by national developments, particularly the Orange Order's official abolition between 1835 and 1845. This happy, if rather tense, calm was not to last.

While the Orange Order was officially reconstituted in October 1845, the key events in Orange renewal occurred in 1848, when the formation of the nationalist Confederate Clubs combined with the news of revolutionary attempts across Europe to create an environment ripe for a loyalist comeback. Saying that these desperate times called for Orange renewal (both the French and Repeal examples were specified), the Order called all Orangemen to march to display their loyalty on the Twelfth of July. At one such gathering in Lisburn, The Revd H. Hodson, after a rousing sermon directed against Repeal, popery and national education, called for Protestants of every class to 'take refuge in our Orange ark'.[11] These loyalty meetings drew thousands of participants from across Ulster (with a large meeting in Dublin as well) and received at least benign tolerance from a Whig government preoccupied with the Irish Famine and the impending threat of nationalist rebellion.[12]

It is this altered national context that tipped the precarious balance forged in south Down. Capitalizing on the rising value of 'loyalty', Rathfriland Orangemen decided to commemorate the Twelfth of July in 1848 by walking in procession through the district for the first time in years. In marching to Tollymore Park, the Earl of Roden's estate near Bryansford, the Orange marchers had their choice of two routes: an old road leading directly through Dolly's Brae and a new more circuitous path. In 1848 magistrates and the police talked the Orangemen into taking the new road, which they believed would prove less contentious with the local Catholic population. The re-routing of the procession seemed to be successful; there were no major incidents in July 1848.

In the wake of the Twelfth celebration in 1848, local Catholics taunted their Orange rivals, circulating a song that condemned the marchers for their cowardice in taking the new road. The first months of 1849 saw a cycle of violence accelerate in the region; on 7 February an Orangeman named David McDowell was beaten to death in Garvaghy parish on his way back from a lodge meeting. A week later, Orangemen marching in McDowell's funeral (some observers reported several thousand participants) wrecked twelve Catholic homes in Tullyorier townland.[13] On St Patrick's Day, processionists fired shots over the head of the magistrate William Beers and his family at his Brook Cottage home.[14] More seriously, partisan marches triggered violent riots in Crossgar and Downpatrick, clashes that claimed at least two lives.[15] In the opinion of one local magistrate these troubles were directly linked to the affray at Dolly's Brae:

> ... a very bad feeling prevails between the parties in the neighbourhood of Rathfriland; the cause of that is that in February last a man named McDowell, an Orangeman, was killed; ... these events increased the bad feeling, which had previously been dying away; indeed, it dies away every year, til about the 17th March and 12th July, and then the devil seems to get into people.[16]

The magistrate's seasonal explanation for sectarian violence aside, there can be no doubt that these local clashes helped forge an environment in which both Orange leaders and the rank and file felt they needed to march through the disputed area in 1849. As another magistrate put it, 'I think it was a point of honour with the Orangemen to go through the Brae'.[17] Whatever the reason, the decision to take the old road through Dolly's Brae created a potentially explosive situation.

Both local and national officials were certainly well aware of the potential for trouble at Dolly's Brae. Several local magistrates petitioned the government for extra police and military resources to preserve the peace and the government quickly complied, sending extra troops, police and two experienced stipendiary magistrates, George Fitzmaurice from Roscrea, and Joseph Tabuteau from Wexford, to prevent party conflict.[18] With all this in mind, Major Arthur Wilkinson positioned his troops on some strategic high ground near Dolly's Brae in the early hours of 12 July 1849. A Ribbon party approached the Brae later that morning, determined to block the passage of the Orange procession. Seemingly surprised by the military presence there, they took up a position in a nearby field. Armed with scythes, pikes and some firearms, two groups made up this Catholic crowd, local men and women and a large number of men from nearby Catholic parishes. In later testimony the local priest, The Revd Patrick Morgan, stated that most of the crowd came from surrounding parishes (a three–four mile area), effectively countering some of the wilder conspiracy theories that had Ribbonmen travelling long distances to get to the party fight at Dolly's Brae.[19] At the very least, it's clear that many of the people in the area were simply villagers determined to protect their homes and ride out the partisan storm caused by the Orange procession through this contested area.

At about eleven o'clock in the morning the Orange procession finally approached Dolly's Brae. Between 1,200 and 1,400 Orangemen reportedly took part in the march, which ran from Ballyward Church to

Lord Roden's demesne at Tollymore Park. The processionists advanced in typical fashion; orange sashes and banners were on display and the air shook with the rhythmic sounds of drumming. One of the banners reportedly read 'No Repeal', nicely underlining the connection between the politics of the street and nation. The marchers clearly expected some sort of trouble; one magistrate estimated that five hundred men had guns with them.[20] Hoping to keep the two parties apart, magistrates and police positioned themselves at the head of the procession. The tactic seemed to work, as the marchers filed through the disputed ground with little trouble. There was a slight disturbance when a group of Catholic women gathered at the roadside to verbally abuse the Orange processionists, but on the whole the authorities seemed pleased with the relative tranquility of the morning. As the procession marched away, Major Wilkinson turned to the local Catholic priest, saying, 'Now that they have got through, I hope the Orange leaders will try and persuade them to return by some other road.'[21] Whatever the answer, the morning had passed as well as could have been hoped.

When the Orange marchers arrived at Tollymore Park, they proceeded to a large meadow, where a tent and platform used the previous day for school children were kept up for the festivities. The proprietor of Tollymore Park, the Earl of Roden, was one of the true grandees of the ultra-Protestant cause in Ireland. Widely known for his active role in advancing Protestant religious education throughout the island, Lord Roden also held the position of Deputy Grand Master of the Orange Order. As the marchers arrived at his estate, Roden's servants provided them with food and beer, which were no doubt welcomed on this exceedingly hot day. One magistrate, George Fitzmaurice, talked with Lord Roden himself, asking him to use his influence with the Orangemen to persuade them to avoid Dolly's Brae on their return march. Roden answered that while he would certainly make the attempt, he feared he had little influence over his plebeian brethren.

Throughout the afternoon several speakers entertained the crowd from the platform. At least three of the orators doubled as magistrates: Lord Roden, William Beers, and Francis Beers. Although each had promised to discourage their followers from returning via Dolly's Brae, none of the speakers did so. In fact, William Beers distinctly advised the Orange party to return home through that contentious space. Giving information before the government investigation that followed the riot, Beers stated that he had not told the Orangemen to change course because he believed that such advice would have split the respectable Orangemen away from plebeian activists determined to force the controversial pass again. Echoing the social control theses regularly given by nineteenth- and twentieth-century Orange elites, Francis Beers stated that by keeping the group together, the respectable members of the march could better moderate the behaviour of their more unruly brethren. Ironically, both Catholic priests offered similar analyses of their relationship with their co-religionists at Dolly's Brae.[22] Depending on your perspective, the deadly fight that ensued either demonstrated the tenuous limits of elite and pastoral social control or a certain economy with the truth.

The marchers approached Dolly's Brae at about five o'clock in the afternoon. Catholic women were again in the forefront of the opposition, labelling the Orange processionists as 'prisoners of the police'.[23] With two-thirds of the procession already through the pass, however, it looked as if the day might pass without serious incident. At this point disaster struck. Someone fired off a squib near the head of the procession. Two members of the Catholic crowd responded with gunfire, aiming several shots at the rear of the parade. Chaos broke loose – Orangemen shot wildly at their Catholic opponents, who returned fire as best they could. Finding themselves under attack from the hill, a body of police under the command of Sub-Inspector James Ponsonby Hill, charged up the slope to dislodge their assailants. The party quickly broke under the assault, and the actual conflict was over in a matter of minutes. Behind the scenes, however, Orangemen remained quite busy. Taking advantage of the confusion of battle, several Orange marchers fired indiscriminately at local Catholic men, women and children. Loyalists also wrecked a number of houses, breaking windows and furniture and setting them ablaze. Seeing the destruction, the police and military rushed back to stop the carnage but were unable to prevent the destruction of these homes. Major Wilkinson recalled 'the houses were evidently fired by stragglers from the main [Orange] body; saw nine or ten houses, on both sides of the road, on fire'.[24] For all their purported efforts, however, the police did not arrest a single Orange perpetrator. The infamous fight at Dolly's Brae was over. In many ways, however, the fight had just begun.

The battle to frame and define the meaning of the deadly violence at Dolly's Brae began in earnest in the immediate aftermath of the conflict. After hearing evidence from a wide range of magistrates, policemen and soldiers, and confirming the deaths of eight Catholic villagers, the coroner's report placed the blame for the clash firmly on the aggressive behaviour of Catholic Ribbonmen. Designed to quell the growing furor over Dolly's Brae, the inquest only fanned the flames of public discontent, particularly the coroner's argument that the Orangemen had the right to march and that the deaths of the four villagers (another four were lying mortally wounded in Castlewellan dispensary) were labelled 'justifiable homicide'.[25] Local anger was echoed in the House of Commons, where several MPs highlighted the Orange Order's role in the deadly affray. Clearly taken by surprise by the continuing uproar, the government announced that Walter Berwick, described by *The Times* as a 'staunch Whig',[26] would lead an investigation into the events at Dolly's Brae. Held in a schoolhouse in Castlewellan in August and September 1849, the inquiry heard testimony from many of the same figures who had participated in the coroner's inquest. While many of the players were the same, the tone of Berwick's investigation offered quite a stark contrast to the coroner's inquest. Berwick's report highlighted the destructive impact of party processions and placed a great deal of blame on the partisan actions of the three Orange magistrates, the Earl of Roden, and Francis and William Beers.[27] After detailing his frustration at William Beers's inability to name more than a single Orangeman after hosting them at his estate and then spending the day with the processionists, Charles William Rutheven, the Crown Inspector for County Down, vented sarcastically to the Under Secretary Thomas Redington: 'You will judge of that simple fact'.[28] Taking its cue from the report, the Whig government stripped the Earl of Roden and Francis and William Beers of their commissions as justices of the peace in County Down.[29] Moreover, the investigation accelerated the government's efforts to pass new legislation designed to permanently ban partisan processions in Ireland.[30] The result, a new Party Processions Act, was passed the following year and remained in place until 1872. If the Rathfriland Orangemen had won back their 'honour' at Dolly's Brae, the price had been quite high indeed.

The importance of writing sectarian violence

As noted earlier, the fight to control the meaning of Dolly's Brae commenced in the immediate aftermath of the thirty-minute long fight. Orange elites and their establishment allies seemed to win a solid victory at the inquest, when the coroner's report labelled the Ribbonmen the primary aggressors. *The Warder*, a hard-line loyalist newspaper, took up the pen, calling the Ribbon attack 'a treacherous stain upon a glorious day' and upping the number of armed assailants from 1,000 on the 14th of July to 2,000 on the 21st.[31] At a celebratory dinner party that week in Downpatrick William Beers waxed eloquent in support of the Orange party:

> They had only lately celebrated the anniversary of the Twelfth and such an anniversary, as it would have been, only for the little blot, if blot he could call it. No, it was a treacherous attempt to betray innocent Protestants of the district, he had been well aware of the plots which had been got up against them, but knew that God was with them. There was nothing contemplated by their enemies but murder and treachery . . . they had the blessing of many clergy and brethren with them at Dolly's Brae, but it was no longer Dolly's Brae, as it had since been christened King William's Hill.[32]

Beers and other members of the Orange elite portrayed the Dolly's Brae fight as the product of Catholic conspiracy and aggression, a discourse with deep historical resonance in the north of Ireland. This narrative had been relatively easy to put forth in the comparatively controlled atmosphere of the coroner's inquest; after all, an armed and organized Catholic body had fired upon the Orange processionists and the police and military at Dolly's Brae, making it quite easy to place the clash in a reductionist narrative of 1641, 1798 and all that. Unfortunately, the combination of outraged public opinion – both nationalist and liberal Protestant – and critically, an unsympathetic Whig government, meant the advent of a formal government inquiry, a much tougher arena in which to write this Orange Dolly's Brae. Here, the militarization of their Catholic opponents as the historic enemy was complicated by the rather tricky fact that the lion's share of casualties were non-combatants. The effort continued nonetheless, and even a brief examination of this process gives us an important insight into the roles these clashes played in the maintenance of communal identities.

It was clear from the outset that the government investigation was not going to be particularly sympathetic to the emerging Orange interpretation of events. Early on the second day of the investigation Walter Berwick made it clear that he viewed both parties in equal terms (particularly galling to Orangemen and their supporters) and that the procession had been illegal: 'both bodies, having these intentions (to force or block the pass), and assembling armed, were evidently illegal'.[33] In this atmosphere the exaggerated rhetoric of *The Warder* was relatively muted, but witnesses still repeatedly referred to their opponents as rebels, emphasizing the military drilling they did under the command of

Captain James Lennon, a veteran who was said to be the Ribbon leader. Moreover, a number of testimonials exaggerated Ribbon numbers and weapons, providing every man with a gun and a pike, itself deeply resonant of sectarian atrocity tales of 1641 and 1798. More pointedly, Orange leaders were silent about the nature of the day's casualties. After playing up the loyal roles that Orangemen had played in helping policemen dislodge their rebel assailants (stories denied by several of the policemen present), William Beers stated that he had not heard that a little boy and an old woman had been killed that day.[34] This particular silence, so essential to the Orange writing of Dolly's Brae, would only deepen in the following decades.

It is important to note that this was very much a minority view within Castlewellan National Schoolhouse, let alone the county, province or island. At the county level, William Sharman Crawford, a liberal Protestant landlord and politician noted for his advocacy of land reform, joined with thirty-two other County Down magistrates in 'deploring the late violence at Dolly's Brae and requesting the government to consider a ban on all party processions in Ireland'.[35] Within the schoolhouse, the dominant interpretation among government and military officials seemed to be that sectarian violence was a natural and almost genetic part of Ulster society. On the one hand, this was definitely a self-interested take, in that it was typically used to absolve the magistrates and military/police for their roles in the affray. After all, if the parties were determined to attack one another, what could the authorities really do but regulate these troublesome people. Walter Berwick took this very tack, stating that if it was not for the 'position taken by the military, hundreds of lives would likely have been lost'.[36] More distressing to Orangemen and their allies was the fact that this interpretation put Ribbonmen and Orangemen on equal footing. Indeed, given the emerging parlance of hardening racialized language in an expanding British empire (Thomas Carlyle's 'Occasional Discourse on the Negro Question' was first published in 1849),[37] it is interesting to note that two soldiers placed Dolly's Brae in a broader imperial context, with one sergeant testifying that if the military had confronted the processionists they would 'have come into collision with the party as with the Sikhs at Ferozeshaw', while another related that he would 'as soon have taken a drink from a black Indian as one of them'.[38] While the editors of *The Warder* made no comments about these colonial comparisons, they were quite bitter about the lack of distinction being made between loyal Orangemen and treacherous Ribbonmen, pointing out that the Lord Lieutenant, the Earl of Clarendon, had found little trouble making such a distinction amidst the revolutionary turmoil of 1848.[39] It goes without saying that the Catholics who appeared at the investigation tended to offer different interpretations of the events entirely, typically centring on their status as the victims of Orange aggression.

It was, of course, this 'two parties' notion that won the day in 1849, resulting in the demotion of the three magistrates and the passage of the Party Processions Act the next year. And indeed, as the tempo of sectarian rioting accelerated in a rapidly growing Belfast, an increasing number of British officials would adopt the view that sectarian clashes were somehow inherent to Ulster society, reflective of the peculiar flaws of these peculiar people. But if the Orange interpretation of the Dolly's Brae did not find broad acceptance in the 1850s, its simple tales of Catholic perfidy, British betrayal and Orange martyrdom made it especially useful and popular within Orange political culture – a minority one among Ulster Protestants until the early 1880s. This can be seen in the proliferation of references to Dolly's Brae in the loyalist press and increasingly in Orange songs and popular histories of the late nineteenth century. Predictably, *The Warder* and various like-minded papers of political Protestantism continued their tales of Orange martyrdom and Lundy-esque British betrayal. More interestingly, this interpretation of Dolly's Brae quickly joined the pantheon of emblematic events in Orange histories. While we do not have the time and space to fully analyse late nineteenth- and early twentieth-century Orange histories for their treatments of Dolly's Brae, even a brief examination of one prominent example, R.M. Sibbett's *Orangeism in Ireland and Throughout the Empire* (first published in 1915), shows the resonant power of this Orange narrative.

Dolly's Brae's importance to early-twentieth century Orangeism is clearly evidenced by the fact that Sibbett devotes nearly twenty-five pages to the clash and the ensuing investigation. Looking closely at his narrative we see the same militarization of the Orange processionists' Catholic opponents, who are described as both threatening and child-ishly incompetent:

> The Ribbon Party, after the Orangemen had disappeared, entertained themselves by exploding their firearms and kindling fires, . . . Ammunition was plentiful, for, in addition to what had been otherwise obtained, they managed to secure a barrel of gunpowder which a carrier was conveying to a merchant in Castlewellan. During the afternoon, . . . they engaged in maneuvers, deploying and forming in column, imitating the

> regular exercises of a regular army. Indeed, as a military spec-
> tator afterwards remarked, they enjoyed a perfect field day.[10]

Sibbett's elaborate militarization of the Orange marchers' Catholic foes clearly echoes (and is closely rooted in) the testimonials of Orangemen and their allies. But this was no mere retelling of an Orange Dolly's Brae. Sibbett's rich and resonant use of the language of empire was driven primarily by the decidedly contemporary needs of Home Rule politics. Like teenagers playing dangerous war games, Sibbett's Ribbonmen clearly were not to be trusted with the responsibilities of self-government. Not surprisingly, his broader narrative centres on the Ribbonmen's murderous intent, Orange gallantry and British betrayal; there is no mention of loyalist violence or a single Catholic casualty.

These same themes are evident in Orange songs. While the version of Dolly's Brae that remains one of the Order's most popular songs was written in the direct aftermath of the clash, Georges Denis Zimmerman lists at least six other ballads on the same subject and John Moulden's more recent treatment lists twelve, testament to the narrative power of the Orange writing of Dolly's Brae. In these musical narratives Catholic villagers, women and children again were simply erased from history, so that the Orange heroes could face a suitably armed and dangerous if craven and easily vanquished masculine foe. A version in *The Crimson Song Book* (1911) takes up these themes with vigour:

> The battle it raged loud and keen along the mountain side,
> To save ourselves as best we could, our ranks we opened wide;
> The volleys from the rebel guns had no effect at all,
> For not a man among our ranks fell by a Papish ball.
>
> As fearlessly we charged on them, their terror it was great,
> Through rocks and whins, to save their shins, they beat a fast retreat,
> The Coolagh Tykes threw down their pikes and boldly ran away,
> And cursed the day they came to fight at fatal Dolly's Brae.
>
> The battle being over, and glorious victory won,
> We reached our homes that evening by the setting of the sun.
> Our wives and sweethearts met us, returning home that day,
> With shouts of joy they greeted us safe back o'er Dolly's Brae.[41]

The image of Catholic foes as both threatening and comically incompetent when faced with Orange bravery certainly echoed the testimonials that Orangemen and their allies had used in 1849 to construct their own Dolly's Brae. In 1911, of course, as the Home Rule Crisis deepened, this narrative had a wider applicability.

By updating and reinforcing the firm boundaries between Protestant and Catholic, so eloquently laid out in the image warehouses of Sir John Temple's *History of the Rebellion of 1641*[42] or Sir Richard Musgrave's *History of the Rebellion of 1798*,[43] Dolly's Brae helped to keep a rich Catholic/Protestant discourse at the centre of Orange political culture. In times of political crisis, of course, this resonated deeply in the broader communities of Irish and British unionists. But it was more than just an updating of communal tropes: Dolly's Brae was even used to reinscribe the Ulster landscape itself. The defining lyric of the most popular version of Dolly's Brae centred on the phrase 'Dolly's Brae no more'. This was a reference to William Beers's famous statement that after the fight, Orange processionists had renamed Dolly's Brae 'King William's Hill', in effect rewriting the south Down countryside to reflect Orange dominance. The geographic description did not take, but the lyric remains resoundingly popular within Orange political culture. While the Orange narrative of Dolly's Brae would not find a ready audience outside this influential Orange minority for quite some time, it helped keep communal identities vital in an era where sectarian divisions seemed to be fading. When the Home Rule Crisis made Catholic/Protestant political divisions central to Ulster and Irish politics, this type of pan-Protestant ideology was available and potent, partly because of sectarian riots like the fight at Dolly's Brae.

Another striking aspect of the various testimonies and cultural productions of the Dolly's Brae fight centres on the ways in which representations of women's participation in the clash were used as markers of communal categorization, separating the respectable Orange and Protestant party from their unruly Catholic opponents. As noted above, Catholic women were important front-line participants in the Dolly's Brae fight, twice challenging the collective manhood of the Orange processionists by labelling them 'prisoners of the police'. What is interesting is how widely this was commented on in the various testimonials that form the basis of Walter Berwick's report. Fully eight of the first ten witnesses provided extensive commentary on how 'shockingly abusive' Catholic women were to the marching Orangemen in the morning and late afternoon. The narrative's implicit contrast between the 'threatening' language of Catholic women and the quiet respectability of the women and children marching with the Orange processionists touched deep cultural nerves in mid-Victorian British political culture, reinforcing prevalent notions of Irish Catholic backwardness – ideas seen in the era's widespread English ethnographies that portrayed the Celts as 'the primitives within'.[44] Of course, this was hardly a British or even modern phenomenon – in many ways these portrayals remind one of nothing so much as the early modern European depictions of women unbridled – hysterical, unregulated and potentially subversive and powerful (the types of images analysed so deftly and productively by Natalie Zemon Davis and a generation of acolytes).

Of the testimonies, Francis Beers's is no doubt the most telling. Facing the crowd in the morning of the Dolly's Brae fight, Beers related how he found 'an immense number of women' amid the crowd determined to block the march and that the women spoke 'very wickedly against the Orangemen'. Beers continued with his testimony:

> I felt exceedingly anxious, fearing that some of them might throw a stone at the procession, and there would be some breach of the peace; . . . one girl, in particular appeared very much excited, and a man in the procession also appeared very much excited: the girl, lifting a stone, said to him: 'I'll jaup your brains out'; I said to her 'On my honour, if you don't throw down that stone, I'll kiss you.'; she threw it down instantly.[45]

The apparent deterrent power of a threatened Orange kiss aside, Beers's fantasy/anecdote reflects an important theme within the Orange magisterial and British military testimonials: for these men, the active and public participation of women in sectarian confrontation was 'shocking' and 'monstrous', and was of great use in marking Irish Catholics off as barbaric or at best uncivil. Here, Beers is clearly playing to the crowd, using the well-worn comic stereotype of the Irish as both threatening and controllable to get a laugh from his Orange supporters. And of course, Beers's fantasy provided both him and his fellow elites with the best of both worlds: his female rioter was not only hysterical and out of control but also proved quite submissive when confronted with Beers's forceful application of Victorian masculinity.

It should not surprise us that this was not a one-way process. Examining emerging notions of British identity in the late-eighteenth and nineteenth centuries, Kathleen Wilson and Anna Clark have each shown how important women were as markers of civility and national progress – between colonizer and colonized, and between the emerging middle and working classes in Britain.[46] In Ulster before 1850 such narratives were also used to differentiate the savage mob from the loyal and more respectable Orange procession. Thus, for one magistrate, the women walking with the marchers at Dolly's Brae were proof of the peaceful intentions of the loyalist processionists:

> ... from so many women and children – respectable women –
> being with the Orange procession, I am satisfied that they did
> not intend to commit a breach of the peace, and were armed for
> self-defence; there were a great many respectable women walking
> with the procession, and some respectable women on jaunting
> cars.[47]

Another magistrate even used the presence of women and children to justify military and police inaction, stating 'that it would have been monstrous to have attempted to stop a procession where there were so many women and children'.[48] As Kathleen Wilson has noted, the notion of the fragile nature of female virtue is characteristically taken up by colonialists. Given the problematic applicability of the imperial framework to the Anglo-Irish relationship, it is perhaps better to say that this type of discourse served the purpose of those trying to differentiate the civil and loyal from the dangerous and uncivil.

Again, it is important to note that these images were hardly monolithic and uncontested. Since the majority of testimonials were from members of the Irish Anglican gentry, British military elites or British soldiers, they were hardly representative of some type of Protestant community in the north of Ireland. After all, there were no middling Presbyterian tenant-farmers from the Ulster countryside or merchants from Belfast – social groups that would long oppose the Loyal Orange Order. Moreover, key figures in the investigation such as Walter Berwick and Charles Rutheven refused to buy into these stereotypes, providing their own portraits of both the participants and the communities they supposedly represented. If the Orange narrative of Dolly's Brae was not an effective tale of pan-Protestant consolidation in the short term, the use of women's public appearance and behaviour as a significant marker of communal hierarchy does, however, seem to have been an important weapon in Orange elite commentary. After all, when R.M. Sibbett wrote his influential history of Orangeism, he used many of these same tropes, contrasting Catholic women's ferocious participation in the Dolly's Brae clash with the more respectable behaviour of Orange women and children. When Orangemen marched back from Tollymore Park they were subjected to 'very abusive language by women and children.' Conversely, when the fighting broke out, Dolly's Brae was punctuated 'with the screams of terrified women and children, and the defiant shouts of enraged men'.[49] For Sibbett, it is clear that a gendered narrative of the Dolly's Brae clash provided indisputable evidence of Orange civility and Catholic incivility. By 1915, of course, this was nothing new. Clearly, this Orange narrative had been built to last.

Conclusion

This brief examination of aspects of the Orange writing of Dolly's Brae shows the complex process involved in the formation of communal public memories – a process that, despite the strength of historically potent binary divisions, both real and imagined, never produced meanings that were uncontested and/or monolithic across the Ulster body politic. Put simply, in the half century after Dolly's Brae, Orangemen and their allies used an increasingly powerful and rich imperial vocabulary to construct gendered narratives of sectarian violence. In doing so they often employed seemingly contradictory images of Catholic participants (women who were both threatening and submissive and men who showed a militarized masculinity devoid of steadfast courage) to support historically resonant Catholic/Protestant divisions and hierarchies, updating vibrant narratives and tropes that kept a powerful sectarian discourse alive and ready for use when needed. This clearly echoes Jill Lepore's notion quoted at the outset of this essay; both the riot and subsequent narratives were designed to demarcate communal boundaries along Catholic/Protestant lines.

One of the most striking aspects of the investigations and reports surrounding the fight at Dolly's Brae is the widespread articulation of binary models of Ulster society. This was not simply a matter of Orange/Green assertion and counter-assertion; a wide and fairly diverse variety of government and military officials all interpreted the Dolly's Brae fight in the simple reductionist terms of communal conflict. Of course, this is more a question of perception rather than reality, for as recent work has shown, the 'two nations' model rarely reflects the complex and often contradictory mosaic of lived relationships in nineteenth-century Ulster.[50] But this perception was important, as Orange processions, and the riots that they often triggered, strengthened the binary model by crowding out alternative readings of northern society, preventing competing discourses from emerging from the not-so-narrow ground. The writing of sectarian violence was crucial to this process. Obviously, these linkages were contested both within and without the Orange Order (class divisions within the Order, non-support from Ulster Presbyterians, British Whig officials, Irish Catholics) and dependent on broader and more important issues of political and economic power relations. The Orange writing of Dolly's Brae was not immediately successful outside of the Order's influential but still narrow constituency. But maintaining the vitality of communal language was important. When the Home Rule Crisis occurred in the mid-1880s, aspects of this pan-Protestant ideology were attractive to a broader Irish Protestant community eager to face down the threat of Irish Home Rule. In this new environment Orange narratives of Dolly's Brae had a wider parlance, a fact attested to by the proliferation of songs and histories that featured the story. Many former Whigs and Liberal Protestants joined (however awkwardly) their former foes in the Conservative Party and the Loyal Orange Order, wielding unionist arguments made all the more resonant by stories like Dolly's Brae – cry 'Dolly's Brae No More!'

Symbolic and Hyperreal Violence in the Irish 'Troubles' Movie

BRIAN McILROY

In an extended response to the surfeit of violence in American films in the early 1990s, critic Henry A. Giroux utilized a rudimentary classification scheme of the kinds of violence depicted.[1] He argues that critics of popular films can distinguish between and among ritualistic, symbolic and hyperreal uses of screen violence. To Giroux, ritualistic uses of violence are the most harmless as they are expected structural elements most often found in classic genres such as the Western film, the Gangster film and the Horror film. Symbolic violence is most valuable because it seeks to tie violent acts to more specific historical and personal causes and circumstances. To Giroux's mind, Oliver Stone reworks the War film from ritual violence to symbolic violence in *Platoon*[2] and Clint Eastwood's *Unforgiven*[3] does the same work for the Western film. Most distressing to Giroux, however, is the wallowing of recent films in hyperreal violence, especially the films of Quentin Tarrantino, where even parodic excessive and controversial violence are divorced from any social engagement, and emphasize instead a world without ethics and morality where to be a drug-pushing gun-toting pimp who is cruel, cynical and murderous is to be deemed 'cool'. Giroux convincingly argues that hyperreal violence (in America at least) is a sign of the success of neo-conservative ideology because, with its veil of black humour, it impedes any thinking through of cultural, social or political issues. As I suggest below, however, this blanket condemnation does not preclude the utility of hyperreal screen violence for seeking answers to crisis situations in other national contexts.

The films that have attempted to tell stories of the Northern Ireland 'Troubles' have mainly fallen into the category of symbolic violence, and that is why they deserve extended treatment as serious works of art that seek to reveal or clarify an unresolved state of affairs. Hyperreal violence has not been heavily present in the corpus of films dealing with

Northern Ireland, although a case might be made for parts of Marc Evans's *Resurrection Man*[4] and David Caffrey's *Divorcing Jack*.[5] More often than not, and this is my main claim here, the films strive for the status of thoughtful symbolic violence, but often fall short into a kind of stunted ritualism of repetition. The reason for this failure is that film-makers and screenwriters have embraced the anti-imperialist myth. One way to provide evidence for this claim is to consider how the Protestant community in Ireland has been represented in these films.

The representation of minorities in narrative film has always attracted critical attention. Good reasons exist for this interest, since it is through such an examination that we can judge how mainstream society (however defined), and from which the works generally come, positions itself against other less central groups, particularly in terms of political and social power relations. Fiction film, therefore, often provides us with exemplars of dominant cultural assumptions. In a critical Utopia, written analyses of minorities, and their visual representation, may indeed lead some filmmakers and producers to rethink stereotypes and previously unquestioned areas. Fiction film also provides an arena where violence is often expressed and even assumed as an essential building block, since it creates a natural pressure that must be released in some way.

Yet violent representations take on a political role when they depict a historical situation whose tentacles of tension remain with us today. This is most certainly the case with the Irish 'Troubles', whether one refers to Northern Ireland from 1968 onwards, or the War of Independence and Civil War of the 1919–1923 period. A review of the range of Irish films made since the 1980s would confirm to a neutral observer that stories focusing on the Catholic nationalist and republican communities have been dominant. Ken Loach's recent award-winning *The Wind That Shakes the Barley*[6] reinscribes this tendency. Of late the focus has been upon the Catholic civilian population caught up in the violent events of the troubles, as seen in Paul Greengrass's *Bloody Sunday*[7] and Pete Travis's *Omagh*.[8] Yet this observation only begs the question: how have their counterparts in the Protestant unionist and loyalist communities been addressed? Or, indeed, what of those Protestants who live in the Republic of Ireland? One of the key difficulties faced when approaching this conundrum are the conflicting definitions of a majority and a minority. Each community in Northern Ireland can see themselves as both. If one stresses the all-Ireland concept, Catholics become part of a 80 per cent majority and Protestants a 20 per cent minority; if one stresses the Northern Ireland state alone, there emerges an approximately 55 per cent Protestant majority and a 45 per cent Catholic minority (this leaves the Republic of Ireland with less than a 5 per cent Protestant population).

Simply put, the Protestant community in Ireland is not one that has attracted filmmakers to any great degree. Many films that do exist are mentioned below, and there are gems among them; however, several impediments to a fuller representation are constantly at play. These include the perception of the unionist and loyalist communities as backward-looking, unduly attached to the status quo, in frequent opposition to left-wing politics and culture, reliant on supremacist thinking, and as holders of more than enough privileges. A film that posits these assumptions is the British Film Institute-funded *Ascendancy*,[9] directed by Edward Bennett. In this work, set at the birth of the Northern Ireland state, unionism is linked inextricably to imperialism, militarism, and sectarianism. *Ascendancy* attempts to show how its traumatized wealthy Protestant heroine is unable to cope with the loss of her brother in the First World War. This familial sacrifice for the British empire is at the base of unionist and loyalist culture, members of which conjure up the Ulster commitment at the Battle of the Somme as evidence of allegiance to the crown. By implication the film seems to suggest that such ties were misplaced, and that clearly such sacrifices did not bring peace to Ireland.

These assumptions also extend beyond the Ulster community. Ironically, despite the long tradition of Protestant nationalists and republicans – Wolfe Tone, Henry Joy McCracken, Roger Casement, W.B. Yeats, and so on – southern Irish Protestants still retain, if we were to extrapolate from visual representations alone, an aura of decayed privilege. The popular history of these so-called Anglo-Irish is one of mansions, estates, servants, and access to the 'joys' of empire. These advantageous conditions were destroyed by the formation of the Irish Free State and the War of Independence in 1921/22. As a community, the Protestants gradually dwindled through migration and intermarriage. To many they had had their day, and given the undeniable grievances of the Catholic population over hundreds of years, they withered in the background to general indifference.

The Irish writer William Trevor has captured this gloomy mood magnificently, so much so that one can almost feel the sepia tones come right off the page. His novel *Fools of Fortune* was translated to film in 1990[10] by Pat O'Connor, and is probably the most powerful visual commentary on the fate of the Protestants in the South. *Fools of Fortune* traces the tragic story of Willie Quinton, whose father is murdered and his home burned by a Black and Tan soldier, Rudkin, during the War of Independence. Willie's sisters die in the fire, and many years later his mother, finally unable to deal with the losses, commits suicide. Driven by revenge, Willie travels to England to seek out Rudkin whom he kills brutally with a knife. Willie goes into exile, only returning to the remains of the family home when he learns that his liaison with his English cousin, Marianne, has resulted in a gifted but troubled child, Imelda, and that he may be free from persecution. Stretching from 1920 to the 1940s and 1950s, the film would seem to be a heritage or period film that relies for much of its effect on costume and setting. But it is a peculiarly Irish heritage film that speaks just as much to the unsettled present as it does to the unsettled past. O'Connor underscores this point by opening the film with slow-motion black and white footage of the Protestant Quinton family, all dressed in their summer whites, having mid-afternoon tea and cakes on the grounds of their estate. That time could be likened to the atmosphere of the *ancien régime* just before the French Revolution. Once the War of Independence begins, the Quin-tons are placed, as representatives of the Anglo-Irish, in an impossible situation. While sympathetic to the aspirations of the IRA, in the spirit of the United Irishmen, and resentful of the repressive British military presence, Mr Quinton has too many vested interests and obligations to provide more than clandestine financial resources. Ironically, his English wife is more supportive of Ireland for the Irish than he.

The marriage between an Irish Protestant man and an English woman is replicated later in the film in the relationship between Willie and Marianne. Here O'Connor suggests how Irish Protestants are inter-connected with Britain perhaps in a more complex way than Irish Catholics. Adding to this complexity is the role of the Quinton's employee Doyle, who fought for the British during the First World War, who informs for the Black and Tans, and yet, who may well be a Catholic. Loyalties are full of shades of grey, and in his historic speech to both houses of the Irish parliament in November 1998, Tony Blair specifically mentioned how unionists and nationalists travelled to Flan-ders to 'remember shared suffering'.[11] As the young Willie is told by his tutor, a defrocked priest, 'The past is always there in the present.'

Very early on in the film Mr. Quinton explains to his son that it is very difficult to be Irish in Ireland, whereas what the film proves is that it was difficult to be Protestant and Irish. The forces of history and vio-lence reduce the Quintons to emotional cripples, a rather sad, gentle, but anachronistic group of people who have been unable to overcome their past heritage. The daughter Imelda is the repository in which this past family trauma resides. Spurred on by discrimination at school, where she is made to feel an outsider because she is not a Catholic, and by a troubled relationship with her mother, who also feels abandoned by her family, the child experiences visions of the violent past, including that of Mr Quinton's murder and Willie's murder of Rudkin. She loses the power of speech and appears to live in a fantasy world where time slippages are seamless. If Imelda is representative of the Protestant future in the Republic of Ireland, it is an ambiguous rendering. To her mother, she has simply gone insane, traumatized by history; to others, she is blessed and has the power to heal the afflicted. We are encouraged to favour the latter reading, but the former is not eliminated from our thoughts. For all its cultural baggage as a troubled heritage piece, *Fools of Fortune* is a powerful film, particularly noteworthy for its suggestive use of landscapes and interiors that dovetail nicely with the melodramatic elements.

As befits the size of population, most representations, however, focus on the Ulster Protestants, and these films are clearly informed by Tom Nairn's 'anti-imperialist' myth.[12] This myth presupposes that the Protestants are suffering from a false consciousness since they wish to remain connected to the origin of imperialism (Britain); that the Protestants are not a 'real' people or nation with legitimate rights and views which happen to diverge from the aspirations of Irish nationalists and British Ministers; that since the Protestants are 'deluded lackeys', they can be 'dismissed from history'. Once the myth is adopted, awkward facts can be elided (for example, the last power-sharing agreement in 1974 was brought down primarily by working-class Protestants, not the unionist elites, and there is reason to think that an equal but less violent resistance may undermine the current efforts to restart a Northern Ireland Assembly). The power of the anti-imperialist myth is indubitably seductive, allied as it is to the romantic, restorative image of Irish unification, with all the suggestive metaphors of harmony, closing the circle and finishing a narrative quest. Only recently have unionists realized that they must repeatedly travel to Britain, continental Europe, and the United States to argue their case, just as their nationalist adversaries have done for years.

This dismissal from history creates at least three kinds of identifiable representation in Irish film. Sometimes elements of all three occur in the same film. First, the Protestants 'appear' as a structuring absence or background filler. Second, the Protestants are collapsed into figures in uniform, thereby strongly linking the community with military-like repression. Third, the Protestants are demonized or decontextualized. In Terry George's *Some Mother's Son*,[13] for example, the two Catholic female protagonists mainly experience their Protestant neighbours as mute, suspicious prison officers, as aggressive, ranting protesters at an election count, or as the people involved in throwing urine at them as they hand out leaflets. Jim Sheridan's *In the Name of the Father*[14] positively excludes Irish Protestants, except for brief visual suggestions of heinous RUC men. In Sheridan's later *The Boxer*,[15] the Protestant population is reduced to two bereaved parents, a policeman who is assassinated, a faceless mob, and a sinister assortment of tattooed 'hard men'. Roger Michel's *Titanic Town*[16] features for thirty seconds or so a group of middle-class Protestant women who, within a few seconds, are pilloried and thrust out of a community meeting. We might even say that Martin Cahill in John Boorman's *The General*[17] seals his fate when he brashly deals with a loyalist organization, thereby flouting the IRA.

Neil Jordan's remarkably successful *The Crying Game*[18] appears to omit Protestants totally, forcing the viewer to see the Irish conflict as a struggle between Britain and Ireland rather than between two ethnic communities within Ireland. If, in addition to pursuing the queer and race themes, Jordan had chosen to have his IRA group arrest a local Protestant policeman or soldier, it would have, perforce, led to a most challenging piece of political dialogue. Such a choice, however, would have invalidated the comfortable anti-imperialist myth at the level of politics that the film relies upon in its Irish section. Jordan's first feature film, *Angel*,[19] made a clear link between Protestant policing and loyalist death squads; his *Michael Collins*[20] featured one Belfast police detective being blown up in his car. In and of itself, this scene is unremarkable, until you realize that it is the only specific Protestant representation in the film. These selective observations naturally appear univocal and reductive, but what they suggest is the exclusionary aesthetics that the anti-imperialist myth determines, consciously and unconsciously, in a screenwriter's and director's mind.

These films place the Protestants in the margins of their narratives, and are easily taken to task. More interesting are the films that seek, on the surface, to confer parity of esteem between the two communities. The notion of parity of esteem emerged in the late 1980s as a cultural nostrum from various governmental bodies eager to find a middle ground in a very divided society. It's one English filmmakers and writers explored in the 1980s. Peter Smith's *No Surrender*[21] was written by Alan Bleasedale and exudes his penchant for biting, black satire. What is unique about *No Surrender* is Bleasedale's setting of the story in Liverpool, where the transplanted Protestant and Catholics maintain a warring enmity. But whereas in their youth the feelings were direct and vital, the antagonism has turned in old age to weary sarcasm and self-doubt.

Bleasedale hilariously heightens their antique nature by having both Protestant and Catholic senior social clubs turn up at the same venue for an evening out, along with incompetent and outrageous comedians and musicians. In amongst this chaos a loyalist gunman is trying to hide out with one of his former comrades, Billy. The political and social impact of the film centres on Billy, once a fierce Protestant loyalist, who has now forsaken his sectarianism, an act underscored by his eventual killing of his former colleague, and by his asking to speak for the first time to his Catholic son-in-law. It's interesting that Bleasedale would see that it is the Protestants who most need to renounce their violence (particularly when one realizes that republican paramilitaries were responsible for up to two-thirds of the deaths in Northern Ireland, and the loyalists one-third).

A more traditional approach to joint representation or apparent parity of esteem is to adopt the Romeo and Juliet storyline. We see this in the poorly distributed film *This is the Sea*[22] directed by Mary McGuckian, in which Hazel, a Plymouth Brethren Protestant meets Catholic Malachy, but both must negotiate difficult family, religious and political objections to the match. The fundamentalist Protestant depiction inevitably pushes the viewer to identify with the more socially relaxed Catholic family. Invariably, in these films, and in others such as *Four Days in July*[23] by Mike Leigh, the Protestants are depicted as if they are all collectively suffering from a joyless upbringing with too much dogma.

Even when the Protestants are the main focus of a feature narrative, the tendency is to give them a disturbing pathology. This is particularly the case with two recent feature films on the 'Shankill Butchers' of the mid 1970s (a loyalist death squad) – Thaddeus O'Sullivan's *Nothing Personal*[24] and Marc Evans's *Resurrection Man*. Both of these films suffered from indifferent distribution, and it is not hard to see why. At a time of tortured negotiations for peace, and efforts to wean the violent paramilitaries into political dialogue, these two films seemingly presented themselves as part of the 1970s' retro movement that was so popular in the 1990s. Unfortunately, in Northern Ireland, this takes us back to the most violent sectarian period of the 'Troubles'. Ginger in *Nothing Personal* and Victor in *The Resurrection Man* are based, in part, on a real-life figure, Lenny Murphy, who encouraged his gang to torture and mutilate their random victims. At the 1995 Vancouver International Film Festival, Ian Hart, who plays Ginger, put forward the theory that this man was the biggest serial killer in Britain, but he escaped detection for a long time because of the general violence.[25]

O'Sullivan's film interrogates the 'cease-fire' period in 1975 when for a few weeks in Belfast there was a modicum of peace.

Kenny and Ginger are the 'hard men' of the Protestant paramilitaries. They are armed defenders of their own community and run a drinking club for the leading loyalist godfather, Leonard Wilson. Both leaders of the Catholic and Protestant paramilitaries appear to want to give peace a chance, and they meet to clear up logistical matters, such as the punishment of petty criminals, similar to what we see at the beginning of *In the Name of the Father*. For most of the film Ginger is trigger-happy, constantly seeking to wreak havoc and violence. It is Kenny's job to settle him down, and then finally to kill him because he is seen as a loose cannon.

The results of the violence have divided families. Kenny has a wife and two children, but he is separated from them, presumably because of his murderous activities, although this is not explained. On the other side of the divide, there is Liam, a Catholic and father of two children. The narrative develops rapidly when Liam, out protecting his community, ends up on the wrong side of the barricades and is beaten up. Kenny's wife, Ann, patches his wounds, and they both take the opportunity to share their feelings concerning marriage, children and relationships. Liam, however, is spirited off the streets by Kenny and Ginger, roughed up again, and subjected to Ginger's Russian roulette gun games. Finally, Liam is deposited near his home, but Ginger prepares to kill him, forcing Kenny to intervene and shoot his comrade in the leg. As they scramble to safety, a young Catholic boy takes out a stolen gun and attempts to shoot Kenny. Liam's daughter tries to stop him and is killed by accident in the scuffle. Seemingly disgusted by Ginger's actions, Kenny murders him, knowing that the British Army, who have been directed to his location by Wilson, will kill them all.

Four levels of discourse are at work in the film: (1) the interactions of the IRA and UDA/UVF leaderships; (2) the discussions among the foot-soldiers of the Protestant paramilitaries; (3) the views of the non-combatants, Liam and Ann; and (4) the children of the 'Troubles'. Of these, perhaps of most importance are the actions and suffering of the children, both Protestant and Catholic. In the loyalist drinking den, Tommy, a teenager, drinks and makes plans to court a blond girl on the dance floor. Eventually, he goes over to dance with her, rescuing her from a rowdy lout, for which action Kenny rewards him by promoting him to doorman, with a handgun at the ready. Feeling like a 'real man' with a gun in his pocket and having used his fists gallantly for his girl, he plucks up enough courage to kiss her. Interestingly, she puts the gun down on the road as he attempts to kiss her, but he picks it up again. Gunplay is obviously a substitute in some measure for repressed sexuality. Carried along by the further promotion to Kenny and Ginger's side, the boy is party to Liam's abduction and ill treatment (even forced by Ginger to press the gun against Liam's head at one point). These events traumatize the boy who clearly is having second thoughts about being a 'hard man'. The reason for Ginger's extreme violence is never fully explored. By implication, he represents the vicious side of loyalism that, the film seems to suggest, is an ideology most likely to support ethnic cleansing. On the Catholic side, Liam's daughter has a suitor. This young boy tries to help her look for her father, even going as far as to steal a gun from one of the IRA men's coats. It is his desire to shoot Kenny at the end that precipitates the young girl's death in the ensuing struggle. Children, and youth in general, suffer at the barricades, where Kenny kills a Catholic boy who has been engulfed in flames.

Throughout the film various (admittedly rather stilted) conversations among the Protestant paramilitaries try to articulate what their overall purpose is: killing the 'enemy'; defending and patrolling their own neighbourhoods; and fighting for their 'country'. But this is as far as such intellectualizing goes. The film does little to displace the moral vacuum of these characters. Very strangely, the film begins with an IRA bombing of a pub. The attempt to kill members of the RUC fails, as we see them leave the pub just as young female and male civilians enter, who are then killed or maimed. In the aftermath of the bombing, as the security forces and the rescue services pick their way through the rubble, we see Liam making his way through the devastation in a way intended to emphasize his sympathy for the victims. The reason why this is curious is because the bomb has gone off in a Protestant area, and here is Liam, a Catholic, blithely walking around at a time when sectarian feelings would be very high. It would make more local sense to have Kenny walking around the bomb-site, as a visual way of making sense of the Protestant paramilitaries' motivation: that of a community that feels itself under siege and subject to random attacks by the IRA. The bombing campaign of the 1970s was the IRA's 'total war' against the Northern Ireland state and (although they officially denied it) against the Protestant loyalist community.

One area of the film that is unfortunately not developed is the relationship between Liam and Kenny. A reference is made to Liam's father having taken Kenny's family to the hills for safety during World War Two's German bombing of Belfast. This reference, added to their previous and presumably pre-1968/69 fights, gives them a connection that the present war seems to have almost completely eradicated. Hints at a more complicated relationship between Protestant and Catholic are no more than that in this film which tends to return to naked violence for its resolution of conflict. Of course, Kenny's 'nothing personal' comment to Liam as he is tortured and nearly killed is far less than the truth, although it is true in the sense of an ideological war between Irish and British nationalism.

O'Sullivan knew that the film would cause controversy, since it shows the loyalists as aggressors and the nationalists as victims: 'I guess it was a political decision [to show the loyalist guerillas] but that was what the book was about, and it was written by a Protestant.'[26] And it is true that *Nothing Personal* came in for less criticism than Marc Evans's *Resurrection Man*, partly because the focus in the latter is on an effort to show the same pathology in a journalist as in the murderous gang he is reporting on. Also, there are no redeeming or fully developed Catholic characters. But what the film does do very well is to create a connection between sectarian violence and self-loathing. To some extent Ginger in O'Sullivan's film was considered by others and himself as 'just a little shite', by which was meant that without the 'Troubles', working-class losers like Ginger would have no status in any part of society. Victor Kelly's pathology attempts to hide this inner hatred, but once the religious persuasion of his father – a Catholic – is mentioned, it's as if a white heat takes over, sending him into a violent but calculated frenzy.

Victor's attachment to Irish-American gangsters, as represented in the James Cagney movies he watches as a child and remembers as an adult, gives him a structure by which to live, however perverse. Evans and McNamee are equally interested in tracing the psychological descent of Victor along with that of fellow paramilitary Darkie and bloodthirsty wife-beating alcoholic Ryan, the journalist. There is a dangerous ideology at work in this narrative that those who report on violence finally become apologists for it, as evidenced by Ryan's killing of Darkie and his refusal to stop the murder of Victor. Evans draws clear parallels between loyalist criminal behaviour and extreme rightism – at one point we see the Godfather McClure put on a Nazi hat and sniff cocaine, while at another point we see him preach religious slogans in the street, conjuring up fundamental Protestant traditions.

As with Ginger, Victor is the mad mutilator (a Protestant version of the mad bomber of the Hollywood films). His actions are gruesome and arguably exploitative, but at least the film seeks to find the seeds of this violence in a strict family background with an overbearing and indulgent mother, coupled with an effectively absent father whose allegiances are questioned by the community at large. This may be bad pseudo-psychology, but at least an explanatory kite is flown. Family is totally absent in Ginger's representation in *Nothing Personal*, and neither he nor his immediate boss is contextualized meaningfully in political terms. Although O'Sullivan has produced a technically more assured film with big name stars, witty dialogue, and superb kinetic energy, it arguably raises more questions than *Resurrection Man*'s Victor.

What is elided in such representations is the belief in secular individualism and in civic society, incorporating a pluralist and federalist British Isles, to which Protestant unionism and culture give voice. Also often missing is the value of a dissenter culture, only part of which manifests itself in Orangeism and extreme loyalism. Yet it is also true to say that more sophisticated representations of Protestantism do exist and are emerging. O'Sullivan's earlier *December Bride*[27] and David Caffrey's *Divorcing Jack* are two possible approaches which defy stereotypes. *December Bride* is based on a famous Ulster novel by Sam Hanna Bell, which is here rewarded by a crisp screenplay by David Rudkin and stupendous cinematography. In the film, set around the turn of the century in northeast Ireland, a young Protestant woman Sarah and her mother Martha are given employment on the Echlins' farm. The two Echlin sons, Frank and Hamilton, compete for the attentions of Sarah, but though she has a relationship with both of them and gives birth to a child, she refuses to marry. Only in old age, at her daughter's pleading, does she give in to marriage to Hamilton with Frank serving as best man.

What is of import in *December Bride* is how the Presbyterian culture of northeast Ireland is analysed. The dissenter beliefs of the Echlins extend in a different direction from the obvious Protestant/Catholic clash. The Echlin brothers choose not to attend church on Sundays and not to be members of the strong local district Orange Lodge. They also choose to accept the unusual living arrangements with Sarah and choose to provide for Catholics on their land. Even the simple matter of Frank playing a Jews' harp becomes a subversive act in a Presbyterian culture that prefers the beat of the Lambeg drum. Of great interest, too, is the way Sarah has healthy but pragmatic ambitions to be more than a domestic servant. She is more sectarian than the brothers, and she is initially surprised by their lack of interest in Orangeism; they, in turn, are surprised by but respect her desire to retain her own name and not to lose it by marriage.

O'Sullivan is also able to give screen time to the Presbyterian clergyman who finds the Echlin arrangement deeply disturbing, since it seems, as Sarah exclaims at one point, that religious men are 'botched on the inside. But smooth on the outside'. So powerful is Sarah's rebuke and so confused is the man's response that he seeks another parish, 'a tidy little town' where he will not have to deal, he thinks, with such matters as fornication and children out of wedlock. Sarah extends, by implication, her negative assessment to all Presbyterian observance. She is, in short, an unmarked or secular Protestant, eager to break with at least some old traditions and to whom land acquisition and personal freedom are paramount.

The notion of the unmarked secular Protestant is a useful way to approach Dan Starkey, the hero in David Caffrey's *Divorcing Jack*. Starkey is a political columnist for a local newspaper, gearing up for the election of a Prime Minister in a new, independent Northern Ireland. At last, a writer and filmmaker have decided to look ahead and to imagine a possible future for Northern Ireland instead of lamenting and working over past wrongs and incidents. The writer and screenwriter Colin Bateman has said that this production is a 'unionist thriller',[28] although Starkey's unionist background is played down in the film, whereas arguably his political credentials are clearer in the novel on which it is based. Starkey occupies that intellectual middle-class centre ground, a man who wishes the warring factions would destroy themselves rather than the innocent people around them.

The baroque style of *Divorcing Jack* relies on black humour – how else can we explain an attachment to a hero who accidentally kills an elderly woman? Caffrey and Bateman also ingeniously recast the paramilitaries and government operatives in terms that render them equally culpable. Most striking is the acceptance that any workable government will comprise former terrorists – in many respects, this likelihood is an underlying assumption for at least part of the future governance of Northern Ireland. Equally striking is the model of an independent state. This idea has always simmered beneath the surface of Northern Irish politics, and with a devolved assembly now in theory in existence, we may be surprised at further turns in this direction. What is so refreshing about Caffrey's film is a willingness to play with clichés in a tense political situation, and to play equally fast and loose with generic codes. To depict the Protestant gun-toting paramilitaries to the strains of the theme music of *The Magnificent Seven* is to reclaim some sanity and ironic distancing in a world that often has neither. In the absence of a thoughtful symbolic use of screen violence, a dose of hyperreal violence may thus have some rewards.

Undoing the Fanaticism of Meaning:
Neil Jordan's *Angel*

KEITH HOPPER

> Why is this subtlety of meaning so crucial? Precisely because meaning, from the moment that it is fixed and imposed and ceases to be subtle, becomes an instrument, a counter in the power game. To make meaning subtle is therefore a second-level political activity, as is any attempt to crumble, disturb or undo the fanaticism of meaning.
>
> (Roland Barthes, 'Dear Antonioni . . ', 1980)[1]

Within the real and symbolic arena of contemporary Irish culture, Neil Jordan is both an icon and an iconoclast. Beginning as a writer of intricate and innovative short stories – Seán O'Faoláin compared him favourably with Joyce – Jordan migrated to the world of film, eventually winning an Oscar for Best Original Screenplay in 1992 (*The Crying Game*).[2] Throughout a prolific and controversial career Jordan has attracted approval and opprobrium in equal measure, especially in Ireland. To some he 'represents "a fence sitter", a bland child of Hollywood, and a feckless dilettante'; to others he is quite simply the most important Irish artist of his generation.[3] Either way, as Fintan O'Toole noted in 1996 (during the controversy over Jordan's *Michael Collins*):

> Neil Jordan is, for modern Ireland, not just a famous movie director, but a peculiarly emblematic figure of cultural change. His work over the last two decades represents not just one man's pursuit of his ideas and ambitions, but a significant shift in a nation's culture. By starting out as a writer of literary fiction and re-inventing himself as a film director, he symbolises a much bigger change in the way the country sees itself.[4]

This is certainly true of Jordan's debut feature film, *Angel* (1982),[5] which in retrospect marked an important turning point in the development of modern Irish cinema. Given its subject matter and treatment – a

revenge parable about paramilitary violence in Northern Ireland, stylis-
tically explored through the generic filters of *film noir* – *Angel* was always
going to be controversial, especially in the emotive aftermath of the
1981 Hunger Strike.[6] However, *Angel* was contentious and challenging
for a variety of other reasons, some of which are worth teasing out
here. For the purposes of this essay, I will briefly track the origins of
the film, and then discuss the broad range of critical responses it provoked (both at the time of its release and in subsequent academic
analyses). I will argue that these profoundly ambivalent and polarized
reactions are an index of much deeper ideological tensions which are
intimately bound up with the issue of violence in Ireland. I also want
to suggest that the aesthetics of ambivalence enshrined in *Angel* serve to
raise some fundamental questions not just about the ideological nature
of criticism and spectatorship but also about the cinematic representation of violence as well.

Brute music: the background to *Angel*

At the 1981 Cannes Film Festival, where *Angel* was first shown outside
of competition in an attempt to attract video distributors, the over-
whelmingly positive critical response was such that extra screenings had
to be arranged to cater for the demand.[7] And after its release in Britain
– in a groundbreaking deal brokered with Channel 4 television[8] –
Jordan won the *London Evening Standard*'s Most Promising Newcomer
Award. Despite these accolades, when *Angel* held its official world premiere in Ireland (31 March 1982) the screening was publicly boycotted
by other Irish filmmakers, who were outraged by the manner in which
it had been funded. Basically, the controversy arose after the newly
established Bord Scannán na hÉireann (Irish Film Board) had allocated
its entire annual production budget for 1981 to *Angel*, and because the
British filmmaker John Boorman – Jordan's mentor, and a Film Board
member – was also the film's executive producer and a director of its
production company. Although Boorman and Jordan insisted that the
IR£100,000 loan allocation was strictly above board – in fact, money
was returned to the Irish Exchequer by the end of 1982 – and even
though this money accounted for only 20% of *Angel*'s production costs,[9]
there was nonetheless a perceived conflict of interest. After an acrimo-
nious public debate Boorman resigned from the Film Board, but
resentment against his protégé continued to linger.[10] Subsequently, as
John Orr has noted,

Some, ignored by the Irish Film Board, denounced Jordan's project as apolitical and colonialist. Others saw it as influenced by the Americanised values of Boorman's *Point Blank*, while other voices thought it self-consciously arty in trying to imitate European cinema. In a pincer movement Jordan was attacked from different directions.[11]

That being said, these ambivalent responses were also a by-product of *Angel*'s oblique style, as well a consequence of Jordan's unconventional approach to filmmaking. *Angel* was shot over a six-week period at the National Film Studios of Ireland and on location in the Wicklow area. Given Jordan's lack of technical expertise, Boorman had secured the services of the highly regarded British cinematographer Chris Menges, who showed Jordan how to set up and orchestrate the shots.[12] Without the benefit of an orthodox film-school training, Jordan knew very little about the conventional 'rules' of filmmaking: he worked entirely from the script rather than storyboards, and instead of the usual multiple takes and complementary cover shots he only filmed what he had written. As Jordan recalled, by the time it came to the editing process, 'the editor had nothing to work with, really. Everything I shot was in the finished film [but] when we cut it together it definitely had its own logic.'[13] In many ways this technical naïvety was also the film's greatest strength, imbuing it with a strong sense of personal vision. As James Park later remarked: 'What Jordan brought to his first film was a perspective on the world which he had developed in his fiction, the sensitivities of an intelligent film viewer, and a clear sense of why he wanted to move into the film medium.'[14]

When Jordan had first started working on the draft outline of the script in 1979, it was provisionally entitled 'Brute Music'. The story was inspired by the notorious 'Miami Showband Massacre', which had taken place four years earlier.[15] At that time Jordan had been working as a professional musician, and he frequently travelled across the border from Dublin to play gigs in the North. As he later recalled, the Miami Showband atrocity was the 'basic stimulus' for the film, but 'at the time I couldn't say that, because it was such a renowned event. . . . But it was the idea of guys in silvery suits being shot down arbitrarily. It was a bit like circus people being assassinated, even though they did no harm to anybody.'[16] In an early draft treatment (June 1980), Jordan outlined the core objective correlative between the theme of violence and the central metaphor of music:

> This film takes the form of an ironic musical. . . . So there is music throughout, there is a male lead saxophone player and a

female singer as in standard musicals. The difference is that the sax-player transforms his obsession with the saxophone into a gun [and] the world of music and the joy and freedom it implies is always contrasted with the world of violent death and assassination.[17]

Later, in a slightly more developed version of this treatment, Jordan added:

The film would start from a quite documentary premise and so proceed in a rather documentary way at first, with the stricter nature of a thriller taking over slowly. The killers would never be revealed – their identity and their part in the sectarian/political conflict would not be made an issue. They would be hidden human beings involved in an act of pure death, pure evil. The hero's discovery of each one would be a discovery of a human being behind that act, not of a political or sectarian reason.[18]

In subsequent draft versions all of these basic elements were retained and refined, but the generic conventions and discursive tropes of the *film noir* thriller gradually came to the fore. However, as Jordan later commented, 'given that I wanted to speak about morality and questions of good and evil and the soul, I didn't want to make it with the speed, and the glitter, and the *distractions* with which action films are normally made. I wanted to do precisely the opposite of that' [his emphasis].[19] The 'opposite of that' is largely achieved by a series of visual and acoustic motifs which undercut the generic conventions of plot. As a result of this deconstructive strategy any straightforward description of *Angel's* surface plot is necessarily limited (and any subsequent analysis that ignores these underlying patterns is bound to be reductive). To begin with though, it is certainly worth trying to separate what Formalists call the *fabula* (the pattern of relationships between characters and actions as they unfold in chronological order) from the *syuzhet* (the artistic organization or deformation of the causal-chronological order of events) in order to begin isolating some of these estranging, counter-narrative patterns. Indeed, as we will see, in its assorted plot details and repetitions the storyline is already strange enough.

Strange fruit: the plot of *Angel*

Angel is set in Northern Ireland (*c.*1975) and tells the story of a professional saxophone player, Danny (Stephen Rea). The film opens outside a rural ballroom called 'Dreamland', where Danny is about to perform with a typical Irish showband of the period (a populist fusion of rock 'n' roll and big band jazz).[20] Danny meets a young deaf-mute woman named Annie (Veronica Quilligan), and invites her to the show. During a song by the lead singer, Deirdre (Honor Heffernan, herself a real-life cabaret singer), a wedding party enters the hall. Danny flirts with the bride (Lise-Ann McLaughlin), much to the annoyance of the groom (Ian McElhinney). Meanwhile, the band's manager, Ray (Peter Caffrey), forcefully ejects a man who apparently has been demanding protection money. When the show is over, Danny goes outside to a modern-day 'wishing tree', hoping to seduce Deirdre. Instead, Annie seduces him, and they make love inside a large concrete construction pipe on a piece of wasteland.[21] Afterwards, Danny witnesses the arrival of four masked paramilitaries who shoot Ray dead. They then murder the angelic and naïve Annie, and blow up the ballroom. The only clue to their identity is an orthopaedic shoe – rather like a cloven hoof – which one of the killers is wearing.[22]

Traumatized and still in shock, Danny wakes up in hospital where he is questioned by two policemen, Bloom (Ray McAnally) and Bonner (Donal McCann), but Danny fails to mention the orthopaedic shoe. After being discharged, he visits his auntie Mae (Marie Kean), the elderly widow who raised him. Mae was once a fortune-teller, and she begins to read Danny's cards. But when the sequence appears entirely in black – the jack, eight, queen and ace of spades – Mae abandons the reading, telling him she's 'lost the knack'.[23] (The four cards foreshadow Danny's eventual pursuit of the four killers, culminating in the final showdown with the gang leader.)

Afterwards, Danny goes to rehearse with the reformed band, under the new management of the drummer, Bill (Alan Devlin). Later, in one of many uncanny coincidences that litter the film, Danny comes across an orthopaedic shoe-shop. The counter assistant (Gerard McSorley) is himself wearing one of these shoes, and Danny follows him to a dilapidated council house. Danny later breaks in and finds an Uzi machine-gun, similar to the one used to kill Annie. When the nameless counter assistant returns home unexpectedly, Danny – much to his own surprise – shoots him dead. After the murder, Danny's sax playing is particularly soulful, and Deirdre becomes more sexually attracted to him. Later on, Danny returns to the scene of his crime and watches while two men enter the house – clearly the dead man's accomplices. Danny hides but catches a glimpse of one of them. Afterwards, Mae reads his cards again, and prophesies the appearance of 'a dark lady and a government man'.[24] In more sinister tones she speaks of 'Nobo-daddy' – the faceless, dark spirit of the cards.

Bloom brings Danny into the police station for questioning: 'By the way', he says, 'in case you're wondering, I'm Jewish.' 'Are you a Catholic Jew or a Protestant Jew?' Danny drolly replies.[25] Bloom shows him a series of mug shots, including one of a man standing outside a seaside cottage whom Danny recognizes as his victim's accomplice. Danny visits the man – George (Tony Rohr) – and after a fraught conversation, he shoots George dead on the beach.

Before the band's first gig at a seaside resort, Danny and Deirdre pose for publicity photographs in their shiny pink costumes (part of the manager's new image for them). Afterwards, they dance together, and end up having sex:

> DANNY: You a convent girl?
> DEIRDRE: I'm a woman, Danny.
> DANNY: Tell me what a sin is.
> DEIRDRE: It's a habit Catholics indulge in.
> DANNY: What about Protestants?
> DEIRDRE: *(Takes his dark glasses off.)* They don't know what sinning is. *(She kisses him.)* You do though.[26]

The next day, in one of several meditative interludes, Danny encounters a Salvation Army band rehearsing on the beach. Later, Bonner and Bloom pick him up for questioning, and show him George's body in the morgue. After an oblique and existential conversation about love and death, Bloom cryptically comments: 'You know, Danny, you can go places I never could. You understand?'[27]

At their next gig – held, bizarrely, in an asylum – Deirdre sings the Billie Holiday anthem 'Strange Fruit', and afterwards she professes her love to Danny. The following day Danny encounters the young bride from the night of Annie's murder, now separated from her abusive husband: 'Och, y'know men', she says, 'start out angels, end up brutes.'[28] She tells him of how her husband disappeared on their wedding night, and Danny suddenly realizes that the groom was a member of the murder gang. He invites her to his next gig and, afterwards, Deirdre watches in dismay as Danny takes the bride home. They have sex, and Danny discovers that her husband works as a forester. Still wearing his pink suit, Danny goes to the forest, where the man is conducting an affair with a Catholic woman: 'I like you Beth', the man croons, 'You've got soul'; 'You're a Prod', she teases, 'they don't have souls.' Danny puts a gun to the man's head, and forces him to drive. When Danny questions him about the murder, the man hints at a deeper conspiracy: 'It's not me you want, you know. There's someone bigger than me.'[29] After an agitated conversation, Danny shoots him dead, and the car careers blindly into a field.

Danny staggers from the wreckage, and goes to the venue for his next gig – a marquee by an estuary. Inside the tent, Bill, the manager, is paying protection money to a stranger. Danny shoots the stranger – executing him in the same manner that Ray was first murdered – and Deirdre witnesses this brutal act: 'Don't touch me – you're dead', she screams, 'You make me feel unclean.'[30] She tells Danny that the police are hunting for him, and he flees. He comes to a deserted farmyard where he meets a Catholic widow named Mary (Sorcha Cusack). Showing her his gun, he orders her to cut his hair and find him some clothes. Mary tells him about her abusive husband, and how much she hated him. Danny falls asleep, and when he wakes up Mary shoots herself in front of him. Distraught, Danny takes her truck and drives to the ruins of the Dreamland Ballroom.

On the wasteland where Annie died, Danny encounters a young boy in a shiny satin suit. The boy, Francie (Macrea Clarke), is a Catholic faith healer – the seventh son of a seventh son. When he lays his hands on Danny, Danny collapses. When he recovers, Bonner is standing over him. The policeman escorts him to the ruins of the ballroom, and pulls out a gun: Bonner himself is the leader of the murder gang. Just as Bonner is about to kill Danny, a shot rings out and Bonner dies: Danny's guardian angel, Bloom, has come to his rescue:

> DANNY: Why didn't you tell me, Mr Bloom?
> BLOOM: I didn't know.
> DANNY: You wanted me to find out –
> (BLOOM *turns and moves out of the burnt-out ballroom, followed by* DANNY: *and* FRANCIE. *The wind* [from an unseen helicopter] *blows posters and dust outside the ballroom.*)[31]

On this eerie and desolate note, *Angel* ends where it first began: in the ruins of Dreamland, but with Danny now transformed from a poetic innocent into a brutal –and brutalized – avenging angel.

In the ruins of Dreamland: critical reception

When *Angel* was first released, both in the cinema and on Channel 4 television, the critical reviews were generally quite positive. In Britain most

critics judged it against the perceived reality of the Northern Irish Troubles, and against more conventional cinematic representations of
violence. Derek Malcolm in the *Guardian*, for instance, thought the
'importance of Jordan's first feature is not the fact that it is an efficient
thriller, but that its superstructure is informed with a genuine feeling for
the misery behind the headlines. It has content, style and imagination.'[32]
Similarly, John Coleman in the *New Statesman* believed that in the context
of 'real corpses [and] real grief almost daily displayed on TV', Jordan
had deftly avoided any 'accusations of political insensitivity' by shifting
the emphasis from the real world to 'a landscape of surreal encounters'.
In search of a suitable reference point, Coleman compared Jordan to
Wim Wenders – 'but a Wenders with more vim, less whim'.[33] On the
other hand, Richard Cook in the *NME* could discern no 'clear cinematic
tradition' and argued that 'Jordan's grasp seems almost entirely instinc-
tual – he gives the appearance of breathing in an elemental attitude to
filmmaking.' For Cook, *Angel* had 'the aura and weight of an authentic
masterpiece', and he argued that 'Jordan's first masterstroke is to divorce
his scenario from the all-engulfing shadow of the Troubles. Aside from a
few flickers in the script the only direct reference is a single, brief shot of
a soldier peering nervously around a street corner.'[34]

Other British critics echoed these sentiments, though not without
making some important caveats. Again, Tim Pulleine in *Sight and Sound*
thought the opening sequence of *Angel* 'pictures a milieu hardly witnessed on our screens: the everyday reality of Ulster behind the media
statistics of death and destruction which dominate "mainland" appre-
hension of the province'. However, Pulleine also felt that this initial
'documentary' impulse – which he compared to the British Free
Cinema movement of the 1950s – was eventually overwhelmed by the
influence of John Boorman's *Point Blank* (1967) 'with its deflection of
thriller material towards the figurative and the abstract'.[35] Nick Roddick
in *Films and Filming* agreed: '*Angel* is a film of implications and reso-
nances, not connections. . . . In the end – probably intentionally –
Jordan's Ireland is no more real than John Ford's, just the reverse image
. . . A metaphysical *film noir* about a political reality is a dangerous
gamble, and Jordan doesn't really bring it off'.[36]

Similarly, in the Republic of Ireland, there was a vague sense of
unease about the relationship between style and substance, especially in
the volatile aftermath of the 1981 Hunger Strike. Ray Comiskey in the
Irish Times, for example, thought that 'the theme of the film – the
destructive power of violence on the individual and the contrast
between it and the healing, uplifting power of art – is developed

cohesively and with total clarity, astutely picked out both visually and by much of the dialogue'. However, he also found 'an opposition between the demands of the genre and the plot, and those of the movie's underlying intent, which is not held in balance. At crucial points both the dialogue and the playing of it are asked to sacrifice naturalism to ensure ... the intellectual development of the theme'. Interestingly, from this emphatically realist perspective, Comiskey believed the film was ultimately 'flawed by the unlikelihood that Danny would have been allowed to progress as far as he did without the intervention of the people who had the greatest motivation to stop him, and who also, as it turns out, had sufficient knowledge to intervene quickly'.[37]

Throughout these contemporaneous reviews, one constant theme emerges: what, exactly, is the connection between *Angel*'s intricate poetics and its peculiarly ambivalent politics? In the years that followed, this question became more and more important, as Irish academic discussions of Jordan grew increasingly fractious in the wake of *The Crying Game* and *Michael Collins*.[38] Although there are several variations of this political critique, the consensus was summed up by Kevin Rockett in *The Companion to British and Irish Cinema* (1996): 'The Irish themes in Jordan's work include a concern with the metaphysics of political violence ... The legitimacy of the state is rarely questioned, and it has been argued that the representation of Ireland in these films is a continuation of a British tradition of dehistoricising Irish political violence.'[39] However, as the Derry filmmaker Margo Harkin remarked,

> [Jordan has] been roundly attacked for his interpretations of the North but I ... think that he was only reflecting quite a commonly held point of view anyway when he talked about the problems of the North being rooted in a sort of psychic violence, rather than looking at other rational explanations for why people behave the way they do.[40]

So, 'psychic violence' versus 'rational explanations': this is the nub of the critical debate. On the one hand we have a text that, in the context of Irish post-colonial history and contemporary politics, 'refuses to decorate its narrative drive with a crass and obvious historical analysis of the Troubles ... knowing too well that the violence has broken free from the tired historical narratives that are supposed to infuse it with meaning'.[41] On the other hand, we have a now-standard academic assessment which – within the same historical and political parameters – insists that *Angel* is part of an on-going tradition of misrepresentation. Or as Louisa Burns-Bisogno articulates it, '[Jordan] gave the audience a frame of reference, Northern Ireland, then narrowed the focus to the extreme. Lacking alternative images, the result unfortunately was reinforcement of the [traditional] stereotype'.[42]

Reinforcing the stereotype: images of violence

In the absence of a native film industry after independence the cinematic depiction of Ireland was left to the commercial designs of British and American companies, which frequently resulted in recidivist, stereotypical projections. In his seminal essay 'Images of Violence', John Hill argues that these stereotypical signs broadly conform to a basic, binary typology: a nostalgic American pastoralism (Ireland as rural, pre-modern and idyllic); and an anxious British neo-imperialism (Ireland as primevally dark and irrationally violent). For Hill, both sets of images share a similar, universalizing discourse which is derived from pre-existing stereotypes of the Irish (lazy, drunken, violent) and the Irish landscape (picturesque but savage). Furthermore, these stereotypes are reinforced and filtered through the dominant conventions of cinematic realism, which 'encourages the explanation of events and actions in terms of individual psychology rather than more general social, political and economic relations'.[43] In terms of the British representation of Ireland, with which Hill is primarily concerned, this ideological discourse manifests itself in one of two ways: 'In the first case, violence is attributed to destiny; in the second, to the deficiencies of the Irish character. . . . It is only metaphysics or race, not history and politics, which offer an explanation of Irish violence.'[44]

Despite the apparent cogency of this thesis, it is worth querying Hill's methodology. Firstly, within the terms of his own argument, Hill admits that given the 'differing histories of America and Britain in relation to Ireland . . . it is the British cinema, rather than the American, which has most consistently chosen to paint its Irish characters black'.[45] This hardly comes as a surprise to an Irish audience, but in practice American representations have always been more publicly influential. Indeed, as Kevin Rockett comments, given the lack of an indigenous industry from the 1930s onwards, 'it is probably true that Hollywood cinema provided an attractive and liberating alternative to official ideologies' – just as it provided a sympathetic alternative to British colonialism prior to independence.[46]

Secondly, Hill's practical analysis presupposes that British and American films share the same narrative model. Theoretically, however, he concedes a quite significant difference, which goes beyond conventional strategies of narrative resolution:

> [W]hile the British cinema has been no less dependent upon narrative than its American counterpart, it has nonetheless lacked the genres which would match the dynamism and energy of the western or gangster film. Far more typical have been the light comedy or domestic drama in which the forward momentum of the American cinema is absent.[47]

If this is true – and I suggest it is – then it radically alters our reading: John Ford's 'Irish western' *The Quiet Man*,[48] for example, comes replete with its own well-established generic values, star personae, iconography, and so on, which are knowingly mapped on to an Irish setting (and subsequently recognized by Irish audiences). To ignore the active intertextuality of this – as Hill does – is to seriously underestimate the narrative sophistication of both filmmaker and audience. Exploring this generic impetus more fully, we might also say that a text like *Angel* is equally complicated by its self-conscious knowledge of *film noir* conventions. In fact, as Hill concedes in an endnote, the 'pessimistic and fatalistic ethos' of *noir* disproves the abstract notion that American genres are always slickly 'affirmative' – but he accounts for this anomaly by noting the genre's 'deployment of a partly "European" aesthetic, in the form of expressionism'. Although he admits that the deployment of this aesthetic in John Ford's *The Informer*,[49] for example, 'makes its representation of Ireland an exception to the typical American model', Hill's binary categories remain firmly fixed and immutable.[50] Yet it is this same expressionistic mode that estranges and deconstructs the stock generic structures of *Angel*, and so we cannot ignore the considerable European influences at work in such a hybrid text.

Thirdly, Hill's general theory of narrative is itself problematic, certainly from a Formalist perspective. Despite his belief in the realist logic of 'consequence' – a narrative drive which is 'not just linear (sequential) but also causal (consequential)' – his analysis focuses almost exclusively on the *fabula* (or story) of the text and virtually ignores its *syuzhet* (or discourse). To insist on the importance of discourse is not simply an 'aesthetic argument', as Hill bluntly puts it, or a diminution of the political in favour of some glib, post-structuralist relativism, but is rather a means of addressing the specifically *filmic* nature of our subject. As David Bordwell points out, 'The primary role of the syuzhet is to present the fabula information that the spectator uses to construct the story'.[51] Nowhere in Hill's analysis does he refer to *mise-en-scène*, montage or the multiple codes of film language (dialogue, sound effects, music and written on-screen material). Thus, by focusing on the *fabula* at the expense of the semiotic colourations of form, Hill might as well be discussing novels instead of films.

As Kevin Barry has pointed out in an important essay on the 1981 film *Traveller* (directed by Joe Comerford, from a script by Neil Jordan),[52] such literary reductiveness is quite common: 'The range of narrative transitions of writing and of film are . . . not symmetrical. Yet we have to acknowledge that film theory (and cinema itself) has relentlessly pursued the novel as its double.'[53] Therefore, the status of *framed image* (the basic cinematic unit) is undermined and diminished, what Barry (following Christian Metz) calls 'the vanishing of the image into the plot'. From this 'novelesque' perspective, 'The narrative (and our desire for a narrative) at once interprets, explains, clarifies and almost annihilates each frame which moves it forward. Narrative, by organising the frame/images in relatively subordinated groups, deflects each one of them.'[54] To counter this totalizing impulse, Barry calls for a critical restoration of the image: a way of reading film – on a vertical rather than a horizontal narrative plane – which would reduce 'subordination and narrative, in favour of sequence and juxtaposition'.[55] This last point is crucial to our understanding of how the surface structure of a narrative is sometimes contradicted and challenged by a deeper structure (the discourse) which functions as a critical counter-narrative. Or as Barry phrases it, in certain films 'the relationships within the frame/image are obviously *in excess of* their relationship in the narrative'.[56]

This brings us to our final criticism of Hill's argument. In assuming that there is no *substantive* difference between British and American narratives (or between story and discourse), Hill presupposes the existence of a universalizing, realist model – which is patently not the case. Ironically, this resurrects itself in a clarion call for a truly 'national' Irish cinema – one which would emphasize the particular and the local – as opposed to an 'international' Irish cinema (exemplified by Jordan), which conforms 'to a long-standing tradition of representing Ireland on the screen'.[57] In other words, as Luke Gibbons has noted, 'The view that truth can only win out in the struggle against myth and prejudice manifest[s] itself . . . in the call for greater realism in the Irish cinema.'[58] However, as Gibbons himself has forcefully argued, 'what passes for realism may often be little more than romanticism in disguise'.[59] Conversely, what often passes for romanticism can sometimes reveal an estranging awareness of social realities, and it 'is this ability of certain strains in Irish romanticism to conduct a process of self-interrogation, to raise doubts at key moments about their own veracity, which cuts across any tendency to take romantic images as realistic accounts of Irish life'.[60] The critical implication of this is clear: we must question all modes of representation – be they realist or romantic – at the level of discourse, for that is where their ideological distortions and political subversions ultimately lie.

The reason for rehearsing these arguments at such length becomes apparent when John Hill turns his considerable critical guns on *Angel*: 'The representations of the Irish characteristically associated with sources outside of Ireland have now apparently become so "natural" and "normal" that they are providing a framework for certain sections of Irish film-making as well'. More specifically, by charting the narrative (*fabula*) progression of *Angel*, Hill apprehends an apolitical, Jungian allegory obsessed with the question of evil. Hill objects to the fact that Danny's motivation for revenge is psychic rather than political, and that the ideological identity of the offending paramilitaries is deliberately withheld: 'this preoccupation with "pure" violence requires a suppression of social and political specifics'. On this basis, Hill condemns *Angel*'s mode of discourse because it is insufficiently realist: it is too vague about politics and place; its texture is too 'dreamlike'; its rhythms are too 'self-consciously poetic'. In the final analysis, by 'attempting to show all violence as the same, irrespective of political context or motivation, the film defies the possibility of any political explanation, and, indeed, any political solution, to the conflicts which are occurring'.[61] This 'realist' critique has long since become the standard model for academic analyses of *Angel* (and for subsequent Jordan films as well). For example, as Matthew Ryan wrote in 2000:[62]

> *Angel* not only dissolves social and political questions in a technical play of surreal lighting, indistinct setting and montaged images, as Hill argues; it also effects this transcendence by thematically combining the binary representations which Hill has identified. *Angel* re-creates Northern Ireland as an American fantasy-land (like the wild west) where individual violence can assume the aura of righteousness. [At] the same time, the figure of the Jewish RUC detective, Bloom, reinstates the British State as the, somehow impartial and legitimate, repository of force by invisibly having the last shot (from outside the frame, like the helicopter we hear throughout the credits)[63] and putting a full stop on this all too Irish excess of passionate vengeance.

An excess of passionate vengeance: *Angel* as counter-narrative

In an elegant and thought-provoking essay on *Angel*, Richard Kearney provides a persuasive counter-argument to these realist critiques.[64] Although equally wary of any indigenous reinforcement of traditional stereotypes, Kearney finds in *Angel* a text that 'works against the romantic grain of traditional Irish cinema [by proposing] alternative models of narrative which challenge the viewer to reassess the dominant myths of national culture'. Contrary to Hill, Kearney approves of *Angel*'s ethical treatment of the mythic unconscious as a means of exploring the personal desires 'which animate ideological violence', and he applauds Jordan's aesthetic strategy, which pitches a 'surface structure' narrative (a conventional detective mystery) against a 'deep structure' counter-narrative (a more expressionistic and 'psychic' discourse).[65] This critical counter-narrative is achieved through a series of synchronic visual and acoustic motifs which cut across the familiar – and therefore expected – conventions of the diachronic plot.

By way of illustration, Kearney briefly outlines some of these motifs. Firstly, the fact that various women invite Danny to dance at crucial plot intervals: Annie (before her murder, and to the tune of 'Blood is Thicker than Water'); the young bride (before her husband deserts her, to the tune of 'I Want to Be Near You [Every Day of My Life]'); Deirdre (after Danny's murder of George, in a comic samba routine); and Aunty Mae (also after George's murder, to the tune of 'Narcissus'). Secondly, there is the constant use of music and song, which is juxtaposed against the action of the revenge narrative: Deirdre's singing of 'Danny Boy' and 'Strange Fruit'; Mae's improvization of a music-hall ditty; the eerie Verdi Requiem, which recurs at key moments throughout the film; the bizarre musical performance in the asylum,[66] and so on. Thirdly, there is the 'healing hands' motif: at key points Danny is touched by Annie, Deirdre, Mae and Mary in an effort to heal him. The significance of this is reinforced at the end when the young faith-healer blesses Danny near the ruins of the ballroom, and a whole series of vertical motifs collide: the burning candles in Francie's caravan evoke the fairy lights of the ballroom and the wishing tree; Danny encounters his nemesis, Bonner, in the ashes of the bombsite; Bonner's dying words – 'stay with me' – echo the final words of the second assassin, and so on. These rhythmic refrains underscore Danny's own movement from healer to killer, and recall the prophetic words of the young bride who warns Danny that men 'start out as angels but end up as brutes'. Finally, there is Jordan's deployment of key 'framing images', which punctuate and deliberately suspend the action: the haunting asylum sequence (before Danny commits his second murder); the elegiac Salvation Army sequence (after the second murder); the eerie mountain sequence (before and after Danny commits his third murder); the uncanny faith-healing rite at the end, and so on.[67]

If anything, Kearney probably underplays this deconstructive process: in virtually every scene of this film an image or phrase will re-occur in another context, and these estranging motifs and leitmotifs connect synchronically to create an alternative field of semantic possibilities. Take, for example, the musical motif: extending Kearney's analysis, Maria Pramaggiore argues that 'the music in *Angel* – dominated by a jazz aesthetic based on repetition and violence – underscores the themes of sexuality, loss and violence, and undergirds the film's formal and narrative circularity'. In the opening sequence, for example, Danny – 'the Stan Getz of South Armagh' – plays a riff from 'Danny Boy', and when Annie touches the instrument it becomes symbolically endowed with 'phallic status'.[68] Given these phallic connotations, it is hardly surprising that after Annie's death Danny temporarily loses his instrument and his ability to play it. In his traumatized memory, music becomes associated with violent death rather than sexual conquest, and his gradual descent into bloodshed 'is marked by an increase in the use of jazz riffs which signal the return of repressed memories' at crucial points: when the police take Danny to the morgue; when the bride tells Danny of her husband's absence on the night of Annie's murder; when Danny finds his new manager making protection payments; in Danny's final confrontation with Bonner. As Pramaggiore concludes: 'Not only are the specific songs Danny performs connected to his struggle against violence and anonymity, but the non-diegetic score, resonant with Danny's replaying and revising the loss of Annie and his innocence, is critical to the film's anti-narrative elements'.[69]

Furthermore, although Richard Kearney notes the influence of Boorman's *Point Blank* and Bertolucci's *The Conformist*,[70] he somewhat underplays the rampant intertextuality of *Angel*, which goes far beyond the use of unmotivated, traumatic flashbacks implicit in these two films. Take, for example, the oft-cited influence of *Point Blank*: 'a highly ambitious film, the first and maybe still the richest merging of an American genre with European art-house aspirations'.[71] Even at the most basic level of plot, there are abundant parallels between *Point Blank* and *Angel*: reluctantly drawn into a robbery, the hero, Walker (Lee Marvin), is double-crossed and left for dead by his wife and his partner, Reese, on the deserted island of Alcatraz. Walker miraculously survives and, skilfully manipulated by the mysterious Fairfax, sets about exacting his revenge. His progress becomes a destructive and paranoid quest through the ranks of an all-powerful criminal organization, which Reese has transformed into a legitimate corporation. However, after Walker begins an affair with his wife's sister, he is forced to consider the deeper reasons for his vengeful pursuit.

In terms of *Angel*, however, it is the formal texture of Boorman's thriller that concerns us here, and not the mere similarities in plot. As Michael Open notes, '*Point Blank* is a work of extraordinary richness. . . . Its structural symmetry is amazingly thorough, and congruences abound. Most obviously, the film begins and ends on Alcatraz, with the same atmosphere of sinister melancholy . . . One might say that Walker has found his way back to a time before betrayal.'[72] The impact of this textual richness on *Angel* extends to its corresponding use of montage flashbacks, its violent jazz score, and its expressionistic use of colour to convey extreme states of mind.[73] But the most significant intertextual trace element is undoubtedly Boorman's dialogic narrative, which uses the conventions of *film noir* to make a philosophical statement about the psychic effects of violence. As Michael Open comments, in 'the details of its construction, *Point Blank* evidences a duality of content. There is a complicated account of [the hero's] rampage . . . and a parallel description of the regeneration of his atrophied life. This simple principle dominates the film, and has caused countless interpretative difficulties.'[74] Indeed, in one quite suggestive reading of *Point Blank*, David Thompson argues that the entire non-linear narrative is actually a dream of revenge on the part of the dying protagonist, and not an objective reality; in any case, it is fair to say that Walker – as much as Danny – is emotionally and spiritually dead.[75] Interestingly, in his introduction to the published screenplay of *Angel*, John Boorman himself noted the stylistic traces of *Point Blank*: 'Most interesting is the dialogue which is composed in a style which I call "poetic cliché". The characters mostly swap platitudes, but by repetition and rhythm, Jordan stylises their exchanges [and plays this] against the tension of realistic staging.'[76]

This counter-realist stylization is all part of a much broader matrix of European art-house influences. In an interview in 1982 Jordan freely conceded the influence of Michelangelo Antonioni's *Blow Up*[77] and *The Passenger*[78] – especially the latter's 'transmutation of identity' (where the protagonist assumes a dead man's identity).[79] More directly significant, though, is *Angel*'s sly verbal and visual allusion to Antonioni's *L'Avventura*.[80]

> DANNY *and* DEIRDRE *are sitting in the dressing-room.* . . .
> DANNY: (*Pointing to a photograph*) Who's that?
> DEIRDRE: Monica Vitti.
> DANNY: Who's Monica Vitti?[81]

Part of the in-joke here is that Monica Vitti – the star of *L'Avventura* – is the spitting image of Deirdre (Honor Heffernan), but the real signifi-cance of the allusion lies in its evocation of Antonioni's strange (and estranging) meditation on cultural alienation. At the level of *fabula*, *L'Avventura* is essentially plotless: a woman goes missing on an island; several characters search listlessly for her; they fail to find her; the quest – and the woman – is eventually forgotten; cue credits. However, as Pauline Kael remarks, 'There's something great here – a new mood, a new emotional rhythm – even with all the affectation.'[82] Moreover, in terms of how 'meaning' – *any* meaning, including moral and political meaning – is generated and transmitted through the cinematic appa-ratus, *L'Avventura*'s 'emotional rhythms' broke entirely new ground. As Geoffrey Nowell-Smith observes: 'If [*L'Avventura*] offers a statement it is a second-order one, a statement about the limits of what it is possible to say. It speaks through silence. It opens up a space for comprehension to enter, without saying (because it cannot) what that comprehension should be'.[83] Interestingly, like Richard Kearney on *Angel* and Kevin Barry on *Traveller*, Nowell-Smith borrows liberally from the narrative theories of Roland Barthes. And as Barthes himself said of *L'Avventura* (though it could equally apply to *Angel*):

> [T]his subtlety of meaning, this conviction that meaning does not stop crudely with the thing being said but always goes further, fascinated by what lies beyond – this subtlety is, I believe, that of all artists, whose object is not this or that technique but that strange phenomenon, vibration. The object represented vibrates, to the detriment of dogma.[84]

To the detriment of dogma: the politics of *Angel*

As I have discussed in detail elsewhere, the dialectic tension in Jordan's work is frequently generated by the provocative clash of competing literary and filmic intertexts.[85] For the purposes of this present discus-sion I will limit my analysis to just two literary allusions in *Angel*. First, and returning to the musical motif, there is Deirdre's soulful rendition of 'Strange Fruit' – an anti-violence poem made famous by Billie Holiday in the 1930s:

> Southern trees bear a strange fruit,
> Blood on the leaves and blood at the root,
> Black body swinging in the Southern breeze,
> Strange fruit hanging from the poplar trees.[86]

As Jordan noted in an interview, 'Strange Fruit' is 'such a horrific poem that when you look at it you could almost transpose the whole lyrics over to Ireland'.[87] But as Jordan was well aware, Seamus Heaney had already done so in 1975 – the very year in which *Angel* is set – as part of a sequence of poems in *North* about prehistoric bodies found ritually executed in a Jutland bog:

> Murdered, forgotten, nameless, terrible
> Beheaded girl, outstaring axe
> And beatification, outstaring
> What had begun to feel like reverence.[88]

Heaney, no more than Jordan, is sometimes taken to task for his perceived refusal to speak directly about the politics of the Northern Irish conflict. As Desmond Fennell has argued, *North* 'says nothing, plainly or figuratively, about the war, about any of the three main parties to it, or about the issues at stake . . . except that it is sad, rooted in history, often ruthless, and connected with the oppression of the poet's people and sacrifice to a goddess'.[89] However, such literal – or realist – criticism often says more about the ideological bias of the critic than about the subject of the critique. Heaney, like Jordan, is painfully aware of the rational and historical reasons for political violence in Ireland, but alongside this knowledge is an understanding that the facts of the world are rarely the end of the matter. As artists, both Heaney and Jordan are interested in discovering the unspoken – and usually unconscious – fears and desires that animate the physical act of violence, whether it be sectarian hatred, corruption, revenge, or jealousy. Moreover, as Heaney noted in an interview in 1982 (the same year as *Angel*'s release):

> Poetry is born out of the watermarks and colourings of the self.
> But that self in some ways takes its spiritual pulse from the
> inward spiritual structure of the community to which it belongs;
> and the community to which I belong is Catholic and nationalist.

> I believe that the poet's force now . . . is to maintain the efficacy
> of his own 'mythos', his own cultural and political colourings,
> rather than serve any particular momentary strategy that his
> political leaders, his paramilitary organization, or his own liberal
> self might want him to serve.[90]

Similarly, as Jordan himself noted, 'the metaphysical language in which [*Angel*] speaks is a very Catholic one of guilt, sin and redemption'.[91] Nonetheless, as Paul Taylor comments, although 'the underpinnings of *Angel* are solidly Catholic (and it obstinately refuses to be drawn into the politics of sectarianism)', Jordan is still 'willing to subject that limiting theological schema to critical tests of reason and humour . . . as he is to counterpose it with mystical echoes of some rare order'.[92] As part of his own exploration of atavistic violence, Jordan employs a second poetic metaphor, namely the 'mystical echoes' of William Blake's 'Nobodaddy' – an archetype first invoked by Aunty Mae when she reads Danny's cards: 'He's got no face. Somewhere between all the other faces'. Nobodaddy – significantly, a portmanteau mix of 'Nobody's Daddy' – is Blake's characterization of the Old Testament god of wrath and hellfire, a dark god jealous of the joy of his own creation:

> Why art thou silent and invisible,
> Father of jealousy?
> Why dost thou hide thyself in clouds
> From every searching eye?
>
> Why darkness and obscurity
> In all thy words and laws,
> That none dare eat the fruit but from
> The wily serpent's jaws?
> Or is it because secrecy
> Gains females' loud applause?[93]

Throughout *Angel*, this living embodiment of evil and unfettered Oedipal desire is constantly invoked: by George ('I'm nobody'); by Bloom ('I know nothing too. You've got to watch nothing. It can take hold of you'); by the deserted bride ('Nobody's touched me since'); by the abused Mary ('Hating is easy, that's what I found out. It can take hold of you'); and even by Danny himself ('It's like a nothing you can feel. And it gets worse'). Unsurprisingly, it is this Jungian, even mystical, personification of evil that most provokes Jordan's more realist critics, but this blanket outrage is surely missing the semiotic and semantic nuances of the metaphor. Nobodaddy in *Angel* is a psychic projection of people's fears in a culture overwhelmed by physical violence – but he is simultaneously a figure of attraction as well as a self-fulfilling prophecy. This psychic metaphor is not entirely without political foundation, or as Richard Kearney notes in 'Myth and Martyrdom I':

> The credibility of [an] attempt to identify a mythological dimension in Ulster terrorism does not presuppose a belief in a Jungian collective Unconscious ... Mythic archetypes of behaviour and thought are as likely transmitted by means of actual and narrated experience as by some form of transhistorical or innate inheritance. It is enough for the Provisional [IRA] to have known and heard of the 1916 martyrs and these to have known and heard of the Fenian rebels and these of the heroes of ancient Ireland etc. for the mythic experience of sacrificial terror to perdure and recur.[94]

In a fascinating ethnographic study of violence in Northern Ireland, anthropologist Allen Feldman argues that the conventional search for the origins of political violence inevitably locates it as a surface expression of deeper ideological contexts, and tends to ignore the act (and effects) of violence itself. Feldman is keen to stress that his own study – based on interviews with one hundred Protestants and Catholics in working-class areas of Belfast – is not an 'event history' but rather 'a genealogical analysis of the symbolic forms, material practices, and narrative strategies through which certain types of political agency are constructed in Northern Ireland'.[95] Consequently, Feldman privileges performative narratives over pedagogic ones, on the grounds that 'the use of history to repress historicity is a central ideological mechanism in the political culture of Northern Ireland'.[96] Central to Feldman's study is the (Catholic) urban myth of the 'Black Man', which first emerged in the early 1970s:

> The Black Man was a rumour, a cultural elaboration of terror. He appeared wearing a black cloak or hood and an upside-down cross, and he 'sacrificed' dogs in arcane rites of black magic. He was simultaneously 'Man', 'Devil' and 'Prod', and was associated with the entry of the First Paratroop Regiment into the Ardoyne, a Catholic area of Belfast known for its militant republicanism. He visited the houses of recently killed IRA men, leaving black candles. He was both elusive and indestructible.[97]

Feldman notes how this mythic bogey man had a material basis, both as a British paratrooper – the First Paratroop Regiment were known to have killed dogs in the area, as dogs were often trained to bark at their approach – and as a sectarian killer (the description evokes the balaclavas worn by paramilitaries). So 'The Black Man', like Jordan's 'Nobodaddy', emerges as a kind of archetypal trickster-scapegoat figure – a brutal, nightmarish projection of a culture enveloped by violence:

> The Black Man is a divided figure . . . .. The fact that he is beaten but not killed indicates that he performs a ritual function. As an operator of sacrificial signifiers he is a necessary presence. He participates equally in the imagery of paramilitary violence and state counterinsurgency. He is victimizer and victim. . . . The Black Man is a theatre of mirror effects that reduces all the forms, agencies, and objects of violence to relations of sameness and value equivalence. In this manner, he personifies the infrastructure of violence as exchange.[98]

Within this 'infrastructure of violence', it is hardly surprising that *Angel* has elicited such violent – and disparate – critical responses. Indeed, as the (pro-unionist) critic Alexander Walker approvingly remarked, *Angel* is 'a truly conceptual film on which nothing is imposed but out of which everything can be read'.[99] Thus, in Richard Kearney's reading, Jordan's counter-narrative strategies enable 'the viewer to delve beneath the ideological clichés of political violence to its unconscious hidden dimension'. Because the narrative gaze is almost exclusively Danny's, we witness the horror of his own violence as he performs it, and then experience his Kafkaesque disorientation at the end when he realizes the depth of the political conspiracy surrounding him. By deconstructing the narratives of classic realism – which encourage passive identification with the hero – *Angel* thus becomes, in Kearney's terms, a 'radical deromanticism of the cult of heroic violence which has fuelled sentimental nationalism in many of its traditional and contemporary guises'.[100]

For John Hill, however, these same aesthetic strategies serve to decontextualize 'the rationale of political violence' (i.e. British and Irish nationalism), and thereby add to 'the legitimacy of the state by de-politicising its activities as well'.[101] In other words, by blurring the ideological identity of the killers and by counter-pointing Danny's graphic acts of violence against more discreet acts of state violence (Bloom's killing of Bonner is performed off-camera), Hill believes that *Angel* effectively obscures political complexity. But as Kearney and others have argued, there *are* hints given – albeit obliquely – as to the identity of the central players: the murder gang, including the policeman Bonner, are Protestant/loyalist; the protection racketeers are Catholic/republican; and Danny himself is probably Protestant, though politically unaligned.[102] However, this materialist reading raises as many questions as it resolves, depending on the ideological standpoint of the viewer. Indeed, for Brian McIlroy, writing from an avowedly Northern Irish Protestant perspective, this particular scenario may well imply a deeply sectarian politics:

> The film's underlying premise is that police corruption and murder (represented by the Protestant community) destroy Danny's humanity and lead him to violent acts. Danny is, then, the IRA, 'the people' radicalised into action. Literally, he is a son without parents, one who finds his voice – first by sax playing and then by gunplay. He eliminates the 'cancer' of Protestantism and contentedly leaves a Jewish head of police – significantly called Bloom (a cute Joycean echo) – to sort out the mess at the end.[103]

McIlroy's interpretation certainly reflects a valid – and often under-represented – ideological anxiety concerning the cinematic representation of Northern Irish Protestantism. For Jordan himself though, writing from the point of view of a Southern Irish Catholic, *Angel* reflects a different set of political and epistemological concerns, or as he commented in an interview in 1982: 'I wanted to speak about a certain kind of violence which has come up in Ireland the past five or six years. . . . Violence which is not directly political, but in some bizarre way is a spin-off of the availability of armaments.'[104] In terms of the politics of *Angel* this suggests two distinct issues: 1) that a certain degree of 'political' terrorism in the North (be it republican or loyalist) is actually a front for criminal racketeering – an observation now generally accepted by political analysts in the wake of the Anglo-Irish Peace Process; 2) Jordan's film implicitly suggests a degree of institutional collusion between the security forces and loyalist paramilitaries in the period under scrutiny – again, a point that is now generally (if not always officially) accepted by many political commentators.[105]

Certainly, at least in terms of the particular sectarian atrocity that originally inspired *Angel*, this theory of state-sponsored terrorism carries some weight – and not just amongst the Catholic community in Northern Ireland. In his controversial maiden speech to the House of Commons in 1987, the Labour MP (and later Mayor of London) Ken Livingstone alleged that the UVF unit that carried out the Miami Showband Massacre was actually led by Captain Robert Nairac, a notorious MI5 agent, as part of a covert black propaganda campaign by British intelligence services.[106] This allegation was never conclusively proven, but it nonetheless remains a narrative 'fact' within certain sections of the nationalist community in the North (and South) of Ireland. Like the modern myth of the 'Black Man' (who is both an image of paramilitary violence and state counterinsurgency), such conspiracy theories may indeed have some basis in fact – but that is not really the point. Instead, these stories symbolize in very powerful ways the paralysing sense of fear and paranoia that emanates from a culture traumatized by years of violence.

Consequently, in this respect alone, *Angel* does reveal a residual political awareness that is both performative and prophetic by turn. More importantly though, by exploring a whole range of unpalatable atavisms that underlie the conflict (sectarianism, corruption, revenge, jealousy), *Angel* displays a wealth of complexity which traditional political narratives and conventional models of criticism have tended to occlude. 'Violence', according to Gilles Deleuze, 'is something that does not speak'[107] – at least not in realist terms. In the final analysis, it is the very ambivalence and open-endedness of *Angel* which makes its muted but multiple messages all the more compelling. Or as Seamus Heaney wrote in 1984:

> 'Pure' poetry is perfectly justifiable in earshot of the carbomb, but it still implies a politics, depending on the nature of the poetry. A poetry of hermetic wit, of riddles and slips and self-mocking ironies, while it may appear culpably miniaturist or fastidious to the activist with his microphone at the street corner, may be exercising in its inaudible way a fierce disdain of the amplified message, or a distressed sympathy with it.[108]

Ciaran Carson:
the New Urban Poetics

ELMER KENNEDY-ANDREWS

The dominant perception of Irish poetry is that it is a rural poetry, yet, as my title implies, there was before the emergence of a '*new*' Irish urban poetics, represented by Ciaran Carson since the late 1980s, an older urban poetry in Ireland. James Joyce was in fact the first to open up the literary potential of the Irish city. The city as a site of discontinuity and difference, of infinite 'plurabilities', became the locus of an alternative vision to Yeats's totalizing, rural-based cultural nationalism. Joyce's influence is clearly seen in succeeding poets such as Austin Clarke and Thomas Kinsella whose work reflects a distinctive Dublin poetic locale and engages with the emerging urban culture of the 1950s and 1960s that resulted from the opening of the South to the economics of modern international capitalism, the shift in the country's population from the country to the city, and the break with the values of an insular, rural, Gaelic past. In his lecture, 'The Irish Writer', Kinsella cites Joyce as the true 'father' of modern Irish poetry, specifically on account of Joyce's inscription of the city rather than the land as the central term in Irish literature, and his understanding of alienation, fragmentation and discontinuity as the essential features of the modern Irish condition.[1] In the North, as Edna Longley notes, Louis MacNeice, 'for whom Belfast was the first city', was 'in the vanguard of absorbing the city into English poetry generally'.[2] MacNeice's receptivity to the city is part and parcel of a vision of the world perceived as 'flux', as 'incorrigibly plural'.[3] Born in Belfast, brought up in Carrickfergus, County Antrim, educated in a preparatory school in Dorset, followed by Marlborough public school, then Oxford, Birmingham and London, while constantly returning to 'Ireland, my Ireland', he wrote from the vantage point of the perennially sceptical, cosmopolitan outsider in whom multiple strains criss-cross in productive tension. His exile's *odi atque amo* relationship with Belfast in particular and Ireland more generally has made him an important example for younger poets such as Carson who have also been interested in exploring hybrid, plural identity in a culture all too prone to fixity and fossilization.

Similarly, Derek Mahon responds to his native Belfast as a place of transit, and sees himself as a tourist in his own country, repelled by its philistinism, its bigotry and its vulgar petit bourgeois materialism. 'Spring in Belfast', the first poem in his *Collected Poems*, points to an alternative to 'the desperate city': 'We could *all* be saved by keeping an eye on the hill / At the top of every street, for there it is, / Eternally, if irrelevantly, visible – '.[4] 'We', as Edna Longley notes, registers 'the poet's implication and complicity in the evil', while 'saved' indicates that 'once more a Protestant writer is turning Protestant orthodoxy, Protestant conscience, against itself, to conceive a very different kind of salvation to that offered by evangelism'.[5] Belfast is not the 'city *on* a hill' of Puritan mythology, but there is a (green?) hill not too far away symbolizing the possibility of salvation, perhaps through a return to a more open and natural religion, or through reclaiming 'original' identity with the land. Such grounding, however, remains elusive or illusory: just as MacNeice acknowledged of his beloved West that 'the pre-natal mountain is far away'[6] (both his parents were from Connemara) so Mahon concedes the 'irrelevance' of his eternal hill. Even while conveying the fragmentation of modernity, these poets display a typically modernist nostalgia for authenticity and wholeness. This tension is just as pronounced in Mahon's recent work, which shifts its urban focus from Belfast to New York and Dublin. Mahon shows an openness to the discontinuous culture of the postmodern city when it is New York (*The Hudson Letter*), but not at all when it is Dublin (*The Yellow Book*). Resisting the homogenizing threat of globalization and postmodern indifference, *The Yellow Book* is an elegy for a lost authenticity, an imaginary past that has been dismissed as 'irrelevant': 'Those were the days; now patience, courage, artistry, / solitude things of the past, like the fear of God, / we nod to you from the pastiche paradise of the post-modern'.[7]

Unlike Mahon, Michael Longley has stayed and worked in Belfast throughout the 'Troubles', both he and Carson holding positions in the Arts Council of Northern Ireland. Contrasting with Mahon's stance of disaffected outsider, Longley identifies with the city, with its shopkeepers, civil servants and linen workers who represent the economic and civic life of the city. Where Heaney, coming from a close-knit rural background, memorializes casualties of the Troubles who were relatives (his second cousin Colum McCartney in 'The Strand at Lough Beg')[8] or at least personal acquaintances (Louis O'Neal in 'Casualty'),[9]

Longley's elegies are tributes to anonymous urban strangers. Longley relates to Belfast not in terms of inherited familial, tribal or religious affiliation (his family connection with the province dates from 1927 when his parents first arrived in Belfast from Clapham Common) but in terms of his own humane, 'baggage-free' sense of place, unencumbered by questions of identity. 'Home' for Longley is always a personal construct, Belfast a subjectively imagined metropolis. 'Wounds'[10] juxtaposes images of his father's experiences on the Somme in 1916 with the deaths of nameless victims of the contemporary Troubles on the streets of Belfast: all wounds are the same. In keeping with this analogizing approach, the situation in Belfast is explored through multiple trans-cultural perspectives: the Warsaw ghetto, First and Second World War battlefields, the Jarama valley, scenes from Homeric epic.

Heaney's statement in his essay 'The Sense of Place' that it is to 'the stable element, the land itself, that we must look for continuity'[11] suggests a basic opposition: the land as timeless constant, the image of the past, the place of traditional ways, of all that is human and natural, the organic society; and the city as flux and change, the engine of progress and modernisation, the route to the future. Referring to the city, Raymond Williams draws attention to how 'within the new kind of open, complex and mobile society, small groups in any form of divergence or dissent could find some kind of foothold, in ways that would not have been possible if the artists and thinkers composing them had been scattered in more traditional, closed societies'.[12] City-life complicates traditional monolithic nationalisms, whether Irish or unionist, because it gives a foothold to other forms of struggle – class or gender, for example – which cut across the traditional divisions and oppositions. Drawn to the 'stable element', Heaney, we can agree with Eamonn Hughes,[13] has difficulty engaging directly with the metropolis, for what is notable about Heaney's treatment of the city is his tendency to mythologize or allegorize it, as seen from the iconic portraiture of the early 'Docker' to the construction of Belfast as the city of plague in 'A Northern Hoard', a suite of Belfast poems in *Wintering Out*, published in 1972 at the height of the Troubles. In a series of hallucinatory images, Belfast is pictured as a diseased and blood-soaked city, 'Out there . . . / Where the fault is opening again'. It is 'old Gomorrah', 'No man's land', 'No sanctuary'. 'What do I say if they wheel out their dead?'[14] he asks himself. His answer is to withdraw from the city, back to the County Derry farm for most of the rest of the poems in this volume and, in Part I of his next collection, *North*,[15] away from Belfast and the contemporary 'massacre' into Scandinavian and Viking myth. Carson, in his well-known review of *'North*, '"Escaped from the Massacre"?', registers his objections: 'Heaney seems to have moved from being a writer with the gift of precision, to become the laureate of violence – a mythmaker, an anthropologist of ritual killing, an apologist for "the situation", in the last resort, a mystifier'. Carson objects to the attempt to impose a trans-historical, totalizing framework within which the contemporary violence is to be understood and ultimately transposed into 'the realm of inevitability'.[16]

In Carson's challenge to Heaney's work, Neil Corcoran reads 'the ground of a Northern Irish poetry of the postmodern beginning to prepare itself'.[17] Carson's own poetry, Corcoran continues, is a search for a way of registering 'the full shock of the challenge to recognised modes and forms represented by the realities of post-1968 Northern Ireland, and more particularly post-1968 Belfast'.[18] It is the purpose of this essay to identify and describe the elements of this new urban poetics which, emanating from the epicentre of the recent Troubles, unsettle the fixed versions of the city we find in Heaney, Mahon and other poets who see Belfast in essentialist terms, as unchanging and monolithic, standing in stark opposition to the pre- or anti-modern land. By experimenting with discontinuous, de-centred or ungrounded forms, Carson presents a city space that is unstable and unreliable yet always susceptible to re-construction and renewal. Exploring this new space leads to the creation of new maps, the formulation of new concepts of identity and place, and the relationships between them. Belfast is no longer merely the place which must be escaped, but the location of post-national, encyclopaedic, labyrinthine, ever-shifting Northern scenarios.

Carson's work exemplifies the ways in which 'open' or discontinuous or broken forms function to represent epistemological attitudes. His gapped, elliptical poems whose parts refuse to combine into unified wholes, constitute a distinctive view of the world, one originating from within a society in the throes of violent breakdown. A broken style reflects a fractured society. As many of the poems demonstrate, discontinuity can place considerable demands on the reader who is left to arrange the elements more or less as he or she sees fit. Incompleteness and indeterminacy in the poem reflect the incompleteness and indeterminacy, and even the necessity of such incompleteness and indeterminacy of our knowledge of reality. Whatever knowledge is available takes the form of disjointed facts or observations with no comprehensive explanations to connect them. Rationalistic metaphysics, and the form in which they are usually presented, are rejected because they give a misleadingly coherent picture of our knowledge of reality.

Take one of his best-known poems, 'Belfast Confetti', which suggests, in its 'stuttering' but powerfully energetic way, a connection between history and poetry, civil disturbance and textual disturbance, the city and the language in which it is (de-)constructed;

> Suddenly as the riot squad moved in, it was raining
>   exclamation marks,
> Nuts, bolts, nails, car-keys. A fount of broken type. And the
>   explosion
> Itself – an asterisk on the map. This hyphenated line, a burst
>   of rapid fire . . .
> I was trying to complete a sentence in my head, but it kept
>   stuttering,
> All the alleyways and side-streets blocked with stops and
>   colons.[19]

No longer able to maintain conventional structure, the poem consists of disjointed lists of things presented without subordination, giving the impression of a discourse unmediated by an ordering rational mind, responding directly to the exigencies of the moment. Relying on an accumulating power of perception, the poem, proceeding through a series of alternating staccato bursts and arrests, speaks emphatically of the here and now. 'Confetti', with its ironic connotations of union and celebration, refers to the missiles hurled by the rioting mob, the disrupted text of the poem, and the confusion of the poet's own shredded thoughts. Against this backdrop of violent disturbance, questions of identity ('What is /My name?'), origins ('Where am I coming from?') and purpose ('Where am I going?') are thrown into confusion. We cannot even be sure who is asking the questions. Is the poet questioning himself? Or has he been stopped by the police or the army? Or is this a similar situation to that described in 'Question Time',[20] where he is watched and followed and then interrogated by local Falls Road vigilantes? Where Heaney's place-names (Anahorish, Broagh, Derrygarve) provide the reassuring co-ordinates of home, Carson's mark out an alienating imperial past: 'I know this labyrinth so well – Balaclava, Raglan, Inkerman, Odessa Street –/ Why can't I escape?' The speaker, though assimilated to the city, cannot dominate the situation but, instead, begins to lose his initial, complacent 'self' in a process which opens the self to the battering assault of otherness and contingency.

Carson replaces the rational, abstract, ahistorical, unified subject with a de-centred consciousness. The subject that emerges is a provisional, historical figure composed through its interaction with the 'other', through remaining 'in play', in movement, a harried *flâneur*. Without a sense of centre, the abstract binaries – subject/object, self/city, inner/outer – which have formed the basis of knowledge and certainty – dissolve into each other, and the subject as autonomous agent is relocated within the networks of historical process, deprived of the distance that would enable him to produce a 'grand narrative' that is without gaps or elisions, without stops or stuttering. As if in response to Nietzsche's words; 'It was out of this pathos of distance that they assumed the right to create values, to coin the names of values,'[21] – Carson's poem proclaims the primacy of lived, historical contingencies over metaphysical abstraction, being over truth.

The first line of 'Night Patrol' – 'Jerking his head spasmodically as he is penetrated by invisible gunfire'[22] – presents an image of what one might expect from the title. But then, it would seem, this is all metaphor and the soldier is actually in bed dreaming or, possibly, masturbating to 'pull-outs from *Contact* and *Men Only*', death on the streets from a sniper's bullet linked with the 'little death' of orgasm. The soldier is in 'a room that is a room knocked into other rooms', just as the poem itself moves uninterruptedly from the soldier's bedroom to remembered rooms 'in Balkan Street and Hooker Street' to the entire Grand Central Hotel (an hotel that was actually 'knocked into' an army barracks), to the streets of the city generally. The image of 'a room that is a room knocked into other rooms' might stand for Carson's poetic methodology which is always challenging arbitrarily imposed demarcations and notions of discrete identity. The objects of the phenomenal world, rather than being distinct, are seen as actually shading into or merging with one another or joining together in a process of promiscuous hybridization. As he puts it in another poem, 'Jawbox', 'one image warps into another, like the double helix / Of the DNA code'.[23] Thus, the masturbatory motif in 'Night Patrol' is extended to the entire city, which is revealed in a state of vulgar dishevelment: 'the whole Victorian creamy façade has been tossed off'. 'Telstar', the name of the communications satellite, is 'knocked into' the name of a taxi firm ('Telstar Taxis'), whose depot is 'a hole' that has, quite literally, been 'knocked into' 'a breeze-block wall' in the material fabric of the city. These multiple conjugations find their lexical enactment in the proliferation of words that have been 'knocked into' each other to form hyphenated compounds. The poem ends with reference to 'a wire grille and a voice-box uttering gobbledygook'. Whose disembodied voice is this? What is this 'gobbledegook'? – merely nonsense, or a soldier's coded message? The discontinuous form of the poem reflects indeterminacy and incomplete knowledge, denying us the possibility of a unified and definitive picture of the world.

All this, of course, relates significantly to those contemporary Belfast actualities where security, whether of the individual, the community or the state, depends on intelligence gathering, surveillance, taking detours and devious routes, exchanging coded messages, using confidential phones. 'Last Orders' has the speaker seeking entry to a late-night drinking-club. We wonder to which paramilitary group the club is linked, and from which religious background the speaker comes. The poem is deliberately unforthcoming: 'I, for instance could be anybody. Though I'm told / Taig's written on my face. See me, would *I* trust appearances?'[24] He could never be just 'anybody' in Northern Ireland's reductive sectarian calculus of 'us' and 'them', though the 'Taig' attribution is as quickly undermined as it is suggested. The world of the poem is one in which 'you never know for sure who's who'. What is palpable is the ever-present suggestion of violence: the speaker squeezes the buzzer 'like a trigger', but it's 'someone else' who has him in 'their sights'. Once inside he orders *Harp*, which 'seems safe enough, everybody drinks it', though the brand-name is decidedly Irish nationalist. He notices the hostile looks of an unidentified 'someone' in 'the *Bushmills* mirror', the brand-name this time linked with the staunchly loyalist north Antrim town where the whiskey is made. The poem's play with pronouns and perspectives leads to complete confusion of self and other, the speaker ultimately identifying simultaneously with both bombers and victims:

> how simple it would
> be for someone
> Like ourselves to walk in and blow the whole place, and
> ourselves, to Kingdom Come.

'Queen's Gambit' is another example of a poem which does not simply tell us about discontinuity; it *is* that discontinuity. Through episodic fragmentation of the narrative, the absence of causal explanations, the disjointing of chronology, Carson achieves a radical discontinuity, which is a function of 'content'. The poem sets up several narrative lines which begin to unfold in different time frames but which fail to cohere into any reliable meaning. The final italicized section offers some putative order when a barber, while giving the speaker a haircut, tells his version of events. But the barber's story leaves much unexplained. Littered as it is with tags such as '*It seems . . .*', and '*If you ask me . . .*', it acknowledges its own provisional, partial and unreliable status:

It looks to me, it was a set-up job, though who
   exactly
Was set up, God only knows . . .

                                                       . . . If you ask
   me,
With these confidential telephones, you never know who's doing who, or
   why[25]

Poetic form is a field of possibilities, like the 'stoolie-pigeon spool', which, when replayed, 'Its querulous troughs and peaks map out a different curve of possibility'.[26] In the continually mutating world of the poem – 'It's all go, here, changing something into something else'[27] – even the speaker at the end, shorn of hair and beard, feels 'like a new man'. Re-entering the outside world, he leaves the barber 'to a row of empty mirrors'.[28] Peter Barry wants to rescue Carson from postmodern 'new narrativism', claiming that the postmodern label 'docs some disservice to the starkness and impact of many of these pieces, which lack the disembodied, ludic, but perhaps ultimately rather pointless complexities of this mode of writing'. In the typical Carson poem, according to Barry, the 'chronotope is always clear, its viewpoint consistent, and all the apparently random details are clicked into place at the end'.[29] The radical instability of 'Queen's Gambit' might be invoked to refute the accuracy of this description. In 'Queen's Gambit', details *are* left 'teasingly untied' rather than 'pushed relentlessly home', ludic *jouissance* is a marked feature of the writing, questions of meaning *are* left unresolved. But the resulting poem is not one of 'pointless complexity': the poem questions the possibility of a true narrative, but does not discount the possibility of *some* truth. By playing with narrative in various ways, Carson challenges ontological and epistemological certainty, but he does this in order to demonstrate the difficulty of constructing a reliable history, not to invalidate the humanist quest for truth and moral value.

In contrast to Heaney's 'untoppled omphalos',[30] Carson's exploded view of the city's secret places in 'Night Patrol' reveals a brutally unromantic viscera of 'cables, sewers, a snarl of Portakabins,/ Soft-porn shops and carry-outs'.[31] Carson's Belfast, viewed as a debased, crudely improvised commodity culture, is the antithesis of Heaney's grounding rural home. Heaney's is a predominantly commemorative poetics, born of a sacral sense of place, and honouring the communal calendar customs and the traditional craft work of digging, ploughing, fishing and thatching, all of which are presented as analogues of the poet's craft rather than expressions of a commercial or economic view of life.

Carson's city is a site of alienation, confusion and violence, to be located as an unstable conceptual or virtual arena as well as an equally unstable physical space. But there is also in his poetry a humane and affirmative vision that refuses to surrender to either irony or pathos. Compulsively, he keeps returning to his native Belfast, providing affectionate portraits of its citizenry (from Horse Boyle in 'Dresden'[32] to the two winos in the poem of that name), and enunciating a postmodern sense of the city as a place of new opportunities, where questions of identity and nationality have to be re-addressed.

'Clearance' describes the kind of 'collapse' which takes place 'under the breaker's / pendulum'.[33] Urban development is both liberating and estranging, allowing for fresh, new perceptions of the city. Through his direct, dramatic address, Carson gives his observations epiphanic force:

> A breeze springs up from nowhere –
>
> There, through a gap in the rubble, a greengrocer's shop
> I'd never noticed until now . . .
>   Everything –
> Yellow, green and purple – is fresh as paint. Rain glistens on
>   the aubergines
> And peppers; even from this distance, the potatoes smell of earth.

If the potatoes still smelling of earth suggest that Belfast people are never far away from their rural origins, the peppers and aubergines intimate the city's implication in wider international currents of exchange. Carson's title recalls Heaney's sequence 'Clearances', in which the poet's quest for an 'omphalos' leads to the space which is 'utterly empty, utterly a source'.[34] Where Heaney concentrates on the moment of transition from the physical world to the 'bright nowhere', the 'placeless heaven' of textual plenitude, Carson's 'Clearance' remains rooted in the physical world which, in the midst of destruction, is nevertheless able to provoke rhapsodic catalogues of urban variousness, hymns to fruitful serendipity.

'Smithfield Market' ends with an ambiguous hint of the possibility of order out of chaos. After the Smithfield fire 'everything [is] unstitched, unravelled'.[35] The speaker feels trapped and disorientated: 'Since everything went up in smoke, no entrances, no exits'. But he spies a 'map of Belfast / In the ruins: obliterated streets, the faint impression of a key'. Does he see the ruins of Smithfield as a map, a simulacrum of the city itself? Or does he see an actual map in the rubble? Is it an actual key he sees, or is it the key to the map which will allow him to find his way through the labyrinth? Will the key help him escape from the labyrinth or merely lead him into greater danger, for 'Something many-toothed, elaborate, stirred briefly in the labyrinth'?

Maps are usually taken to be scientific, objective, impersonal, authoritative, seemingly able to provide firm ground on which to stand, a sense of security for those who like to know where they are. Maps figure importantly in Carson's work but, like other texts (including Carson's own), their meanings are shown to be neither fixed nor singular. It is impossible to write Belfast: 'No, don't trust maps, for they avoid the moment: ramps, barricades, diversions, Peace Lines'.[36] The recitation of street names in poems such as 'Belfast Confetti' suggest the poet's own desire to map the city, to try and hold it together, even while it is collapsing around him. This is why he can identify so readily with the Irish-Australians, the emigrants of the 1950s and 60s who meet every Thursday in the Wollongong Bar to reconstruct from memory and the latest news reports the Falls Road they have left. The poem is delicately poised between acknowledgement of the human desire to fix reality and recognition of the ever-changing, teeming complexity of that reality. No map, no form of representation, can accommodate the flux of life, particularly the life of a city in a constant process of destruction and re-construction. Maps contradict the peculiarly human qualities of the urban landscapes that they reference. They can never capture truly the reality inherent in a city's historical memory or its convoluted array of cultures, stories, languages and experiences. The city can be caught, as Carson's poems acknowledge, only in fragments, in the economy of disorder. 'Linear B', a kind of poetic manifesto, records his fascination with the man with the 'cracked lens' and 'staccato walk': 'From years of watching, I know the zig-zags circle: / He has been the same place many times, never standing still'.[37] Glimpsing the man's notebook, the speaker sees 'Squiggles, dashes, question-marks', and wonders if it's 'nonsense, or a formula – for . . . the collapsing city'. In his own poetic mapping of the city, Carson too refuses simple linear progression, opting for zig-zag circles and cracked lenses. The city disrupts traditional ideas of single, homogenous truth and promotes the view of truth as deriving from our being-in-the-world, from our continual becoming in the languages in which we are inscribed. The past survives not as traces of a unique tradition, but as elements of different histories that can be continually reconfigured. Fragmentation does not imply an original unity that has been lost: Carson's postmodern fragmentation is dissemination, a scattering of origins, centre, identity, presence and belonging. He maps a world where nothing stands still, where there are no absolute fixed points, where boundaries are always porous, and where it is always possible to envisage the possibility of change. 'Turn Again' concentrates on the unreliability of maps and texts, the poem informed by the postmodern understanding of the inevitable mis-match between reality and its representation. In this poem, 'The linen backing is falling apart'[38] – an image which subtly links textual collapse with historic disintegration resulting from the decline of Belfast's linen industry. But the immediately preceding poem, 'Patchwork', offers an emblem of stitching and mending – the grandmother's patchwork quilt that she made for a wedding that never took place. Though time has unravelled the family, there remain connective traces, evidenced most particularly in the patchwork (*'your father's stitched into that quilt,/ Your uncles and your aunts'*), which has passed down to 'some one of us'.[39] The poem itself is a patchwork made out of fragments of memory and speech, that is, something new made out of old bits and pieces.

Formalists see the work of art as possessing a symmetry, a completeness that life lacks. As Henry James put it in *The Art of the Novel*:

> Really universally, relations stop nowhere, and the exquisite problem of the artist is eternally but to draw by a geometry of his own, the circle which they shall happily *appear* to do so. Where, for the complete expression of one's subject, does a particular relation stop – giving way to some other not concerned in that expression?[40]

The parts earn their place in the whole according to the nature of their contribution to the truth toward which the work is pointing. A form that is orderly rather than digressive is founded upon the principle of relevance to the truth. But if there is no central truth to be presented, the rationale for seeing the work of art as a closed circle collapses. Unable to impose a transcendent perspective, the poet is unable to control his material by subordinating the parts to such a perspective. His only hope is to include everything. But art cannot do that. Seeking to capture the truth of reality, but unable to know the truth, the poet can only digress. Digressiveness, then, is the embodiment of an epistemological dilemma, and Carson's whole *oeuvre* reads like a fabric of digressions, ranging from apparently arbitrary details to long interpolated narratives. Things are continually seen from more than one point of view. No detail seems to be irrelevant; each is worthy of elaboration. The poet refuses to allow himself to be recruited to any one version of reality, preferring to 'walk between the story lines'.

'Dresden' is a longish, meandering, apparently pointless poem made up of a series of narratives that disrupt and intersect each other. The poem begins by introducing Horse Boyle, his brother Mule, and the caravan they live in:

> Horse Boyle was called Horse Boyle because of his brother
>   Mule;
> Though why Mule was called Mule is anybody's guess. I
>   stayed there once,
> Or rather, I nearly stayed there once. But that's another story.
> At any rate they lived in this decrepit caravan, not two miles
>   out of Carrick.[41]

Identities are uncertain, a Saussurian matter of establishing relationships among signs without there being any absolute terms. We listen to the speaker working with his materials, initiating narrative, then retracting and qualifying it, then dismissing it altogether – but eventually returning to it at the end of the poem where, for a second time, the story of why he did not stay the night is abruptly rejected: 'there's no time/ To go back to that now; I could hardly, at any rate, pick up the thread'.[42] The caravan, associated with itineracy, temporariness and pro-visionality, symbolizes an aesthetic as well as a life-style – the unsettled, serial mode of the whole poem. The caravan reminds the speaker of an old-fashioned shop, then, as Muldoon would say, 'of something else, then something else again'.[43] Questions about the daughter of the shop-owner lead back to Horse who not only knew all the local news but was a great storyteller. One of his stories is about 'young Flynn', an IRA man in the 1920s whose recollection of the scraping sound he made when digging a reclaimed tip of 'delph and crockery ware' reminds him of chalk squeaking on a blackboard, which reminds him of Master McGinty, who came from Narrow Quarter, a place which Horse knew well. Only at this point does the poem pick up its 'major', titular narra-tive, the story of Horse as a rear gunner in the RAF: 'Of all the missions, Dresden broke his heart. It reminded him of china'.[44] As a memento of that awful experience, Horse has kept a china milkmaid from his childhood. The poem ends with Mule's 'careful drunken weaving / Through the tin-stacks' as he makes his way to the caravan, while the speaker, unable to pick up the thread of the 'Mule' story, leaves the caravan home and 'wandered out through the steeples of rust, the gate that was a broken bed'.[45] All is contingency. We cannot be sure that the end is indeed what the rest of the poem was leading towards. This is 'open' poetry, poetry which eschews resolution or even definition. But, as 'Dresden' powerfully demonstrates, it is also a warmly humanistic poetry that scrutinizes individual lives with compassionate understanding.

Underlying Carson's fragmented, temporally and spatially mobile, digressive poetics is his intuition of centrelessness. He radically undermines the idea of a centre capable of providing discursive unity and fixity, and the claims of any culture to possess a pure and homogeneous body of values. 'Snow' begins with recollection of playing ping-pong as a child. Despite the speaker's efforts to recreate the actuality of the past as clearly and accurately as he can, he is forced to recognize the emptiness at the heart of experience: 'I broke open the husk so many times / And always found it empty; the pith was a wordless bubble'.[46] In Heaney emptiness is transformed, by the power of imagination, into wordless plenitude, as the poet discovers a space which is 'utterly empty, utterly a source'. Contrastingly, in Carson, 'Though there's nothing in the thing itself, bits of it come back unbidden'. Heaney's poetry allows him to affirm transcendent wholeness: Carson makes do with postmodern patchwork. Carson, like Wallace Stevens's poet in 'The Snowman',[47] is trying to make something out of nothing, relying on the prompts provided by ordinary everyday objects and experience. One such prompt is 'this thirties scuffed leather sofa', which the speaker finds particularly redolent of childhood. Carson is no doubt thinking of Heaney's 'A Sofa in the Forties'. In Heaney's poem, the sofa is transmogrified into 'ghost train' and 'death-gondola'.[48] A transformative dynamic is at work, the 'engine' of imagination capable of turning what is 'earthbound, for sure' into the 'potentially heavenbound'. In Carson, however, the sofa remains itself, the poet insistent that 'anything's too much when you have nothing'. Rather than a transformative, otherworldly aesthetic, Carson's is 'earthbound, for sure', childhood memory leading finally to the scene of a wake and the unavoidable fact of human mortality. The closing line is ambiguous: 'Roses are brought in, and suddenly, white confetti seethes against the window'. The whole poem, but this line especially, recalls MacNeice's 'Snow', which begins: 'The room was suddenly rich and the great bay-window was / Spawning snow and pink roses against it / Soundlessly collateral and incompatible: / World is suddener than we fancy it'.[49] Like MacNeice's 'spawning snow', the image of seething white confetti, synthesizing 'incompatible' ideas of life and death, wedding and wake, heat and coldness, anger and celebration, connotes ferocious organic process, incorrigible plurality, 'the drunkenness of things being various'. The great task facing the poet is to find an ordering structure that nevertheless will not violate 'plurality' or unduly confine 'drunkenness'. Both Mahon, in his elegy on MacNeice, 'In Carrowdore Churchyard', and Muldoon, in 'History',[50] refer to MacNeice's 'Snow', but, as Edna Longley has pointed out, Mahon departs from MacNeice and Muldoon, and we might add from Carson, in the way he 'goes on to claim that poetry can in some sense "solve" or at least sieve the "inrush" of phenomena and history'.

> This, you implied, is how we ought to live –
>
> The ironical, loving crush of roses against snow,
> Each fragile, solving ambiguity. So
> From the pneumonia of the ditch, from the ague
> Of the blind poet and the bombed-out town you bring
> The all-clear to the empty holes of spring;
> Rinsing the choked mud, keeping the colours new.[51]

As Longley concludes, 'Rhythmically and rhetorically it [the above stanza] moves beyond "ambiguity"'.[52] Contrast Mahon's teleologism and Heaney's transcendentalism with MacNeice's, Muldoon's and Carson's desire to remain open to the flux of consciousness and history.

The 'spawning' 'seething' snow is also present in Carson's 'Loaf', the poem immediately preceding 'Snow'. The speaker is 'muffled by forgotten drifts / Of flour', the white dough reminds him of snow, he and his workmate write their names 'on the snowed-up panes'.[53] Like the bread which is being baked, 'Loaf' rises from the yeasty ferment of the poet's memories of a summer job in McWatters' bakery, the poem repeatedly suggesting a connection between writing and the work in the bakery: empty flour-sacks are 'cloudy caesurae', bread is like blotting-paper, the speaker and his mate write on the floury windows. The young worker has to submit to the discipline of the factory but still finds plenty of time for skiving, talking, writing, making up stories, just as the poet, within the general structures of his poem, finds room for all kinds of digressive and transgressive textual play. Much of this playfulness is generated by the attempt to 'pin down' an elusive reality. There is a constant awareness that words are not up to the job of capturing or encoding a 'spawning', 'seething' world: 'the nib keeps skidding off. Or the ink won't take'.[54] Reality refuses to let itself be written. It cannot be contained within the given structures and discourses and ready-made formulae, but overspills or eludes the received categories. As MacNeice put it, 'World is suddener than we fancy it. / World is crazier and more of it than we think'. 'Loaf' reiterates Carson's 'in-between' subject position, his sense of identity, meaning and imaginative power as lying between, rather than in, things:

> Blue-black
> *Quink* is what I used then. I liked the in-between-ness of it,
>   neither
> One thing nor the other. A *Conway Stewart* fountain-pen,
>   blue-ish green
> Mock tortoiseshell . . .[55]

'Snowball' breaks down the difference between significant and trivial, high and low, central and peripheral, to consider 'All the signs'.[56] These signs are never fully explained; they are suggestive rather than definitive. Specificity promises precise meaning ('An Audi Quattro sidles up in first gear past the loading-bay of Tomb Street / GPO – a litter of white plastic cord, a broken whiskey bottle –') but does not deliver, and simply 'revs away'. Desired connections don't get made, unions fail to materialize, the parts do not add up, though everything is potentially connected to everything else. 'All the signs' accumulate with accelerating rapidity, snowballing. But the thing about snowballs is that they melt. In the words of the poem, 'Like a fish-net stocking, everything is full of holes'. The fragments remain disconnected and unconnectable. The poem authorizes multiple combinations but, since we can never be sure how the elements ought to be arranged, none of the possible interpretations is validated or sustainable.

The difficulty of holding together a coherent narrative is repeatedly emphasized in Carson's poetry:

> As someone spills a cup of tea on a discarded
> *Irish News*
>
> A minor item bleeds through from another page, blurring
>   the main story.
> It's difficult to pick up without the whole thing coming apart
>   in your hands[57]

Minor items not only blur but also threaten to displace the main story, so that the difference between 'major' and 'minor' dissolves. Narrative is always palimpsestic: 'Like the names on a school desk, carved into one another till they're indecipherable'; '. . . the sketch that's taking shape on the Army HQ blackboard, chalky ghosts / Behind the present, showing what was contemplated and rubbed out, Plan A / Becoming X or Y; interlocked, curved arrows of the mortgaged future'.[58] If narrative cannot escape the past, neither should it close itself off to the future, but remain open to change and revision, to chance and the unpredictable:

> What comes next is next, and no one knows the *che sera* of
> it, but must allow
> The *Tipp-Ex* present at the fingertips. Listen now: an angel
> whispers of the here-and-now.

> The future looms into the mouth incessantly, gulped-at and
> unspoken;
> Its guardian is intangible, but gives you hints and winks and
> nudges as its broken token.[59]

Given a world of flux and contingency, the great challenge is to 'pin down' the uniqueness of experience, the precise nature of the 'here-and-now': 'Aromas, sounds, the texture of the roads, the heaviness or lightness of the air – / All these contribute to the sense of place. These things are what we are, / Though mitigated by ourselves'.[60]

Carson's aesthetic requires a return to concrete particulars as the basis of knowledge. The question is how to give structure to the array of particulars without violating their particularity. With Carson, systematic arrangements, whether those of individual poems or 'chapters' of prose, serve merely to undermine themselves, to reveal their affinity with the artificial arrangements of dictionaries. The alphabetical format used in *Opera Et Cetera*[61] gives primacy to the parts at the expense of the whole. Encyclopaedic form signifies a turn away from unity and universals. According to John Locke, parts rather than wholes conform more closely to external reality and are therefore to be prized more highly:

> General and universal belong not to the real existence of things, but are the inventions and creatures of the understanding, made by it for its own use, and concern only signs, whether words or ideas. Words are general . . . when used for signs of general ideas, and so are applicable indifferently to many particular things: but universality belongs not to things themselves, which are all of them particular in their existence . . . When therefore we quit particulars, the generals that rest are only creatures of our own making: their general nature being nothing but the capacity they are put into, by the understanding, of signifying or representing many particulars.[62]

But while this may be so, there is still value in establishing connections between parts. This faith is attested to by Carson's compulsive cross-referencing, echoing and pattern-making; by the way, for example, the alphabetical format of the opening section of *Opera Et Cetera*, 'Letters from the Alphabet', is repeated in the distorting mirrors of the closing section, 'Opera', which is based on the radio operator's alphabetical code. The alphabetical arrangement itself is an image of the stubborn particularity of things, while the 'careful drunken weaving' of connections within and among poems represents a countervailing impulse towards unification. Carson's aesthetic is poised between anti-essentialism and organization. His encyclopaedic form, with its discontinuous, apparently arbitrary arrangement of particulars and its artificial patternings, at once proclaims the unity of the whole and undermines that unity. The resulting narrative is historical *and* fragmentary, structured *and* open, continuous *and* discontinuous.

He takes fragmentariness even further in his most recent collection, *Breaking News*, the first part of which is remarkable for his abandoning the long line for an extremely short-lined, broken format which owes a good deal to William Carlos Williams. The title works on several levels. It alludes to the continuous stream of reportage that brings the most up-to-date news of what is happening around the world, but also refers to the convulsions of war in the poet's home place and around the world, and to the breaking-up of conventional poetic form under pressure of violent events. The collection title is broken across two poems which appear on facing pages. The first, 'Breaking', contains the image of a car 'about to disintegrate'[63] in an eerily silent street. The second, 'News', concerns the aftermath of the car-bomb. The actual explosion falls into the gap between the two poems, unrepresented and unrepresentable. In 'News' the sign above the *Belfast Telegraph* shop now reads *'fast rap,'*[64] reminiscent of the situation described in the earlier 'Gate', where a boutique called 'Terminus' has lost its 'T' and 'r' as a result of a bomb, leaving *'e minus'.* Writing, like maps, is never adequate, especially in times of rapid, violent change:

Difficult to keep track:
Everything's a bit askew . . .[65]

It's that frottage effect again: the paper that you're scribbling on is grained
And blackened, till the pencil-lead snaps off, in a valley of the broken alphabet[66]

The collection opens with 'Belfast', a poem gesturing towards Williams's rhythms of speech and living, in which Belfast is enveloped in an unreal silence – except for the whistling of a blackbird. Carson's poem, with a painterly vividness and concrete precision similar to that one finds in Williams's 'The Red Wheelbarrow',[67] emphasizes patterns of colour, the relationship of the parts of the picture to each other. No one thing stands for something else; it is uniquely itself: 'No ideas but in things'.

BELFAST

east

beyond the yellow
shipyard cranes

a blackbird whistles
in a whin bush

west

beside the motorway
a black taxi

rusts in a field
of blue thistles[68]

Here, William Carlos Williams and American Imagism meet early Irish Gaelic nature poetry. Carson's poem, written with haiku-like precision and clarity, exhibits the kind of freshness and directness, the kind of watchfulness towards nature, that we associate with early Irish nature poems. Indeed, 'Belfast' closely echoes the well-known 'The Blackbird of Belfast Lough', written by a seventh-century Irish monk in the margins of an illuminated manuscript. Mentioning this poem specifically in his essay on early Irish nature poetry, 'The God in the Tree', Heaney referred to the 'tang and clarity of a pristine world' in this poetry, and used Wordsworth's phrase, 'surprised by joy', to describe the way these poems 'combine suddenness and richness'.[69] In his own compact concrete lines, Carson similarly aims to convey sudden 'little jabs of delight in the elemental',[70] for the archaic powers of the Celtic god in the tree, manifest in blackbird and thistle, continue to hover over the modern metropolis with its motorways, black taxis and shipyard cranes. 'Belfast' presents a curious social ecology, a heterogeneous discursive field of fluctuating languages and contexts in which the imagery of an exhausted metropolis gives way to the semiotics of nature, suggestive of a wider frame for re-thinking and re-presenting the city. The yellow shipyard cranes and black taxi may now be redundant, but the blue thistles and blackbird's whistles (picked out by the poem's only rhyme), are testimony to nature's irrepressible vitality in the midst of desolation.

The blackbird is heard again in 'Wake', another poem about the immediate aftermath of a bomb going off. In 'the lull' after the explosion, 'a blackbird / whistled in / a chink / of light / between that world / and this'.[71] Breaks, lulls, gaps, moments of suspension, in-between states are of crucial importance in this collection. The constant sound of the army helicopters over the poet's home in north Belfast is the subject of two short revs of poems, 'Spin Cycle' and 'Spin Cycle 2'. In the first, the sound of the helicopter is like the whir of a washing-machine. Carson perhaps alludes to vorticism, Pound's notion of the poem as 'a VORTEX, from which, and through which, and into which, ideas are constantly rushing'.[72] Significantly, 'Spin Cycle' ends after the speaker 'put in / the ear-plugs' and 'everything went / centrifugal'.[73] In the companion poem, 'Spin Cycle 2', the lyric 'I' has disappeared completely, obliterated by or assimilated into a world of objects: 'gun-gun / ear-plugs in / blank-blank'.[74] 'Blank-blank', alluding not only to the sound of gunfire but to the limits of the poem's own capability, marks an ironic coincidence of word and world, the poem itself become merely another object. In 'Breath', once the noise of the helicopter overhead stops, 'I feel / rinsed / clean', as 'when the / washing-machine/ stops / shuddering'.[75] Here, the poem opens onto a moment of visionary calm, of self-presence and composure, a Heaneyesque 'clearance'. A similar defamiliarizing effect is recorded in 'Minus' where the sudden silence of the helicopter seems to galvanize the speaker into perceiving the world in a fresh new William Carlos Williamsian way, with preternatural vividness, though (as the title would suggest) not an unambiguously positive one. In 'Home', the poet, 'hurtling' down the airport road, stops to look down over Belfast, as if reading a map: 'motionless / at last / I see everything'.[76] Once again, clearance or distance is at least momentarily achieved. The spectacle of the orderly laid-out city below, with its reassuring landmarks, offers a sense of security, a contrast to the disorder of the 'fields of scrap / and thistle / farmyards' he has passed. All of these short, pared-down, minimalist poems, shorn of punctuation and using flexible line lengths, line breaks and line spacing as a kind of musical notation to suggest pauses and breaks, embody with particular acuity and precision the tensions between sound and silence, motion and motionlessness, vitality and decay, order and disorder, presence and absence that characterize the disjunctive and unsettling conditions of the metropolitan terrain.

If the danger in a localist or particularist focus is that poems might become a series of isolated fragments unable to speak beyond their own moment, it is through the sheer intensity of the poet's concentration and the degree of imaginative responsiveness that he brings to bear, that his detailed vignettes of particular incidents or scenes assume universal dimensions. Small, apparently insignificant details disclose far-reaching insights, parts contain wholes, fragments tell a bigger story. 'Fragment' refers to a bit of a Tupperware lunchbox from which 'they could tell / the bombmaker wore / *Marigold* gloves',[77] the single word '*Marigold*' suggesting a whole conspectus of orders – natural, domestic and religious – that the bombmaker has violated.

Belfast itself becomes a site of transit, an intersection, part of a wider story. As the last and title poem of *The Ballad of HMS Belfast* emphasizes, Belfast, set loose from her moorings, begins to drift, to enter other places, other stories. The city does not stand for a rational, firm referent, but slips through the predictable circuitry of 'both Catestants and Protholics'[78] to become a floating signifier, moving through diverse interpretations and narratives. Whether caught in the modes of hallucinatory fantasy, as in 'The Ballad of HMS Belfast', or in the mythical half-light of imagined foreign battlefields, as in *Breaking News*, Belfast, in Carson's account, is a more open and extensive place than the one we have been accustomed to inhabiting. *Breaking News* testifies to the centrality of the battlefield in the figural economy of Carson's Belfast. Poems about Belfast and the ' Troubles' are interspersed with poems about the Russian Revolution, the Indian Mutiny and the Crimean War, the depiction of scenes of different wars reverberating against each other. Diverse histories intersect and open up the space of an encounter, a dialogue, in which no history is reduced to another. Narrowly focused snapshots of battle scenes and their immediate aftermath convey the dehumanization of entire societies. Such is 'Waste Not', a macabre close-up of a Crimean battlefield where the women are 'harvesting'[79] gold buttons shorn from dead soldiers' uniforms. 'Harvest' is the bitterly ironic title of another poem where wounded soldiers crawl through the harvest fields 'like mutilated bees',[80] an image of a terrible metaphysical bleakness. 'Some Uses of a Dead Horse' dramatizes a cold and inhuman aestheticism. The poetic voice is withdrawn in its meticulous calm. Observation, even of the horrific, is unemotive and the tone undeclamatory, avoiding the public modes of historical generalization or moral comment. It might seem, as Lionel Trilling said of the short stories of Isaac Babel (to whom Carson dedicates his poem 'Russia') that Carson's poetry is itself 'touched with cruelty'. Carson deals with extreme violence and destruction, yet describes it, as Trilling believed Babel did, 'with a striking elegance and precision of objectivity, and also with a kind of lyric joy, so that the reader cannot be sure how the author is responding to the brutality he records'.[81] While conceding that Carson's poetry is a relentless detailing of mutilation, desecration and destruction, the reader experiences the predictable human feelings of shock, horror and moral outrage all the more powerfully precisely because of the poet's cool postmodern style – its ironic detachment and objectivity, its apparent indifference to 'depth', 'meanings' and 'values', its refusal of explicit human sympathy.

The collection concludes with a sequence of poems based, sometimes verbatim, on dispatches from the Crimean War sent back by the Anglo-Irish journalist William Howard Russell. Carson's versions of Russell's versions of nineteenth-century Gallipoli, Varna, Dvno, Balaklava, Kertch, Tchernaya and Sedan reflect on his native city which, as he repeatedly emphasizes, is closely linked with Britain's imperial heyday, particularly the Crimean adventure. In 'Exile' he walks 'the smouldering / dark streets / Sevastopol / Crimea / Inkerman / Odessa / Balkan / Lucknow'.[82] Belfast, as Carson goes on to say in the same poem, 'is many / places'. The 'War Correspondent' sequence returns to many of his favourite themes, in particular that of nature's fragile beauty, continuance and promise. 'Tchernaya' echoes 'Belfast' with its description of the birdsong and the colourful flowers enlivening degraded surroundings: 'Strange to hear them sing about the bushes / in the lulls between the thud of the bombs, / or to see between the cannon-flashes / the whole peninsula ignite with blooms'.[83] 'Sedan', the last poem in the sequence, ends with a final affirmation of both nature and art. The speaker, making his way through the 'debris' of 'a ruined empire', as the poet made his way through the ruined streets of Belfast in 'Smithfield Market', comes upon the tokens of hope for the future:

> even the bomb-shelters
> ransacked, though in one dug-out
> I found a music-book
>
> With a woman's name
> In it, and a canary bird,
> And a vase of wild flowers.[84]

Suffering has not extinguished music and song. Though it foretells danger, the canary bird with its bright splash of yellow stands out more prominently against dark surroundings than the blackbird of 'Belfast'.

Wild flowers are still found in the midst of the rubble. Where the bat tlefield flowers in 'Tchernaya', like Keith Douglas's 'desert flowers' or Isaac Rosenberg's poppies in Flanders fields, represent the pathos of nature's enduring innocence and piercing beauty amidst the collapse of civilization, Carson's vase of flowers, retrieved and preserved by human hand, signifies faith in the *human* potential to transform a violent and debased present. 'Sedan' merges images of the battle of Sedan (1870) fought during the Franco-Prussian War with scenes of the siege of Sevastopol (1854) which took place during the Crimean War, and places in the midst of these bloody encounters the vase of flowers which, like Wallace Stevens's jar in Tennessee, symbolizes the aesthetic sense, our only guarantee of the future.

What all of these poems have in common is their privileging of the fragmented detail, the specific event, the body, the voice, with the inevitable consequence of dispersing unified identity, universal subjectivity and continuous narrative. The variousness of our being-in-the-world is given precedence over positivist, universalist or hermetic modes of discourse. In rewriting the grammar of urban historiography in terms of discontinuity and centrelessness, Carson is not simply writing in the margins of dominant discourses. By moving from a poetics of margins to a poetics of differences, he dissolves the relationship between power and knowledge on which our understanding of what is central and what is marginal has traditionally been founded. By doing away with the centre, the authorizing principle, he does away with those binary oppositions in which one term is always privileged over the other. Instead, he wants to open us to considerations beyond ourselves, beyond the usual hegemonic structures of understanding and representation, to what exists only as trace or echo or shadow. Heidegger alerts us to the significance of the shadow as ghostly portent of 'otherness':

> Everyday opinion sees in the shadow only the lack of light, if not light's complete denial. In truth, however, the shadow is a manifest, though impenetrable, testimony to the concealed emitting of light. In keeping with this concept of shadow, we experience the incalculable as that which, withdrawn from representation, is nevertheless manifest in whatever is, pointing to Being, which remains concealed.[85]

Thus, Carson's 'Edward Hopper: *Early Sunday Morning,* 1939' concentrates on the concrete details of the street scene, including the long shadow which falls across the picture: 'another shadow / falls / from what / we cannot see / to what / we cannot see / dawn / before the War'.[86] The picture/poem occupies the interstitial space between the twin mysteries of origins and destiny which lie forever outside the bounds of what is known and representable.

Similarly, 'Last Effect' asks us to consider a bullet-dented watch-case, its hands arrested at the exact moment the owner was saved from death, yet curiously pointing to the 'incalculable', that which remains 'withdrawn from representation': 'O what is time / my friend / when faced with / eternity'.[87] 'Detail' describes a similar incident and frames it in a similar way: a war veteran opens his Bible to reveal the way the bullet 'stopped at Revelation'.[88]

The Carson poem is typically gapped or holed: an excess without a centre, yet with redemptive potential. In its breaks and lulls, it registers its sometimes stunned awareness of other stories, languages and identities. Categories leak and spill; they cast shadows over one another; they interpenetrate each other. Identity is always open, never finite nor resolved. This new urban poetics implies a very different sense of 'home' from that which we find in the older generation of Heaney or Mahon. Carson's 'home' is neither fixed nor closed, but mobile, mutable, constructed in the movement of language that constitutes the sense of place, belonging and identity. Dwelling is sustained, not by roots but by dialogue with other histories, other places, other people. The sense of place that is constructed is always contingent, in transit, with neither origin nor end.

Memory, History, Story:
Between Poetics and Ethics

RICHARD KEARNEY

In this paper I want to explore the relation between poetics and ethics as it pertains to the remembrance of time through place. I take as my guide here the hermeneutic model of 'exchanging memories' advanced by my friend and mentor Paul Ricoeur.[1] So doing, I will suggest that certain topographical memorials of historical trauma (and the violent histories behind such trauma) can epitomize an ethics of hospitality, flexibility, plurality, transfiguration and pardon. My chosen example will be the Irish Hunger Memorial in Battery Park in New York City, an interactive monument designed and installed by Brian Tolle in 2001 to commemorate the Great Irish Famines of the 1840s and the subsequent emigrations to North America.

Commemoration is a complicated act; it is imbued with ways of remembering that are neither straightforward nor simple. Commemoration takes shape in both verbal and non-verbal media and it is clearly the physical memorial or monument that elicits the most controversy. Because a physical memorial is basically static, because it has a solidity of presence, issues surrounding the meaning and interpretation of the object (as well as the experience of the viewer) are myriad. At root of the difficulty in commemoration – a difficulty most recently articulated in the struggle to plan a 9/11 memorial – is the question: what is to be remembered? Will the memorial speak to actions of people, or towards a different future? When commemoration is the result of trauma and/or an act of violence, then those root questions become much more ethically complex. The tension at the heart of the ethical difficulty resides in the possibilities of not remembering a significant, traumatic event at all, or remembering in an inappropriate way, a way that devalues or misconstrues the victims of trauma and violence.[2]

These ethical difficulties find a most potent and continuing articulation in ways of remembering the Holocaust. Films such as Stephen

165

Spielberg's *Schindler's List*[3] and Claude Lanzmann's *Shoah*[4] and the Fortunoff Video Archive[5] for Holocaust Testimonies are but three diverse ways of commemorating the Holocaust and none are without critical controversy.[6] All planners, creators and viewers of Holocaust museums and memorials struggle with the need to recognize individual pain and loss, to become part of the memorializing impulse, but also to not ignore the political, historical and ideological conditions of the violent trauma. Commemoration of the Vietnam War is involved in similar difficulties. Interestingly, two scholars who write about the Holocaust and Vietnam celebrate those memorial projects that refuse closure. In 'The US Holocaust Museum as a Scene of Pedagogical Address' Elizabeth Ellsworth examines the pedagogical project of the Holocaust Memorial Museum in Washington DC.[7] The memorial resists closure, a single narrative, a strategy for complete understanding. Ellsworth determines the very success of the Holocaust Memorial in its refusal to overcome the difficulties inherent in such a commemoration. The attempt of such memorials to teach understanding is identified as one of the main pedagogical problems. The permanent exhibit transcends the goal of simple perception by offering a place between the binary of history and memory. In refusing a single narrative, the project opens up the possibility to teach students a relation to the catastrophe that can generate many meanings. Ellsworth praises the memorial as a 'pedagogical masterpiece' in that it can avoid closure: it succeeds in drawing students into its moral imperatives without 'pre-scribed' responsibility. Like Ellsworth, Maria Sturken sees the Vietnam Veteran's Memorial as something that stands between the public and private discourse. Marita Sturken proposes the duality of the word 'screen' in exploring the place of the Memorial. In one sense the screen is a shield to protect American imperialism from the disastrous implications of a futile and violent reality. The other 'screen' is represented apolitically in the bareness of names on black granite. This screen reflects the individual pain and loss, and allows for a possible renegotiation of 'cultural memory'. Sturken's argument, set up in this way, exposes how the construction of a unique memorial provides the veterans with a new voice within the official, national discourse. So it is that issues of discourse, ethics, memory, aesthetics and politics all intertwine in any commemorative project. The Irish Hunger Memorial in Battery Park is no different.[8]

An invitation to mourning

First, a word about the memorial itself. The installation basically consists of an Irish stone cottage transplanted from the west coast of Ireland
to Battery Park City at the very heart of downtown New York, not far
from where the Twin Towers once stood. The memorial does not
attempt some nostalgic retrieval of a quaint Irish past – so often represented by picture postcard versions of the traditional thatched cottage.
On the contrary, it seeks to re-imagine the past in its present condition
of destitution and ruin. As such, Brian Tolle's installation might best be
described as a hybrid construct which serves as both 1) a commemoration of the great Irish famine of the nineteenth century and 2) a
site-specific art installation in metropolitan New York in the third mil-
lennium marking the ongoing tragedy of world hunger. This double
fidelity to separate moments in time provokes a sense of disorientation
that prevents the act of memory regressing to some kind of sentimental
fixation with the past (what Ricoeur calls 'blocked memory').[9] By the
same token it also prevents the exhibit from serving simply as an exotic
curiosity of tourist voyeurism in the present.

This is a famine memorial with a difference. Whereas most conventional commemorations of the Famine featured 'people without land'
(usually leaving on ships from Ireland or arriving off ships in the new
world), we are confronted here with an uncanny experience of 'land
without people'. Though the installation is located at the very heart of
one of the world's most populous cities, there are no human beings represented here. As such it recalls the 'deserted village' of Slievemore in
Achill Island, County Mayo, which was one of the artist's primary
sources of inspiration for the work: a haunting depopulated row of
abandoned and decayed stone huts facing out towards the Atlantic. And
it is reminiscent in its way of other monuments of historical rupture and
ruin – for example, the bare walls of Machu Picchu in Peru or the
floating hulk of the *Marie Celeste*. It is a far cry in any case from the idealized portraits of rural Irish cottages by romantic landscape painters
such as Paul Henry or James O'Connor.

Tolle's installation resists mystification and mystique by presenting
us with a powerful and disturbing sense of material 'thereness'. As we
enter the site we are confronted with a fieldstone cottage, transplanted
stone by stone from Ireland, and here reconstructed on its own quarter
acre of soil in New York City. But it is impossible to feel at home here.
This could never be a dwelling for us, contemporary visitors to the
cottage. The most obvious reason for this sense of homelessness is no

doubt the memorial's location at the core of a bustling metropolitan cityscape where it is clearly *out of place*, misplaced and dislocated literally and symbolically. And the fact that the cottage and surrounding potato drills are themselves planted on a suspended limestone and concrete base doubly confirms the sense of not belonging. This sentiment of spatial disorientation provokes us, in turn, to reflect on the paradox that our sense of identity and placement in the world often presupposes an acute sense of loss and displacement. As when the Irish Captain McMorris asks 'What ish my nation?' in Shakespeare's *Henry V*,[10] his question betraying the fact that he is preoccupied with his national identity precisely because he has *forfeited* it – he is speaking in the English language and wearing an English army uniform. Likewise, it has often been noted by Irish critics such as Declan Kiberd, Roy Foster and Luke Gibbons that Irish tradition is in many respects an *invention* by modernity.[11] Just as our sense of the past is almost always constituted and reconstituted by our present historical consciousness.

This sense of spatial and temporal inversion is compounded here by the fact that the roofless cottage remains un-restored and is exposed to local weather conditions. Unlike most works of art, this installation is half construct and half nature – it is an artificially contrived synthesis of 'real' stone and soil and architectural-sculptural design. The underground tumuli and passageways, by which one enters the cottage from beneath, are further reminders that the cottage has a dark and buried history – recalling not only the Neolithic Irish burial chambers of Newgrange, Knowth and Dowth in County Meath but also the unmarked mass graves of thousands of famine victims in Ireland and elsewhere. The fact that these subterranean passageways are themselves panelled with glass panes covered in various texts and subtexts – historical, political, fictional, rhetorical, spiritual, apologetic, testimonial – further adds to the sense of a plurality of voices and interpretations. Tolle's memorial refuses to yield any quick fix. There is no single, assured access to this placeless place, this timeless time. It cannot be 'naturalized' in the sense of celebrating some literal recovery of a landscape. Yet it cannot be explained away either as a purely 'aestheticized' sculpture residing in some museum space – for the site alters continually with the surrounding weather and climate, one season covered with weeds, potato shoots and wildflowers, another with snow or mud, and at all times registering the odours, reflections, shadows and sounds of the surrounding city. We are thus palpably reminded of the passing of time, of historical fluidity and transience that no monumental fixation can bring to a full stop. The myth of an eternal Celtic-Mist landscape is demystified before our very eyes.[12]

Not that there were not efforts by certain officials and politicians to perpetuate the myths. On opening the site, for example, Governor Pataki of New York spoke of the opportunity offered here 'to touch the sod of our heritage'; while Mayor Giuliani concluded his inaugural speech with the words: 'May this beautiful Memorial, like Ireland itself, be forever free, forever green.' And some members of the Irish Tourist Board praised the installation's capacity to evoke the 'rolling hills of old Ireland' – conveniently forgetting that the quaint potato field is planted over a slab of concrete and surrounded by High Rises! Certain Irish-American societies and groups were also quick to contribute their own gloss to this sentimentalizing process. Even the Irish government weighed in, at one point offering an authentic 'stone' from every county in Ireland (thirty-two in all, along with an ancient pilgrim standing stone). While Tolle initially resisted such appropriations, he soon came to acknowledge that these readings should not simply be dismissed as inappropriate or misguided. Instead he realized that any *interactive* installation of this kind must learn to incorporate such views into the actual process of the work itself as an open text of interpretation and re-interpretation. Tolle decided, accordingly, to inscribe the deep aspiration of many visitors to relocate the old counties of Ireland by accepting the stones and then placing them at random throughout the landscape. The stones scattered throughout the site thus served to reiterate the role of the stones in the walls and lintels of the cottage itself – that is, to function as 'indices' for the lost meanings and bearings of forgotten dwellers rather than as 'icons' that claim to restore the fetish of an original presence.

Tolle's installation is an invitation to 'mourning' (acknowledging that the lost object is lost) rather than 'melancholy' (refusing to let go of the lost object by obsessively fixating on it).[13] By soliciting visitors' active involvement with the site, as part of an on-going drama of semantic and symbolic reinvention, Tolle manages to insure that the work remains a work in perpetual progress, intertextually open and incomplete by definition. The fact that new readings and reactions are regularly included onto both the audio-sound track of voices, which visitors hear as they traverse the underground tunnel, and the visual inscriptions on the glass panels, are powerful tokens of Tolle's determination to maintain a process of active and responsible memory. Robin Lydenberg captures this radically hermeneutical sense of Tolle's design in her essay 'From Icon to Index: Some Contemporary Visions of the Irish Stone Cottage' and is worth quoting at length:

Tolle designed the memorial to invite and incorporate the viewer's active engagement with the land and its history rather than with vague nostalgia or the iconography of fixed and sentimentalized stereotypes. One entrance into the memorial leads visitors through an underground passageway up into the ruined cottage . . . The walls of the passageway are constructed of alternating sedimented bands of stone and frosted glass on which official and unofficial testimonies from those who experienced the Famine are cast in shadows. This sculptured layering evokes the geologically and historically sedimentary aspect of the Irish landscape. Hunger is not naturalized or aestheticised here but contextualized historically and politically, giving forceful articulation, for example, to the failure of British officials to alleviate massive starvation. Entering the quarter acre of Ireland through this buried history, viewers cannot simply delight in the landscape as idealized icon: the cottage interior is cramped and exposed, the 'rolling hills' are the remnants of uncultivated potato furrows. Visitors may enter the installation by stepping directly onto the sloping earth and climbing up through the landscape to the ruined cottage and its prospect; there they discover, belatedly, the textual history buried below. Whether the memorial is entered from above or from below, the charm of the landscape and its violent history exist in productive tension.[14]

By deterritorializing the stone cottage from rural Ireland and reterritorializing it amidst the alien urban bustle of New York, Tolle is reminding us that the place of trauma is always haunted by a no-place of mourning. Such mourning calls for a letting go of the literal landscape of the past in order to give this past a future, in order to open it to new possibilities of interpretation. In this we could say that the artist is conjuring up the emancipatory potential of the 'Fifth Province'. Ireland, as everyone knows, has four provinces – Munster, Ulster, Leinster and Connaught – but the Irish word for province is *coiced*, meaning a fifth. So where, one might ask, is the fifth since there are only four actually existing as geographical places? The Fifth Province is a placeless place, a place of disposition rather than of position, of detachment rather than attachment. Since the beginnings of Irish myth and folklore it has been acknowledged that it is precisely this Fifth Province that provides a dimension of peace, wisdom and catharsis to the otherwise warring parts of Ireland.[15] Tolle's memorial might thus be said to remind us that all our lives – whether we are Irish or not, emigrants or natives, survivors or victims – are always haunted by an irretrievable sense of absence and loss, ghosted by a longing for some 'irrecoverable elsewhere.'[16]

Tolle attests to the Fifth Province by insuring that his poetical text – the site as work of art – remains answerable to an ethical context of responsibility. And he brings this about by turning his famine memorial into an intertextual play of multiple readings and perspectives. The hold of a single Meta-narrative of Irish history is thus loosened and liberated into a polyphony of discontinuous and competing narratives. Tolle juxtaposes, in both the written and audio commentaries; statistics about the Irish Famine with equally perturbing facts and figures about other famines and world hunger generally. He mixes snatches of Irish history and politics with snippets of song and poetry. He blends together a variety of vernacular and postmodern art styles – Naturalism, Folk Craft, Conceptual Art, Hyper-Realism, Landscape Architecture, Theme Sculpture, Pop Art, Earth Art etc. Moreover, the fact that the installation can grow and mutate – thanks to the use of climactically sensitive organic materials, and to the deployment of flexible, alterable texts (silk-screened onto strips of clear Plexiglas) – illustrates Tolle's conviction that historical memorials are themselves subject to change according to the addition of new and alternative perspectives. As Lydenberg writes:

> This memorial makes no claim to enlighten visitors with a totalizing narrative of the Irish Famine; the texts create a mixture of facts, political propaganda, and personal experience – the imaginative work of fantasy, desire, and hope. Tolle's design offers a transitional passageway through fragmented, often anonymous, voices in the embedded texts and an accompanying audio collage, both of which will be revised, updated and expanded periodically in response to continuing crises in world hunger. The narrative is discontinuous, full of gaps and silences; Tolle teases out multiple meanings by placing fragments in shifting juxtapositions rather than in fixed narrative sequence. A heritage industry presentation of history as a recoverable and repeatable past to be fixed 'like a fly in amber' is displaced here by . . . a 'preposterous history' that multiplies uncertainty and doubt. This alternative mode of history calls for an alternative mode of memorial, one that would . . . defy easy readability and consumer satisfaction to communicate instead dissatisfaction, complexity, and a sense of loss.[17]

The transatlantic exchange between Mayo and New York, between abandoned stone cottage and postmodern concrete megapolis, solicits a response of profound questioning and curiosity in most viewers to the site, reminding us that if we pass *from action to text,* in entering this memorial, we return *from text to action* again as soon as we exit the installation – bringing the heightened poetics of remembering that we experience in this placeless place to bear on our ethics of remembering in the real life-world around us.

Finally, we might add that if Tolle's memorial is an intertext in so far as it brings together the diverse idioms of poetics and ethics, and the diverse disciplines of history and geography, it also functions intertextually by relating to a number of what might be termed 'counter-texts' in the immediate or not so immediate environment.[18] One thinks of Ellis Island and the Statue of Liberty visible to the south of the waterfront Memorial – both symbols of aspiration and expectation for so many Irish emigrant survivors of the Famine. One thinks of the giant Twin Towers, in whose shadow in lower east Manhattan the memorial was originally constructed and in whose wake it now stands vigil in commemorative commiseration. One thinks of the other Irish Famine memorials in Boston and different emigrant ports of North America, so different and so similar; or the memorials to other historical traumas and tragedies from the Holocaust to Vietnam – in particular the Museum of Jewish Heritage; A Living Memorial to the Holocaust also housed in Battery Park City; or Maya Lin's famous Washington Monument to the Vietnam War dead. One might, indeed, even extend the scope of intertextual reference to include the fictional testimonials of writers like Tomas O'Flaherty and Tom Murphy; or of filmmakers like Scorsese whose representation of Irish emigrant warfare in the *Gangs of New York*[19] reminds us that within earshot of Battery Park stood the old site of tribal battle called the Five Points, a notorious battleground where blocked, fixated memories of vengeance and obsession played themselves out in bloody conflict in the 1860s – Nativists and Hibernians locked in hatred, impervious to the work of mourning, catharsis and forgiveness. It is just such a process of therapeutic working-through (*Durcharbeitung*) that, I would argue, Memorials such as the Battery Park City Famine installation solicit.[20]

In sum, Tolle's memorial serves, I submit, as a model for a healing exchange of memories. The exchange in question here involves that between indigenous and emigrant, Irish and Irish-American, Irish-American and ' Anglo-American, Irish-American and non-Anglo American (Asian, African, Middle-Eastern, Hispanic etc). It also involves an exchange between home and abroad, between the old world and the new, between Achill Island and Manhattan Island. And of course, to move from geography back to history, it involves an exchange – in both directions – between past and present. By refusing to either naturalize or aestheticize memory, Tolle keeps open a crucial critical 'gap' that prevents history from collapsing back into a frozen past. His memorial resists being obsessively reified and replicated. Instead, Tolle preserves the gap between Now and Then, Here and There, enabling both poles to transit back and forth between the everyday reality of New York life today and an imaginary place in the minds of those famine emigrants who left it behind over a century and a half ago. It is in this 'between' that contemporary visitors to the site may experience what we might properly call a *poetical ethics of memory*.

Ethics, narrative and memory

So how might we relate the case of the Famine Hunger Memorial in New York to a specifically hermeneutic paradigm of memory exchange, mentioned at the outset? In an essay entitled 'Reflections on a New Ethos for Europe', Paul Ricoeur outlines just such a paradigm. He shows, first, how this can provide a basis for an *ethic of narrative hospitality* that involves 'taking responsibility in imagination and in sympathy for the story of the other, through the life narratives which concern the other.'[21] In the case of memorials such as Tolle's this takes the form of an exchange between different people's histories such that we practise an art of transference and translation that allows us to welcome the story of the other, the stranger, the victim, the forgotten one.

Second, Ricoeur shows how this calls in turn for an *ethic of narrative flexibility*. Memorials face the challenge of resisting the reification of an historical event into a fixed dogma by showing how each event may be told in different ways by different generations and by different narrators. Not that everything becomes relative and arbitrary. On the contrary, acts of trauma and suffering call out for justice, and the best way of achieving this is often to invite empathy with strangers and adversaries by allowing for a plurality of narrative perspectives. The resulting overlap may thus lead to what Gadamer calls a 'fusion of horizons' where diverse horizons of consciousness may at last find some common ground.[22] A reciprocal transfer between opposite minds. 'The identity of a group, culture, people or nation, is not that of an immutable substance', writes Ricoeur, 'nor that of a fixed structure, but that, rather, of a recounted story'. A hermeneutic exchange of stories effectively resists an arrogant or rigid conception of cultural identity which prevents us from perceiving the radical implications of the principle of narrativity – namely, 'the possibilities of revising every story which has been handed down and of carving out a place for several stories directed towards the same past'.[23]

This entails, by implication, a third ethical principle – that of *narrative plurality*. Pluralism here does not mean any lack of respect for the singularity of the event narrated through the various acts of remembering. It might even be said to increase our sense of awareness of such an event, especially if it is foreign to us in time, space or cultural provenance. '*Recounting differently* is not inimical to a certain historical reverence to the extent that the inexhaustible richness of the event is honored by the diversity of stories which are made of it, and by the competition to which that diversity gives rise.'[24] And Ricoeur adds this critical point:

> the ability to recount the founding events of our national history in different ways is reinforced by the exchange of cultural memories. This ability to exchange has as a touchstone the will to share symbolically and respectfully in the commemoration of the founding events of other national cultures, as well as those of their ethnic minorities and their minority religious denominations.[25]

This point applies as much to events of pain and trauma (like that commemorated in the Famine memorial) as to events of triumph and glory.

A fourth aspect of the hermeneutic exchange of memories is the *transfiguring of the past*. This involves a creative retrieval of the betrayed promises of the past, so that we may respond to our 'debt to the dead' and endeavour to give them a voice. The goal of memorials is, therefore, to try to give a future to the past by remembering it in the right way, ethically and poetically. A crucial aspect of reinterpreting transmitted traditions is the task of discerning past promises which have not been honoured. For 'the past is not only what is bygone – that which has taken place and can no longer be changed – it also lives in the memory thanks to arrows of futurity which have not been fired or whose trajectory has been interrupted'.[26] In other words, the unfulfilled future of the past may well signal the richest part of a tradition; and the emancipation of 'this unfulfilled future of the past is the major benefit that we can expect from the crossing of memories and the exchange of narratives'.[27] It is especially the founding events of a community – traumatic or dramatic – which require to be reread in this critical manner in order to unlock the potencies and expectancies which the subsequent unfolding of history may have forgotten or travestied. This is why any genuine memorial involves a certain return to some seminal moment of suffering or hope, to the original events and textual responses to those events, which are all too often occluded by Official History. 'The past is a cemetery of promises which have not been kept', notes Ricoeur. And Memorials can, at best, be ways of 'bringing them back to life like the dry bones in the valley described in the prophecy of Ezekiel'.[28]

A fifth and final ethical moment in the hermeneutics of memory-exchange is *pardon*. If empathy and hospitality towards others are crucial steps in the ethics of remembrance there is something *more* – something which entails moving beyond narrative imagination to forgiveness. In short, the exchange of memories of suffering demands more than sympathy and duty (though these are essential for any kind of justice). And this something 'extra' involves pardon in so far as pardon means 'shattering the debt'. Here the order of justice and reciprocity can be supplemented, but not replaced, by that of 'charity and gift'. Such forgiveness demands huge patience, an enduring practice of 'working-through', mourning and letting go. But it is not a forgetful forgiveness. Amnesty can never be based on amnesia. Amnesty remembers our debt to the dead while at the same time introducing something other, something difficult almost to the point of impossibility, but something all the more important for that reason. One thinks of Brandt kneeling at Warsaw, Havel's apology to the Sudeten Germans, Hume's preparedness to speak with the IRA, Sadat's visit to Jerusalem, Hillesum's refusal to hate her hateful persecuters. All miraculous moments where an ethics of reciprocity is touched by a poetics of pardon. But I repeat: one does not replace the other – both justice *and* pardon are equally important in the act of remembering past trauma. 'To the degree that charity exceeds justice we must guard against substituting it for justice. Charity remains a surplus; this surplus of compassion and tenderness is capable of giving the exchange of memories its profound motivation, its daring and its momentum.'[29]

It is not difficult to see how this hermeneutical model of memory-exchange relates to the Irish Famine Memorial in New York that we analysed in the first part of this paper. The one thing to add perhaps is that Memorials that are located in places far removed from the original trauma, serve the extra purpose of seeking pardon not only from the victims and survivors of that particular event, but from all visitors to the site. This is where a poetics of narrative fantasy may usefully complement a politics of historical judgement. For when we dare to visit the memorials dedicated to other peoples and communities (not our own), we are suddenly all famine sufferers, we are all Holocaust victims, and we are all casualties of the Vietnam War. At least for a special, impossible, fleeting moment.

Notes on Contributors

DANINE FARQUHARSON is Assistant Professor of English Literature at Memorial University of Newfoundland. She has published and presented papers on Brian Friel, Seamus Deane, Roddy Doyle, Robert McLiam Wilson, Edna O'Brien and Neil Jordan. Her current research is devoted to literary representations of the Easter Rising.

SEAN FARRELL is Associate Professor of History at Northern Illinois University. He is the author of *Rituals and Riots: Sectarian Violence and Political Culture in Ulster, 1784–1886* (University Press of Kentucky, 2000) and has written a number of essays on various aspects of eighteenth- and nineteenth-century Irish political culture. His current research project examines the links between late eighteenth-century Belfast and the West Indies.

PETER HART holds the Canada Research Chair in Irish Studies at Memorial University of Newfoundland. He is the author of *Mick: the Real Michael Collins* (Macmillan, 2005), *The IRA and Its Enemies* (Oxford, 1998), and other books.

KEITH HOPPER is a tutor at Kellogg College, Oxford, where he teaches Literature and Film Studies. He is the author of *Flann O'Brien: A Portrait of the Artist as a Young Post-Modernist* (Cork University Press, 1995; second edition forthcoming in 2007) and general editor of the *Ireland into Film* series (Cork University Press, 2001–2006). Keith is currently writing a book on the writer and filmmaker Neil Jordan, and is co-editing a new collection of essays on Flann O'Brien.

RICHARD KEARNEY holds the Charles B. Seelig Chair of Philosophy at Boston College and has served as a Visiting Professor at University College Dublin, the University of Paris Sorbonne and the University of

Nice. He is the author of over twenty books on European philosophy and literature (including two novels and a volume of poetry) and has edited or co-edited fourteen more. His most recent work in philosophy is a trilogy entitled 'Philosophy at the Limit' and the three volumes are: *On Stories* (Routledge, 2002), *The God Who May Be* (Indiana University Press, 2001) and *Strangers, Gods and Monsters* (Routledge, 2003).

ELMER KENNEDY-ANDREWS is Professor of English Literature at the University of Ulster at Coleraine, Northen Ireland. His books include *The Poetry of Seamus Heaney: All the Realms of Whisper* (St Martin's, 1988), *Contemporary Irish Poetry* (Macmillan, 1992), *The Art of Brian Friel* (Macmillan, 1995), *The Poetry of Seamus Heaney: A Reader's Guide to Essential Criticism* (Icon Books, 2nd edition, 2000), *The Poetry of Derek Mahon* (Colin Smythe, 2002), *Fiction and the Northern Ireland Troubles: (De-)Constructing the North* (Four Courts, 2003) and *Paul Muldoon: Poetry, Prose, Drama* (Colin Smythe, 2006).

BRIAN MCILROY is Professor of Film Studies at the University of British Columbia. He is the author of *Irish Cinema: An Illustrated History* (Anna Livia Press, 1988), *Shooting to Kill: Filmmaking and the 'Troubles' in Northern Ireland* (Steveston Press, 2001), and editor of *Genre and Cinema: Ireland and Transnationalism* (Routledge, New York, 2007).

TIMOTHY G. MCMAHON is Assistant Professor of History at Marquette University in Milwaukee, Wisconsin. He is the editor of *Pádraig Ó Fathaigh's War of Independence: Recollections of a Galway Gaelic Leaguer* (Cork University Press, 2000), as well as the author of the forthcoming book, *The Gaelic Revival and Irish Society*. A specialist on national identity, popular culture, and empire, he is past History Representative for the American Conference for Irish Studies.

BERNICE SCHRANK is Professor of English Literature at Memorial University of Newfoundland. She has published extensively on the drama and prose of Sean O'Casey as well as on the work of such other Irish writers as Brendan Behan, Edna O'Brien, W.B. Yeats, Brian Friel, George Bernard Shaw and Frank McGuinness. She also works in the field of American literature and has written about Erica Jong, Hortense Calisher, E.L. Doctorow, Israel Horovitz and William Faulkner.

Notes and References

INTRODUCTION

1 Peter Hart, *The IRA and its Enemies* (Oxford: Clarendon, 1998), p. 21.
2 For Hart's searching examination of the various constructions of the Kilmichael Ambush, see *ibid.*, pp. 21–38. Few memoirs have been more influential than Tom Barry's classic and entertaining account of his exploits in the War of Independence. For his take on Kilmichael, see Tom Barry, *Guerrilla Days in Ireland* (Dublin: Irish Press, 1949), pp. 48–68.
3 See for example the impassioned letters that followed a March 2005 interview with Hart in *History Ireland,* 13, 3, May/June 2005.
4 In *Interpreting Northern Ireland* (Oxford: Clarendon, 1990) John Whyte notes that 7,000 books and articles had been written about the Troubles in Northern Ireland, making it, in proportion to size, 'the most heavily researched area on earth' (viii). That was in 1990 and, to put it diplomatically, the literature on the Troubles shows no sign of slowing down anytime soon.
5 Richmond Lattimore (trans. and intro.), *Aeschylus I: Oresteia* (Chicago: University of Chicago Press, 1953).
6 Gilles Deleuze, 'The Language of Sade and Masoch', in Becky McLaughlin and Bob Coleman (eds.), *Everyday Theory: A Contemporary Reader* (New York: Pearson, 2005), p. 518.
7 Hannah Arendt, 'A Special Supplement: Reflections on Violence', in *The New York Review of Books*, 12, 4, 27 February 1969. This long essay by Arendt is the preliminary version of what would become her book *On Violence* (New York: Harcourt Brace, 1970). 'Reflections on Violence' is a distilled and pointed argument that is elaborated in the book-length text, but the essay is more straightforward.
8 Carl von Clausewitz, *On War*, ed. and trans., Michael Howard (Princeton: Princeton University Press, 1976). Friedrich Engels, *Herrn Eugen Dührings Umwälzung der Wissenschaft* (1878, repr. London: Electric Books, 2001), part II, chapter 2. John Keegan, *The First World War* (London: Hutchinson, 1998).
9 Glenn Bowman, 'The Violence of Identity', in Bettina E. Schmidt (ed.), *Anthropology of Violence and Conflict* (London: Routledge, 2001), pp. 25–46.
10 Beatrice Hanssen, *Critique of Violence: Between Poststructuralism and Critical Theory* (New York: Routledge, 2000).

11 Walter Benjamin, 'Critique of Violence', in Peter Demetz (ed.), *Reflections: Essays, Aphorisms, Autobiographical Writings* (New York: Harcourt Brace, 1978).
12 *Discipline and Punish* (Harmonsworth: Penguin, 1977) was first published in French in 1975 by Éditions Gallimard as *Surveiller et Punir: Naissance de la Prison*. Cass R. Sunstein, 'Is Violent Speech a Right?', in *American Prospect* 22 (New York: Vintage, 1979), Summer 1995, pp. 34–7.
13 Obviously, contemporary study of these issues is too vast to summarize here. For a selection of recent work, please see note 24 below.
14 René Girard, *Violence and the Sacred* (Baltimore: Johns Hopkins University Press, 1977).
15 Göran Aijmer and Jon Abbink (eds.), *Meanings of Violence: A Cross-Cultural Perspective* (Oxford and New York: Berg, 2000).
16 Ibid., p. xv.
17 Lattimore, 1, 734.
18 Ibid., 1, 987.
19 See, for example, the influential collection by Samuel Clark and James S. Donnelly, Jr., *Irish Peasants: Violence and Political Unrest, 1780–1914* (Dublin: Gill & Macmillan, 1983). For Donnelly's influential articles on agrarian violence from the late 1970s and 1980s are recently republished in *Irish Agrarian Rebellion* (Dublin: Irish Academic Press, 1997). For an important examination of violence in Irish film, see John Hill's 'Images of Violence', in Kevin Rockett, Luke Gibbons, and John Hill, *Cinema and Ireland* (Syracuse, New York: Syracuse University Press, 1988).
20 For Veena Das, see *Mirrors of Violence: Communities, Rioters and Survivors in South Asia* (Delhi and New York: Oxford University Press, 1988); for Steger and Lind, see *Violence and its Alternatives* (New York: St Martin's Press, 1999).
21 Margot Backus, *Gothic Family Romance: Heterosexuality, Child Sacrifice and the Anglo-Irish Colonial Order* (Durham, North Carolina: Duke University Press, 1999) and Angela Bourke, *The Burning of Bridget Cleary* (London: Pimlico, 1999 and New York: Viking, 2000)).
22 Sebastian Barry, *A Long Long Way* (New York: Viking, 2005).
23 Kevin Kenny, *Making Sense of the Molly Maguires* (New York: Knopf, 1998).
24 Jill Lepore, *The Name of War: Philip's War and the Origins of American Identity* (New York: Oxford University Press, 1998), x.
25 See David William Foster, *Violence in Argentine Literature: Cultural Responses to Tyranny* (Columbia: University of Missouri Press, 1995); Linda Colley, *Britons: Forging the Nation, 1707–1837* (London: Pimlico, 1992); Aníbal González, *Killer Books: Writing, Violence, and Ethics in Modern Spanish American Narrative* (Austin: University of Texas Press, 2001); Rosemary Jane Jolly, *Colonization, Violence, and Narration in White South African Writing: Andre Brink, Breyten Breytenbach, and J.M. Coetzee* (Athens: Ohio University Press, 1996); Gyanendra Pandey, *Memory, History, and the Question of Violence: Reflections on the Reconstruction of Partition* (Cambridge: Cambridge University Press, 2001), and *Remembering Partition: Violence, Nationalism and History in India* (Cambridge: Cambridge University Press, 2001).
26 For a recent example, see Joseph Lennon, *Irish Orientalism: A Literary and Intellectual History* (Syracuse: Syracuse University Press, 2004). For a provocative examination of the broad links between imperialism and Irish culture, see

Stephen Howe, *Ireland and Empire: Colonial Legacies in Irish History and Culture* (Oxford University Press, 2000)

27 Thaddeus O'Sullivan, dir., *December Bride* (British Screen and Film Four Productions, 1990).

28 David Caffery, *Divorcing Jack* (Scala Productions, 1998).

ON THE NECESSITY OF VIOLENCE IN THE IRISH REVOLUTION

1 Peter Hart, *The IRA at War 1916–1923* (Oxford: Oxford University Press, 2003), p. 31.
2 Hart, *Mick: the Making of Michael Collins* (London: Macmillan, 2005), p. 153.
3 Hart, *IRA at War*, pp. 100–02.
4 For a discussion of the political impact of the Rising (and its necessity), see Charles Townshend, *Easter 1916: the Irish Rebellion* (London: Penguin, 2006), pp. 300–59.
5 Michael Laffan, *The Resurrection of Ireland: the Sinn Féin Party, 1916–1923* (Cambridge: Cambridge University Press, 1999), pp. 68–121.
6 Michael Wheatley, *Nationalism and the Irish Party: Provincial Ireland 1910–1916* (Oxford: Oxford University Press, 2005).
7 John Coakley, 'The Election that Made the First Dáil', in Brian Farrell (ed.), *The Creation of the Dáil* (Dublin: Blackwater Press, 1994).
8 David Fitzpatrick, *Politics and Irish Life: Provincial Experience of War and Revolution 1913–1921* (Dublin: Gill & Macmillan, 1977), p. 13.
9 Charles Townshend, 'The Irish Railway Strike of 1920: Industrial Action and Civil Resistance in the Struggle for Independence', *Irish Historical Studies*, 1979, pp. 21, 83.
10 See the ground-breaking study by Declan Martin, 'Migration Within the Six Counties of Northern Ireland, with Special Reference to the City of Belfast, 1911–37', MA thesis, Queens University of Belfast (1977); and Alan Parkinson, *Belfast's Unholy War: The Troubles of the 1920s* (Dublin: Four Courts Press, 2004).
11 Michael Hopkinson, *The Irish War of Independence* (Dublin: Gill & Macmillan, 2002), pp. 177–91.
12 For another view of this scenario, see Alvin Jackson, 'British Ireland: What if Home Rule Had Been Enacted in 1912?', in Niall Ferguson (ed.), *Virtual History: Alternatives and Counterfactuals* (London: Papermac, 1998).

SEAN O'CASEY AND THE DIALECTICS OF VIOLENCE

1 Sean O'Casey, 'I Knock at the Door', *Autobiographies I* (London: Macmillan, 1963), p. 3.
2 Frank McCourt, *'Tis* (New York: Scribner, 1999), p. 151.
3 See, for example, his chapter on the hawthorn tree in 'Pictures in the Hallway', *Autobiographies I* (London: Macmillan, 1963), pp. 179–402.
4 Sean O'Casey, 'Drums Under the Windows', *Autobiographies I* ((London: Macmillan, 1963), pp. 572–90.
5 Bernice Schrank, 'Studies of the Self, Irish Autobiographical Writing and the Discourses of Colonialism and Independence', *a/b, Auto/Biography Studies*, Fall, 1994, pp. 260–75.

6 Ronald Ayling, *Sean O'Casey's Theatre of War* (Vernon, British Columbia: Kalamalka Press, 2004), p. 1.

7 Bernice Schrank, 'A Portrait of the Artist as an Irish Socialist, Ideology and Identity in the Autobiographical Writings of Sean O'Casey', *Works and Days, Essays in the Socio-Historical Dimensions of Literature and the Arts*, Fall, 1993, pp. 45–60.

8 Sean O'Casey, 'Purple Dust', *Complete Plays, Vol., 3* (London: Macmillan, 1984), pp. 1–122.

9 I found a copy of this letter in a pamphlet belonging to my father, who was a veteran of the Abraham Lincoln Brigade. The pamphlet was put together for a dinner tribute to Dr Barsky on the occasion of the thirtieth Anniversary of the War in Spain in 1967 (some seventeen years after O'Casey wrote his letter). The pamphlet has no date, no place of publication, no notice that its contents are protected by copyright and no author. Its cover bears a picture of Dr Barsky, and beneath it, his name, 'Edward K. Barsky, M.D.', which, presumably, is also the title of the pamphlet. As well as the letter from O'Casey, the pamphlet also includes letters and greetings from Dolores Ibarruri, Paul Robeson, Ring Lardner, Jr., Lazaro Cardenas and A.J. Muste among others. The original letter may be found in the Abraham Lincoln Brigade Archives 125, Joint Anti-Fascist Refugee Committee Correspondence, Box 1, Folder 20, Tamiment Library/Robert Wagner Labor Archives, Elmer Holmes Bobst Library, New York University Libraries.

10 'Unpublished Letter from Sean O'Casey to the Veterans of the Abraham Lincoln Brigade', *Canadian Journal of Irish Studies*, 25 1/2, 1999, pp. 216–18.

11 I use the term 'audiences' in the broadest sense to include not only those present in the theatre on a particular night, but also the public at large amongst whom are to be found theatre reviewers, politicians, clergy and academic critics.

12 See Sean O'Casey, *The Green Crow* (New York: George Braziller, 1956) and *The Flying Wasp* ((London: Macmillan, 1937).

13 Sean O'Casey, *The Story of the Irish Citizen Army* (1919, Dublin: Talbot Press, 1971).

14 O'Casey's portrayals of the British in his plays range from the positive, even noble, English characters of *Oak Leaves and Lavender* (in *Complete Plays of Sean O'Casey*, Vol 4 (London: Macmillan, 1984), pp. 1–116), to the downright inept and silly Stokes and Poges in *Purple Dust*. His autobiographical writings demonstrate the same variability.

15 Sean O'Casey, 'The Plough and the Stars', *Collected Plays, Vol., I* (London: Macmillan, 1963), pp. 159–261.

16 Ibid., p. 170.

17 Ibid., p. 171.

18 Ibid., p. 197.

19 The Jenersky reference suggests a generic socialist text that one feels ought to exist. It is, of course, possible that no such author or text does exist. If indeed the reference is not merely obscure but non-existent, then O'Casey was having a private joke at the Covey's expense by increasing the absurdity of his claims to socialist expertise. Few members of any audience, though, would be likely to know whether or not the reference was accurate. No library I use has the work.

After several days and many hours googling title and author and finding neither separate from references to *The Plough*, I am persuaded that O'Casey made both up.

20 *The Plough*, p. 149.

21 Bernice Schrank, *Sean O'Casey A Research and Production Sourcebook* (London: Greenwood Press, 1996), pp. 51–2.

22 See O'Casey's 'Letter to the Editor', *Irish Independent* (Dublin), 20 February 1926 and 'Letter to the Editor', *Irish Times* (Dublin), 19 February 1926.

23 Sean O'Casey, 'Letter', *The Times*, 19 February 1926.

24 For a report of this debate, see David Krause, *Sean O'Casey The Man and His Work* (1960, London: Macmillan, 1975), pp. 177–80.

25 For a full treatment of the event, see Robert Lowery, *A Whirlwind in Dublin, 'The Plough and the Stars' Riots* (Westport, Connecticut and London: Greenwood Press, 1984).

26 *Within the Gates* (*Complete Plays of Sean O'Casey*), *Vol. 2* (London: Macmillan, 1984), pp. 113–238, like its predecessor, 'The Silver Tassie' (*Collected Plays, Vol. II*, London: Macmillan, 1964), pp. 1–112, marked a shift in O'Casey's work from the conventions of slice of life realism to a more lyrical and symbolic theatre.

27 For the enthusiastic reviews, see J.T. Grein, 'The World of the Theatre', *Illustrated London News*, 3 March 1934, p. 320 and Willson M. Disher, 'A New Sort of Play, Sean O'Casey's Genius, Raw Life', *Daily Mail*, 8 February 1934, p. 17. For the disastrous, see J.G.B., 'An Irish Man's General Grouse, Sean O'Cascy's Play on a London Park Theme', *Evening News*, 8 February 1934, p. 9; G[ordon] B[eckles], 'A Challenge to Sean O'Casey, What Is His Play Really About?' *Daily Express*, 8 February 1934, p. 3; Desmond McCarthy, 'Hyde Park', *New Statesman and Nation*, 17 February 1934, pp. 226–7; and 'London Theatres, *Within the Gates*', *Scotsman*, 8 February 1934, p. 8.

28 Christopher Murray, *Sean O'Casey Writer at Work* (Dublin: Gill & Macmillan, 2004), p. 232.

29 See Bosley Crowther, 'Who Is Then the Gentleman? A Few Notes on Sean O'Casey, the Irish Dramatist, Who Is Here With His Play *Within the Gates*', and 'Started From Scratch, Sean O'Casey, Irish Playwright Here with New Play, Traveled Hard Road', both clippings: O'Casey file, Billy Rose Theater Collection, Lincoln Center for the Performing Arts Library, New York.

30 O'Casey, 'From Within the Gates', *New York Times*, 21 October 1934, sect. 9, pp. 1, 3.

31 Brooks Atkinson, 'The Play, Fantasy of the Seasons in Hyde Park in Sean O'Casey's *Within the Gates*', *New York Times*, 23 October 1934, p. 3; Robert Garland, '*Within the Gates* Surges with Power', *New York World-Telegram*, 23 October 1934; Edith J.R. Isaacs, 'Playhouse Gates, Broadway in Review', *Theatre Arts Monthly*, December 1934, pp. 894–9; and George Jean Nathan, 'Nathan Digests the Plays, *Within the Gates*', *American Spectator*, December 1934, p. 12.

32 Arthur Ruhl, 'The Theatres, *Within the Gates* by Sean O'Casey', *New York Herald Tribune*, 23 October 1934, p. 14.

33 John Mason Brown, '*Within the Gates*', *New York Post*, 23 October 1937, p. 17.

34 Leon Alexander, 'Sean O'Casey Tilts a Dull Lance Against Puritanism in Play *Within the Gates*', *Daily Worker*, 27 October 1934, p. 5; Stark Young, 'Theatre

Gates, *Within the Gates* by Sean O'Casey, National Theatre', *New Republic*, 7 November 1934, p. 369.

35 Euphemia van Rensselaer Wyatt, *Within the Gates, Catholic World*, December 1934, pp. 338–40; Elizabeth Jordan, 'Sean O'Casey's Crawling World', *America*, 24 November 1934, pp. 160–1.

36 Murray, p. 238.

37 Was the play a Broadway success? Murray notes that despite O'Casey's initial sense that the play would ease his financial troubles, he eventually realized that it 'was not going to be a smash hit' (p. 237). Murray leaves the impression that the play was something of a flop. This does not seem to me to be the case. To have run for 101 performances at the height of the Depression, when money for entertainment was a luxury few could afford, suggests that the play had popular appeal. To have taken the show on the road with its large cast bespeaks a commitment by the producers to the value of the material as well as to the money-making possibilities of further productions. The producers surely did not take the play on tour in order to lose money. Murray notes that O'Casey earned some £500 from the New York performances, the equivalent of US $2,500, which was, for those times, a tidy fortune. In the Depression years, my mother earned $10 a week, and she regarded that salary as an excellent wage.

38 *New York Herald Tribune*, 13 January 1935, Clipping, O'Casey file, Billy Rose Theater Collection, Lincoln Center for the Performing Arts Library, New York.

39 See Atkinson 'Mansfield Bans *Within the Gates* on Clergy Protest, Quincy Will Bar It', *Boston Herald*, 16 January 1935, pp.1 and 4, and E[dwin] F. M[elvin], 'Beside Grave Boston's Uncommon Common', *New York Times* 27 January 1935, sec. 8, p. 1.

40 I examined Fr Connolly's papers at the library of Boston College and found his notes on his Irish literature course, amongst them a section on O'Casey's early plays. It would be fair to infer that Fr Connolly was familiar with and influenced by the criticism of O'Casey in Ireland.

41 'Fr Connolly Condemns Play by Sean O'Casey, Authority on Irish Literature Writes Criticism of *Within the Gates* Which Mayor Mansfield Has Prohibited in Boston', *Boston Traveler*, 16 January 1935, p. 25.

42 Ibid., and 'Fr Connolly Calls *Within the Gates* Book of Common Smut', *Boston Globe*, 21 January 1935, p. 2.

43 See, for example, 'Watch-Ward Head Says Friends OK O'Casey Play', *Boston Traveler*, 16 January 1935, pp. 1, 25; 'O'Casey's Play "Not Bad Enough to Be Banned"', *Boston Evening Transcript*, 16 January 1935, pp. 1, 3; and 'Current Comment, It Was a Way Out, From the *Baltimore Sun*', *Boston Evening Transcript*, 21 January 1935, p. 12.

44 'Harvard Dramatic Club Against Ban, Calls *Within the Gates* Suppression Criticism of Religion Not of Play', *Boston Evening Transcript*, 17 January 1935, p. 5; 'Protest of Students Against Play Ban Bears 300 Names, Hillyer, Atkinson Scorns Censor of *Within the Gates*', *Harvard Crimson*, 25 January 1935, pp. 1, 3.

45 'Play Ban By Mayor Contested', *Boston Evening American*, 22 January 1935, p. 11.

46 See Eric Fessenden, 'Modern Drama Stresses Sordid Things of Life', *Boston Herald*, 7 February 1935, p. 14, 'Letters That Come on the O'Casey Play, Reactions of Correspondents To the Banning of *Within the Gates*', *Boston Evening*

Transcript, 17 January 1935, pp. 9–10, and 'Letters to the Editor', *Boston Evening Transcript*, 21 January 1935, p. 12.

47 'Playwrights Plead for Lifting of Ban', *Boston Post*, 18 January 1935, p. 2.

48 'Mayor Moves to Ban O'Casey in Book Form', *Boston Traveler*, 17 January 1935, pp. 1 and 9; 'Move to Bar O'Casey Book in Hub, Police Head Reading It With View to Halt Sales', *Boston Post*, 18 January 1935, pp. 1–2; and George Sprague, 'Mayor Bans Book of O'Casey Play, Book of O'Casey Play "Rotten" Says Mayor', *Boston Record*, 18 January 1935, pp. 1, 2.

49 'O'Casey Banned in Cambridge, Chief Leahy Warns Sellers of Book Are Liable to Prosecution', *Boston Traveler*, 19 January 1935, p. 4.

50 '*Within Gates* Book Sold Out, Police Are Told, King and Men, Possibly Planning Court Action, Visit Stores in Vain', *Boston Evening Transcript*, 18 January 1935, p. 2; 'Copy of Book on O'Casey Play Can't Be Found', *Boston Daily Record*, 19 January 1935, p. 4.

51 'Banned Play Read in Pulpit, Church of the Redemption Bases Sermon on O'Casey's Work, *Within the Gates* Ruling Denounced', *Boston Herald*, 21 January 1935, p. 5; 'Police Censor Sermon in Hub', *Boston Post*, 21 January 1935, p. 1; and 'Police Note Down Sermon, Ban on Play Assailed at Church of Redemption', *Boston Globe*, 21 January 1935, pp. 1–2.

52 'Banned Play Showing Sean, Church Dramatic Group Presentation Indicated on O'Casey Play', *Boston Traveler*, 21 January 1935, p. 14.

53 See 'Dana "Acts" *Within the Gates* in Home', *New York Times*, 22 January 1935, Clipping, O'Casey file, Billy Rose Theater Collection, Lincoln Center for the Performing Arts Library, New York; 'Barred Out of Hall, Reads Play in Home', *Boston Post*, 22 January 1935, p. 9; and 'To Contest Banning of O'Casey Play, Committee Will Meet Tonight to Plan Action Against Mansfield's Order', *Boston Evening Transcript*, 22 January 1935, p. 6.

54 'Dr Skinner to Speak on *Within the Gates*', *Boston Herald*, 26 January 1935, p. 9 and 'Hub Church to Test Ban on O'Casey, Play to Be Interpreted by Theologian at Service', *Boston Post*, 23 January 1935, p. 23.

55 'Censorship Law Revisions Urged, Dean Skinner of Tufts Takes Issue with Catholics on O'Casey Play, License Changes Also Demanded', *Boston Herald*, 28 January 1935, p. 18.

56 'Mayor to Refuse Advance Opinions on Plays of "Doubtful Propriety"', *Boston Herald*, 7 February 1935, p. 4.

57 '*Within the Gates* Ends Tour Tonight, Boston's Ban on Sean O'Casey's Play Responsible for Producer's Decision', *New York Times*, January 1935, and '*Within the Gates* to Continue', both clippings from O'Casey file, Billy Rose Theater Collection, Lincoln Center for the Performing Arts Library, New York.

58 See Edwin F. Melvin, 'Miss Gish to Meet Pilgrims from Boston', *Boston Evening Transcript*, 30 January 1935, Part 2, p. 3 and 'O'Casey Via an Excursion to Manhattan, *Within the Gates* and the Expedition from Boston to See It', *Boston Evening Transcript*, 4 February 1935, p. 10.

59 Schrank, *Sean O'Casey A Research and Production Sourcebook*, pp. 282–3.

60 The term 'later plays' is elastic, but often denotes the plays O'Casey wrote after *The Silver Tassie* (1929) and *Within the Gates*. The phrase 'late O'Casey plays' often refers to the plays O'Casey wrote in his old age: *The Bishop's Bonfire* (1955), *The Drums of Father Ned* (1960), *Behind the Green Curtains* (1962), *The Moon*

Shines on Kylenamoe (1962) and *Figuro in the Night* (1962). Whether 'later' or 'late', the plays on which the most critical scorn falls are *The Star Turns Red* (1940), *Oak Leaves and Lavender* (1946), and O'Casey's last five plays.

61 Jack Mitchell, a British-born scholar who lectured in British and Irish literature at Humboldt University in the former East Germany is an exception. A committed Marxist, Mitchell's study of O'Casey is an old-style doctrinaire Marxist analysis, with a great many interesting things to say about O'Casey's politics and art. It is unsurprising that Mitchell's work is rarely cited by critics writing about O'Casey.

62 Robert Brustein, *The Theater of Revolt, An Approach to Modern Drama* (Boston: Little, Brown, 1964); David Daiches, *A Critical History of English Literature, Vol. IV* (London: Secker and Warburg, 1968).

63 Schrank, *Sean O'Casey A Research and Production Sourcebook*, pp. 14–20, 27–30, 32–3, 42.

64 Terence Brown, *Ireland, A Social and Cultural History 1922 to the Present* (London: Cornell University Press, 1985).

65 The seminal studies of O'Casey by David Krause and Robert Hogan, *The Experiments of Sean O'Casey* (New York: St Martin's Press, 1960), appeared in 1960, when McCarthyism was still a feature of the American political landscape. It is not surprising that Hogan's study of O'Casey's experimental technique floats free of any analysis of the politics that infuse those techniques. Krause's more comprehensive study essentially redefines O'Casey's Communism as primitive Christianity allied with a desire for social justice. I would not like to be understood as saying that either Hogan or Krause consciously trimmed his views of O'Casey to fit the cloth of McCarthyism. What I believe is that the political climate of the United States at the time unconsciously framed their views of O'Casey and made it attractive and easy for them to depoliticize his work. Their great strength is that, unlike Brustein, they found a vocabulary in which to deal with O'Casey's achievement and did not condemn him on the questionable ground of aesthetic failure.

66 Ellen W. Schrecker, *No Ivory Tower, McCarthyism and the Universities* (Oxford University Press, 1986).

67 It should be clear that I am arguing that O'Casey's treatment as an academic subject began with American critics who were not Marxist and unlikely to be sympathetic to O'Casey's Marxist approach to violence. Does this position mean that O'Casey's plays will receive a more sympathetic treatment by Marxist scholars? It needs to be said here that 'Marxist scholar' is not an essentialist category. Marxist scholars carry their own sectarian biases, and their own strengths and weaknesses as literary critics. Two Marxist scholars have written full-length studies of O'Casey, and they come to opposite conclusions about the value of his art and politics. In endnote 61 I refer to the work of Jack Mitchell, an English scholar, whose 1980 study of O'Casey's major plays from a Marxist perspective finds much to admire. A year before Mitchell's work appeared, the Irish socialist historian Desmond Greaves produced a study of O'Casey, *Sean O'Casey, Politics and Art* (London: Lawrence and Wishart, 1979). Greaves's work on O'Casey is, like his previous book on James Connolly (*The Life and Times of James Connolly* [London: Lawrence and Wishart, 1972], primarily a political analysis, but whereas Greaves treats Connolly with the utmost

delicacy and understanding, he is hostile to O'Casey's ideas and lacking in perception about his art. With an eye to reinvigorating Irish socialism, Greaves aims to mainstream Connolly as central both to the Irish labour and the Irish nationalist movements. Such a political position would immediately make Greaves unreceptive to O'Casey's assessment of the Rising as inimical to the development of the Irish labour movement. Indeed, Greaves faults O'Casey for his failure to appreciate the potential of the Rising for Irish socialism. Greaves's study of O'Casey goes on to criticize the later works for what he dismissively calls their stylistic mannerisms about which, in Greaves's view, nothing good can be said (see, in particular, his off-the-mark comments about the alliteration in *Star* p.150) and their propagandizing. With so little sympathy for O'Casey's politics it is not surprising that Greaves finds almost nothing good to say about O'Casey's art. To return to the question about whether Marxists are likely to be more sympathetic to O'Casey than non-Marxists, based on the differing assessments of Mitchell and Greaves, I would have to say that it depends on the Marxist.

68 It is not that the early plays had a thirty-year head start on the later plays. Scholarly articles on O'Casey did not start appearing until the expansion of American universities in the late '50s. By that time, *Bonfire* and *Drums* had appeared on the page and then the stage. The last three were soon to appear.

69 Schrank, *Sean O'Casey A Research and Production Sourcebook,* pp. 20–1.

70 See I.M., 'O'Casey's Premiere at the Gaiety', *Irish Independent,* 1 March 1955, p. 7, and K., 'The Bishop's Bonfire in Gaiety Theatre', *Irish Times,* 1 March 1955, p. 4.

71 See Seamus Byrne, 'The Shadow of an O'Casey', *Standard,* 4 March 1955, p. 3, 'If Critics Did Their Duty', *Standard,* 25 March 1955, p. 6, 'People and Principles', *Standard,* 25 March 1955, p. 6, 'Sean O'Casey's Play, Au B For Whose Sake?' *Standard,* 25 February 1955, p. 1, and 'Sean O'Casey's Play, The "Gods" Can't Be Fooled!' *Standard,* 4 March 1955, p. 1.

72 See 'Between the Acts', *Irish Tattler and Sketch,* April 1955, p. 66, both of J.J. Finegan's, 'Dublin's Advice to O'Casey', *Evening Herald,* 5 March 1955, p. 6 and 'Sean O'Casey Out of Touch', *Evening Herald,* 1 March 1955, p. 6, and X., 'Sean O'Casey', *Leader,* 12 March 1955, pp. 17–18.

73 Sean O'Casey, 'Tender Tears for Poor O'Casey', *The Green Crow* (New York: George Braziller, 1956), pp. 177–90 and 'Bonfire Under a Black Sun', *The Green Crow* (New York: George Braziller, 1956), pp. 130–59.

74 Schrank, *Production,* 27–31; Krause, 212–17.

75 O'Casey also corresponded with the English-born Ronald Ayling, who became a professor of English literature at the University of Alberta, Edmonton, Canada. Examples of correspondence with American academics include: letters to Robert Hogan acknowledging receipt of Hogan's dissertation, to Harry Ritchie and to David Krause concerning an article about O'Casey (*The Letters of Sean O'Casey 1955–58, Vol. III,* ed., David Krause, Washington DC: Catholic University Press, 1989.

76 Michael Sheridan, 'Father Ned's Drums Hollow at the Abbey', *Irish Press,* 10 May 1985, p. 4.

77 See Heinz Kosok, *O'Casey the Dramatist* (Gerards Cross Bucks and Totowa, New Jersey: Colin Smythe, Barnes and Noble, 1985), pp. 258–85, Krause

pp. 202–24, Jack Mitchell, *The Essential O'Casey, A Study of the Twelve Major Plays of Sean O'Casey* (New York: International Publishers, 1980), pp. 267–300, and Bobby L. Smith, *O'Casey's Satiric Vision* (Kent, OH: Kent State University Press, 1978), pp. 116–70.

78 'Illusion and Actuality in the Later O'Casey', written by the Irish critic John Jordan in Ronald Ayling, ed., *Sean O'Casey, Modern Judgments* (London: Macmillan, 1969, pp. 143–61), then teaching at Memorial University of Newfoundland (Canada), is, I think, the most sympathetic article to be written about the late plays. Yet Jordan does not give any attention to either *Figuro* or *Moon*, and provides a mixed review of *Curtains* and *Bonfire*. Jordan is at his best on *Drums*. Jordan's study appears in a collection of essays on O'Casey, and not in the scholarly journals. I emphasize the absence of coverage of the later plays in scholarly journals because some of the most widely circulated and prestigious of these journals (i.e., *PMLA*, *Modern Drama*) are less specialized than an essay collection on a specific author, and therefore may potentially be seen by a wider audience.

SEXING THE RISING: MEN, SEX, VIOLENCE AND EASTER 1916

1 Liam O'Flaherty, *Insurrection* (1950, Dublin: Wolfhound Press, 1993), p. 29.
2 Ibid., p. 59.
3 Ibid., p. 117, 121.
4 Ibid., p. 123.
5 Seamus McSwiney, 'Taking the Gun Out of Irish Politics: An Interview with Neil Jordan', *Cineaste*, May 1997, p. 20.
6 Just as Jim Sheridan's *In the Name of the Father* (Universal, 1994) came under fire for distorting historical facts, so too did *Michael Collins* endure harsh criticism. In his article, 'Cat-Calls from the Cheap Seats: The Third Meaning of Neil Jordan's *Michael Collins*' (*Irish Review*, Fall 1997, pp. 1–16), Keith Hopper documents many responses to the film, and the diversity of opinion is telling. Focusing on the many British critics who condemned it for historical 'inexactitude', Hopper notes the heavy weather that has been made of the anachronistic car-bomb, the armoured tank shooting at Croke Park and other scenes in the film which do not conform to historians' versions of events. Critical response in America was 'generally luke-warm' and the mass of letters to the editor of the *Irish Times* speaks to a divided reception in Ireland. Hooper notes that rarely has 'any film elicited such schizophrenic responses from historians and critics'. In the end, Hopper correctly comments that the question to provide the most interesting avenues into the film is 'how does film construct a historical world?'
7 In her article, 'Demythologizing/Remythologizing the Rising: Roddy Doyle's *A Star Called Henry*', Jose Lanters argues that Doyle's approach to history and Easter 1916 is satirical (*Hungarian Journal of English and American Studies*, 8, 1, 2002, pp. 245–58). In that vein, she also persuasively articulates the fact that 'Henry Smart challenges the accepted view of Irish history . . . but while doing so, his own position also becomes discredited' (p. 246). Lanters concludes that the novel does not ultimately succeed as either a satire or as a revisionist history, but I would add that the novel also throws into question the success of any history, any satire to fully articulate the experience or the relevance of the Easter Rising.

8 Dermot McCarthy, *Roddy Doyle: Raining on the Parade* (Dublin: Liffey Press, 2003), p. 196.

9 Lanters, p. 248.

10 McCarthy, p. 191.

11 Quoted in McCarthy, p. 197.

12 Ibid., p. 223.

13 Ibid. (italics in original), p. 205.

14 Roddy Doyle, *A Star Called Henry* (London: Jonathan Cape, 1999), pp. 120–1.

15 Ibid., p. 220.

16 Ibid., p. 221.

17 Ibid., p. 52.

18 Ibid., p. 89.

19 Lanters, p. 255.

20 Ibid., p. 255.

21 *Star Called*, p. 122.

22 Ibid., pp. 122–3.

23 Consider women such as Kitty Mellett in Liam O'Flaherty's 1928 novel *The Assassin* (Dublin: Wolfhound Press, 1993) or Isabella in Eugene McCabe's 1976 short story 'Victims' (*Christ in the Fields*, London: Minerva, 1993) or Jude in Neil Jordan's 1992 film *The Crying Game* (Miramax). They are unnatural and dangerous women, pushed to the periphery of the 'organization', whether that be the Irish Volunteers or the IRA. They very often die.

24 Kim McMullen, 'New Ireland/Hidden Ireland', *The Kenyon Review*, 26, 2, Spring 2004, p. 130.

25 Ibid., p. 130.

26 A sample of such reviewers commenting on O'Neill's literary influences include Adam Mars-Jones in *The Observer* writing: 'The cathedral is *Ulysses*, and the overwhelming influence on *At Swim, Two Boys* is Joyce' and 'Jim is like Stephen Dedalus with a heart' ('His Master's Joyce', *The Observer Review* 16 September 2001, p. 17). In the same vein, Justine Jordan opens her review in *The Guardian* with: ' "It is quite difficult for an Irish writer to have Joyce standing there," Jamie O'Neill remarked after 10 years of working on *At Swim, Two Boys* during shifts as a night porter. All the more so, one imagines, when your agent insists on touting you as his natural successor – and Samuel Beckett's and Flann O'Brien's into the bargain. But there is no question that O'Neill has stepped boldly and knowingly into the company of the Irish high modernists, from his titular nod at O'Brien's piece of fierce experimental whimsy, *At Swim-two-birds*, to his wordily associative Joycean prose' ('Rebellions of the Heart', *The Guardian: Saturday Review*, 22 September 2001, p. 8).

27 Jamie O'Neill, 'Paperback Writer', *The Guardian*, 3 August 2002.

28 Joseph Valente, 'Race/Sex/Shame: The Queer Nationalism of *At Swim, Two Boys*', *Éire-Ireland*, 40, 3/4 Fall/Winter 2005, p. 59.

29 Michael Cronin, '"He's My Country": Liberalism, Nationalism, and Sexuality in Contemporary Irish Gay Fiction', *Éire-Ireland*, 39, 3, Fall/Winter 2004, p. 266.

30 Michael Cronin, *Romantic Ireland Revisited*, only available from: www.sussex.ac.uk/cssd/courses/michael's diss/pdf, p. 4.

31 Editor's note, *Walt Whitman: Leaves of Grass* (ed.), Scully Bradley (New York: W.W. Norton & Company, 1973), p. 117.

32 Valente, p. 82.

33 Cronin, pp. 265, 267.

34 Jamie O'Neill, *At Swim, Two Boys* (London: Scribner, 2001), p. 440.

35 Ibid., p. 441.

36 Ibid., p. 501.

37 Ibid., p. 44.

38 Ibid., p. 159.

39 Ibid., p. 508.

40 Richard Kearney, *Postnationalist Ireland: Politics, Culture, Philosophy* (London and New York: Routledge, 1997), pp. 122–3.

41 Ibid., p. 123.

42 *At Swim*, p. 329.

43 Ibid., p. 435.

44 Augustine, *The Confessions of St Augustine* (trans. Rex Warner) (New York: New American Library, 1963), p. 74.

45 O'Neill (or his editors) actually misquote Augustine. The epigraph reads '*ecce abstulisti dominem*' and according to all the texts of Augustine's *Confessions* I could find, the original should be: '*ecce abstulisti hominem*'. While O'Neill may be making a comment about the divine in man (is he playing with domine or dominum?), I would argue it is just a misprint.

46 *At Swim*, p. 535.

47 Ibid., p. 643.

'DASH AND DARING': IMPERIAL VIOLENCE AND IRISH AMBIGUITY

1 I am particularly grateful to members of the Midwest Region of the American Conference for Irish Studies, who listened to an earlier version of this chapter at a meeting in Dubuque, Iowa, in October 2005. Their comments, both during and after that session, helped immensely to improve the final product.

2 *Freeman's Journal*, 17 July 1900. Hereafter the *Freeman's Journal* will be cited as *FJ*.

3 Ibid.

4 See *Belfast Newsletter*, 16 July 1900; *Irish Times*, 18 July 1900. Hereafter the *Newsletter* will be cited as *BNL*, and the *Irish Times* will appear as *IT*.

5 The relief of the legations led Queen Victoria to offer a public statement of rejoicing. *BNL*, 21 August 1900.

6 'Opinion shapers' are thus similar to the Gramscian concept of intellectuals, in that they help to organize and express the culture of a society. I contend, however, that Gramsci's focus on intellectuals emerging from a single class to establish cultural hegemony is too limiting. As I am using the term, 'opinion shapers' can emerge from various strata in society. Further, the material in the present chapter has addressed this issue through looking at press sources, but readers should not assume that I am giving primacy to one set of opinion shapers over another. Other scholars – including especially Dr Paul A. Townend in a series of provocative papers at recent meetings of the North American Conference on British Studies and the American Conference for Irish studies – have applied anthropological techniques in intriguing ways to discuss the influence that popular activists had on parliamentary and press spokesmen with regard to imperial questions. See Paul A. Townend, 'Between Two Worlds: Irish Nationalists and Imperial Crisis, 1878–1880', *Past and*

Present, 194: 1 (February 2007), 139–174. I am grateful to Dr Townend for making a draft copy of this article available to me as I prepared the present chapter. Cf., Antonio Gramsci, *An Antonio Gramsci Reader: Selected Writings, 1916–1935* (ed.), David Forgacs (New York: Schocken Books, 1988).

7 I am particularly grateful to Professor Emmet Larkin for his admonition on this point.

8 Joseph Lennon, *Irish Orientalism: A Literary and Intellectual History* (Syracuse: Syracuse University Press, 2004), pp. 149–50. See also Alvin Jackson's comments about the Empire acting as both 'a lock and a key' for the Irish in the nineteenth century. Alvin Jackson, 'Ireland, the union and the empire, 1800–1960', in Kevin Kenny (ed,), *Ireland and the British Empire* (Oxford: Oxford University Press, 2004), p. 136. Several essay collections have appeared in the last fifteen years that provide useful introductions to Ireland and its place in the empire. For example, see Kevin Kenny (ed.), *Ireland and the British Empire* (Oxford: Oxford University Press, 2004); Keith Jeffrey (ed.) *An Irish Empire? Aspects of Ireland and the British Empire* (Manchester: Manchester University Press, 1996); Michael Holmes and Denis Holmes, *Ireland and India: Connections, Comparisons, Contrasts* (Dublin: Folens, 1997); and Stephen Howe, *Ireland and Empire: Colonial Legacies in Irish History and Culture* (Oxford: Oxford University Press, 2000).

9 Michael W. de Nie, *The Eternal Paddy: Irish Identity and the British Press, 1798–1882* (Madison, WI: The University of Wisconsin Press, 2004), p. 33.

10 Contemporary spelling for the territory known today as the Sudan was 'Soudan'. I have silently amended the text of newspaper quotations to reflect modern-day spelling.

11 One potential problem arising immediately with this strategy was that the *Nation* ceased publication several years before the Boxer rising in China. See below, footnote 34. Numerous studies have been done about the press, especially the nationalist press, in nineteenth- and early-twentieth-century Ireland. Two worthwhile introductions are: Mary Louise Legg, *Newspapers and Nationalism: the Irish Provincial Press, 1850–1892* (Dublin: Four Courts Press, 1999); and Virginia Glandon, *Arthur Griffith and the Advanced-Nationalist Press in Ireland, 1900–1922* (New York: P. Lang, 1985).

12 On Ahmed, see Fergus Nicoll, *The Sword of the Prophet: The Mahdi of Sudan and the Death of General Gordon* (Gloucestershire: Sutton Publishing, 2004).

13 *Nation*, 22, 29 July, 23 September 1882.

14 *IT*, 12, 13 July 1882; 7 Feb. 1884.

15 The term refers to Strachey's enduringly influential account, 'The End of General Gordon'. See Lytton Strachey, *Eminent Victorians* (ed.), John Sutherland (Oxford: Oxford University Press, 2003).

16 Scholarship on the so-called 'Dervish wars' is voluminous, and ranges from biographical (sometimes hagiographical) essays of British military figures to studies of the impact of the campaigns on Sudanese history. See, for example, Alice Moore-Harrell, *Gordon and the Sudan: Prologue to the Mahdiyya* (London: Frank Cass, 2001); Michael Barthorp, *Blood-Red Desert Sand: the British invasions of Egypt and the Sudan, 1882–1898* (London: Cassell and Co., 1984); Brian Robson, *Fuzzy-Wuzzy: The Campaigns in the Eastern Sudan, 1884–85* (Tunbridge Wells: Spellmount, Ltd., 1993); Robin Neillands, *The Dervish Wars: Gordon and Kitchener in the Sudan, 1880–1898* (London: John Murray, 1996);

and Edward M. Spiers (ed.), *Sudan: the Reconquest Reconsidered* (London: Frank Cass, 1998).

17 For an overview of the rising of the I-ho Chu'an, see Chester C. Tan, *The Boxer Catastrophe* (New York: Columbia University Press, 1955); The Compilation Group, History of Modern China Series, *The Yi ho Tuan Movement of 1900* (Beijing: Foreign Language Press, 1976); David D. Buck (ed.), *Recent Studies of the Boxer Movement: Chinese Studies in History*, xx: nos. 3–4, Spring/Summer 1987; Jane E. Elliott, *Some Did it for Civilization, some Did it for their Country: A Revised View of the Boxer War* (Hong Kong: The Chinese University of Hong Kong, 2002); and Lanxin Xiang, *The Origins of the Boxer War: A Multinational Study* (London and New York: Routledge Curzon, 2003).

18 Cf. *IT*, 12 July, 14 September 1882, 7 Feb. 1884, 19 July, 20, 22 August 1900; *BNL*, 5, 19 July 1900; *FJ*, 14 February, 15 May 1884, 17, 18 July 1900; *Nation*, 29 July 1882, 9, 16 February 1884.

19 *IT*, 14 September 1882.

20 *Nation*, 22 March 1884.

21 *FJ*, 29 January 1885.

22 *Nation*, 15 July 1882.

23 Ibid., 22 March 1884.

24 Ibid.

25 Ibid. Three weeks earlier, the *Nation* also spoke of 'English duplicity, hypocrisy, and wholesale murder'. Cf. *Nation*, 1 March 1884.

26 *FJ*, 29 January 1885.

27 Cf., Edward Said, *Orientalism* (New York: Pantheon Books, 1978). On race and racialist assumptions in nineteenth-century Britain and Ireland, see L. Perry Curtis (ed.), *Apes and Angels: the Irishman in Victorian Caricature* (London: Smithsonian Institution Press, 1997), especially chaps. 1 and 2; de Nie, *Eternal Paddy*, Introduction; and Cora Kaplan, 'White, black, and green: racialising Irishness in Victorian England', in Peter Gray (ed.), *Victoria's Ireland: Irishness and Britishness, 1837–1901*, (Dublin: Four Courts Press, 2004).

28 *IT*, 14 July 1882.

29 Ibid., 15 July 1882.

30 Ibid., 14 Sept. 1882.

31 *Nation*, 22 July 1882. Emphasis added.

32 *FJ*, 12 March 1884.

33 Ibid.

34 Ibid., 5 June 1900. It is impossible to be certain how the *Nation* might have covered the Boxer rising, as it ceased publication in the early 1890s; however, periodic comments about China and the Chinese people suggest that its assumptions would mirror those of the *Freeman*. See, for example, *Nation*, 3 Jan. 1885: 'For ways that are dark the heathen Chinee [*sic*] is a model of simplicity and ingenuousness when compared with the officials of Dublin Castle'.

35 *FJ*, 5 June 1900.

36 *BNL*, 4 July 1900.

37 See, for example, *FJ*, 17, 18 July 1900.

38 *BNL*, 5 July 1900, *FJ*, 4 July 1900.

39 *FJ*, 17 July 1900.

40 See Patrick Maume, 'Standish James O'Grady: Between Imperial Romance and

Irish Revival', *Éire-Ireland*, xxxix, 1–2, Spring–Summer 200), pp. 30–2. O'Grady's novel appeared originally in serial form as *The Tyranny* in 1899 in the *Kilkenny Moderator* and the *Irish Weekly Independent*. It appeared in book form: Luke Netterville, *Queen of the World or Under the Tyranny* (London: Lawrence and Bullen, 1900).

41 *IT*, 19 July 1900.

42 *FJ*, 10 July 1900.

43 Ibid.

44 *IT*, 17 May 1886.

45 Ibid.

WRITING AN ORANGE DOLLY'S BRAE

1 'Dolly's Brae' (1849) from Georges-Denis Zimmerman, *Songs of Irish Rebellion: Political Street Ballads and Rebel Songs* (Dublin: Allen Figgis, 1967), pp. 311–12.

2 The clash is featured prominently in Orange histories. For a representative sample, see R.M. Sibbett, *Orangeism in Ireland and Throughout the Empire*, Vol. 2 (London: Thynne and Co., 1938), pp. 347–74; M.W. Dewar, *Orangeism: An Historical Appreciation* (Belfast: Grand Orange Lodge of Ireland, 1967), pp. 136–8. On the level of public or popular history, Dolly's Brae's importance is probably even more vital to Orange political culture. For a recent sampling of partisan songs about the clash, see John Moulden, *12 Songs of the Twelfth: Dolly's Brae 1849* (Portrush and Ennistymon: The Library, 1999).

3 Christine Kinealy, 'A Right to March? The Conflict at Dolly's Brae', in D.G. Boyce and Roger Swift, (eds.), *Problems and Perspectives in Irish History Since 1800* (Dublin: Four Courts Press, 2004), pp. 54–79.

4 W.J. Martin, *The Battle of Dolly's Brae, 12th July 1849* (Belfast: Grand Orange Lodge of Ireland Publications, 2001).

5 Perhaps the most insightful work has been done by Donald Harman Akenson, David W. Miller, A.T.Q. Stewart and Frank Wright. For Akenson, see *Small Differences: Irish Catholics and Irish Protestants, 1815–1922: An International Perspective* (Montréal: McGill-Queen's University Press, 1988); for Miller, see *Queen's Rebels: Ulster Loyalism in Historical Perspective* (Dublin: Gill & MacMillan, 1978); for Stewart, see *The Narrow Ground: The Roots of Conflict in Ulster* (London: Faber & Faber, 1977); and for Wright, see *Two Lands on One Soil: Ulster Politics Before Home Rule* (New York: St Martin's Press, 1996). Of these, only Stewart really deals directly with the violence itself, the others focusing on important questions of ideology and politics. Specific episodes in the history of modern sectarian violence have received thorough treatment. For the Armagh Troubles, see Miller, 'The Armagh Troubles,' in Samuel Clark and James S. Donnelly, Jr., (eds.), *Irish Peasants: Violence and Unrest, 1784–1914* (Dublin: Gill & MacMillan, 1983), pp. 155–91 and Sean Farrell, *Rituals and Riots: Sectarian Violence and Political Culture in Ulster, 1784–1886* (Lexington: University Press of Kentucky, 2000), pp. 10–31. For the evolution of urban sectarianism, see A.C. Hepburn's essays in his study of Belfast Catholicism, *A Past Apart: Studies in the History of Catholic Belfast* (Belfast: Ulster Historical Foundation, 1996).

6 Allen Feldman's work is an important exception. See Feldman, *Formations of Violence: The Narrative of the Body and Political Terror in Northern Ireland* (London: University of Chicago Press, 1991).

7   The surveys mentioned here are my own *Rituals and Riots*, and Catherine Hirst, *Religion, Politics and Violence in Nineteenth-Century Belfast: The Pound & Sandy Row* (Dublin: Four Courts Press, 2002).

8   Jill Lepore, *The Name of War: Philip's War and the Origins of American Identity* (New York: Knopf, 1998), p. x. I would like to thank Rachel Hope Cleves for this reference.

9   Kevin Kenny, *Making Sense of the Molly Maguires* (Oxford University Press, 1998). For representative works of scholars mentioned above, see Gyanendra Pandey, *Remembering Partition: Violence, Nationalism and History in India* (Cambridge University Press, 2001); Linda Colley, *Britons: Forging the Nation* (London: Yale University Press, 1993); Kathleen Wilson, *The Island Race: Englishness, Empire and Gender in the Eighteenth Century* (London: Routledge, 2002); Lepore, *The Name of War*.

10 *Northern Whig*, 19 July 1849.

11 *The Protestant Watchman*, 21 July 1848.

12 For sympathetic accounts of the 1848 loyalty meetings, see *The Warder*, 8, 15, 22 July 1848.

13 *Northern Whig*, 3 July 1849.

14 Letter Re: Ribbonism in County Down, 17 March 1849 (Public Record Office of Northern Ireland [hereafter P.R.O.N.I.], D.682/146).

15 Newspaper reports on the Crossgar riots and ensuing trials can be followed in the *Northern Whig*, 20, 22–24 March, 24 April and 23 and 26 June 1849.

16 Evidence of Thomas Scott, *Battle of Magheramayo. Report of the Evidence Taken Before the Government Commissioner, Walter Berwick, Esq., Q.C., at a Court Held in Castlewellan from 30th July to 4th August, and by Adjournment, on Tuesday, 18th September 1849.* (Newry: James Henderson, 1849), 27: hereafter cited as *Berwick Report*.

17 Evidence of Joseph Tabuteau, ibid., p. 15.

18 See the Earl of Clarendon to Sir George Grey, 20 July 1849 (Public Record Office, London [hereafter P.R.O.], HO 45/2603/154).

19 Evidence of the Rev. Patrick Morgan, P.P., *Berwick Report*, p. 114.

20 Ibid., p. 70.

21 Evidence of Major Arthur Wilkinson, ibid., p. 4.

22 See evidence of Francis Beers, ibid., p. 63; evidence of Thomas Scott, ibid., 28 and evidence of the Earl of Roden, ibid., p. 72. For earlier examples of Orange social control arguments, see evidence of Stewart Blacker, *Report from the select committee to inquire into the nature, character, extent, and tendency of Orange lodges, associations, or societies in Ireland, with minutes of evidence and appendix.*, H.C. 1835 (377), XV, 144. For a Catholic parallel, see evidence of the Rev. Patrick Morgan, *Berwick Report*, p. 105.

23 Evidence of Major Arthur Wilkinson, *Berwick Report*, pp. 4–5.

24 Ibid., p. 9.

25 *Inquest and Depositions into the Deaths at Magheramayo, 14–18 July 1849* (National Archives of Ireland [hereafter N.A.I.], CSORP, 8/332 and /357).

26 For Berwick, see Kinealy, 'A Right to March?'.

27 For a good summary of Berwick's views, see Walter Berwick to the Earl of Clarendon, 22 September 1849, P.R.O., HO 45/2603/58–81).

28 Charles Rutheven to T.N. Redington, 2 August 1849 (N.A.I., CSORP, Registered Papers, 1849/8/363).

29 Maziere Brady to the Earl of Roden, Francis Beers and William Beers, 6 October 1849 (P.R.O., HO 45/2603/88–91). The Earl of Clarendon was quite reluctant to punish the Earl of Roden, calling it the 'most painful act I ever performed'. See the Earl of Clarendon to Lord Monteagle, 27 November 1849 (Monteagle Papers, National Library of Ireland, MS 13,199).

30 These intentions clearly predated the investigation: see Charles Greer to the Earl of Clarendon, 24 July 1849 (N.A.I., CSORP, 8/343).

31 *The Warder*, 14 and 21 July 1849.

32 *Downpatrick Reporter*, 21 July 1849. William Beers's line that it was Dolly's Brae no more would later become the tag-line of the famous Orange song 'Dolly's Brae'.

33 Statement of Walter Berwick, *Berwick Report*, p. 21.

34 Evidence of William Beers, ibid., p. 64.

35 *Petition of County Down Magistrates, 1849* (P.R.O., HO 45/2603/180–182).

36 Statement of Walter Berwick, *Berwick Report*, p. 21.

37 It is interesting to note that Carlyle had just returned from Ireland when he wrote the essay. For an excellent discussion of the decline of abolitionism and the emergence of a 'new' racial discourse, see Catherine Hall, *Civilising Subjects: Metropole and Colony in the English Imagination, 1830–1867* (University of Chicago Press, 2002), pp. 338–79.

38 Evidence of St John Dobbin, *Berwick Report*, 31; evidence of Colour Sgt. Stanfield, ibid., p. 69.

39 *The Warder*, 27 October 1849.

40 Sibbett, *Orangeism*, vol. 2, 356. While Dewar's more modern history of Orangeism only devotes two pages to the Dolly Brae clash, it is interesting to note that his chapter on Orangeism in mid-Victorian Ulster is entitled 'Over Dolly's Brae and on to Bangor – and beyond'. See Dewar, Brown and Long, *Orangeism*, pp. 132–44.

41 Quoted in Zimmerman, pp. 312–13.

42 Sir John Temple, *History of the Irish Rebellion* (London: R. White, 1646).

43 Sir Richard Musgrave, *Memoirs of the Different Rebellions in Ireland* (Dublin: J. Milliken and J. Stockdale, 1801).

44 For an interesting discussion of this theme, see Wilson, p. 87.

45 Evidence of Francis Charles Beers, *Berwick Report*, pp. 56–7.

46 Wilson, *Island Race*, pp. 22–3; Anna Clark, *The Struggle for the Breeches: Gender and the Making of the British Working Class* (Berkeley: University of California Press, 1995), pp. 7, 25–26.

47 Evidence of Joseph Tabuteau, *Berwick Report*, p. 16.

48 Evidence of Thomas Scott, ibid., p. 29.

49 For examples, see Sibbett, *Orangeism*, vol. 2, pp. 349, 354, 358–9.

50 See, for example, Kevin Whelan's typically insightful comments in Bartlett et al., *1798: A Bicentenary Perspective* (Dublin: Four Courts Press, 2003), pp. 189–94. For a model case study, see Kyla Madden's award-winning *Forkhill Protestants and Forkhill Catholics* (Montréal: McGill-Queen's University Press, 2005).

SYMBOLIC AND HYPERREAL VIOLENCE IN THE IRISH 'TROUBLES' MOVIE

1 Henry A. Giroux, 'Racism and the Aesthetic of Hyperreal Violence: *Pulp Fiction* and other Visual Tragedies', *Social Identities*, 1, 2, 1995, pp. 333–354.

2   Stone, Oliver, wr./dir, *Platoon* (Orion Pictures, 1987).

3   Eastwood, Clint, dir, *Unforgiven* (Warner Brothers, 1992).

4   Evans, Marc, dir, *Resurrection Man* (Revolutions Films, 1998).

5   Caffrey, David, dir, *Divorcing Jack* (Scala Productions, 1998).

6   Loach, Ken, dir, *The Wind That Shakes the Barley* (Pathé International, 2006).

7   Greengrass, Paul, dir, *Bloody Sunday* (Hell's Kitchen Films, 2002).

8   Travis, Pete, dir, *Omagh* (Hell's Kitchen International, 2004).

9   Bennett, Edward, dir, *Ascendancy* (BFI, 1982).

10 O'Connor, Pat, dir, *Fools of Fortune* (Channel Four Films, 1990); the novel on which the film is based is: Trevor, William, *Fools of Fortune* (London: Bodley Head, 1983).

11 Blair, Tony, http://www.historyplace.com/speeches/blair.htm; the quote is from the film *Fools of Fortune* (see note 10 above).

12 See Tom Nairn, *The Break-Up of Britain: Crisis and Neo-Nationalism* (London: Verso, 1981), p. 222.

13 George, Terry, dir, *Some Mother's Son* (Columbia, 1996).

14 Sheridan, Jim, dir, *In the Name of the Father* (Universal, 1993).

15 Sheridan, Jim, dir, *The Boxer* (Universal, 1997).

16 Michel, Roger, dir, *Titanic Town* (BBC/Alliance, 1998).

17 Boorman, John, dir, *The General* (Sony Brothers, 1998).

18 Jordan, Neil, wr./dir, *The Crying Game* (Miramax, 1982).

19 Jordan, Neil, dir, *Angel* (Miramax, 1992).

20 Jordan, Neil, dir, *Michael Collins* (Geffen Pictures, 1996).

21 Smith, Peter, dir, *No Surrender* (Channel Four Films, 1984).

22 McGuckian, Mary, dir, *This is the Sea* (Paramount, 1997).

23 Leigh, Mike, dir, *Four Days in July* (BBC, 1984).

24 O'Sullivan, Thaddeus, dir, *Nothing Personal* (Channel Four Films, 1995).

25 See Martin Dillon, *The Shankill Butchers: A Case Study of Mass Murder* (London: Hutchinson, 1989), which details the murderous escapades of Lenny Murphy.

26 Quoted by Claudia Parsons for Reuters, and published on the Web 4 September 1995. The novel by Daniel Mornin is *All Our Fault* (London: Hutchinson, 1991). The incredibleness of *Nothing Personal*'s story-line is well observed by Shane Barry when the film was provisionally entitled 'Fanatic Heart'. See his review in *Film Ireland*, 48, August/September 1995, p. 30.

27 O'Sullivan, Thaddeus, dir, *December Bride* (Channel Four Films, 1990).

28 Bateman, Colin, http://www.colinbateman.com/faqs.html.

UNDOING THE FANATICISM OF MEANING: NEIL JORDAN'S *ANGEL*

1   Roland Barthes, 'Dear Antonioni . . .', *Cahiers du Cinéma*, 311, May 1980, repr. and trans. Geoffrey Nowell-Smith in Rob White (ed.), *L'Avventura*, BFI Film Classics series, (London: BFI, 1997), p. 67.

2   Seán O'Faoláin, Introduction, *Night in Tunisia*, by Neil Jordan (1976; Dublin: Irish Writers' Co-operative; Kerry: Brandon, 1982), i–ii; Jordan, Neil, wr./dir, *The Crying Game* (Miramax, 1982).

3   See Kevin Maher, 'From Angel to Vampire', *Film Ireland*, 45, February/March 1995, p. 16.

4   Fintan O'Toole, 'The Man Who Shot Michael Collins', *Independent on Sunday*, 3

November 1996, Magazine section, p. 21; Jordan, Neil, wr./dir, *Michael Collins* (Geffen Pictures, 1996).

5 *Angel*, dir./wr. Neil Jordan (Ireland and GB: Motion Picture Company of Ireland in association with Bord Scannán na hÉireann for Channel 4; First Independent Video, 1982), 92 mins.

6 During the making of *Angel* Jordan received threats from republican paramilitaries in Dublin: 'I was scared, even though I'd realised that to tackle such a political subject would be dangerous. So I called in the Special Branch and had some protection for a while.' Neil Jordan, quoted in Caroline Boucher, 'How We Met: Neil Jordan and Stephen Woolley', *Independent on Sunday*, 8 November 1992, Magazine section, p. 77.

7 In a series of reports for the *Irish Times*, Ray Comiskey recorded the growing critical acclaim for *Angel* at Cannes: see 'Bravura Retreat', 21 May 1982, 10; 'Open Race for Prizes', 25 May 1982, 10; and 'Honours Shared', 28 May 1982, 10. Significantly, perhaps, two other films about the effects of political and sectarian violence were jointly awarded the Palme D'Or that year: *Missing* (dir, Costas-Gavras, Universal, 1982) and *Yol* (dirs, Yilmaz Güney and Serif Gören, Triumph Films, 1982).

8 At the time the newly launched Channel 4 was developing a radically new funding policy whereby low-budget, independent British film productions – rather than the usual made-for-television dramas – would become a central plank in the station's broadcast schedule. These films would be partly financed by Film on Four, and after being first shown on television they could then be released in cinemas. (See Nick Roddick, 'New Audiences, New Films', and Martin Auty, 'But is it Cinema?', in Martin Auty and Nick Roddick (eds.), *British Cinema Now* (London: BFI, 1985), pp. 19–30 and pp. 57–70. However, after *Angel* was screened at Cannes, Stephen Woolley, the chief executive of a vibrant new distribution company, Palace Pictures, was so impressed that he persuaded Channel 4 to give *Angel* a limited theatrical release prior to its televized transmission. As Angus Finney later noted: 'Albeit modest in terms of box-office success, this move was to have a far-reaching significance, pioneering the way for Channel 4's films to play for the cinema long before they reached the British living-room.' (See Angus Finney, *The Egos Have Landed: The Rise and Fall of Palace Pictures* [London: Mandarin, 1997], p. 6.) Stephen Woolley went on to produce Jordan's second feature film, *The Company of Wolves* (dir. Neil Jordan, Cannon Film, 1984), and has produced virtually every Jordan film since then.

9 80 per cent of *Angel's* eventual £420,000 (IR£490,000) budget came from Channel 4. See Antoinette Moses, 'British Film Production 1981: Survey', *Sight and Sound*, 51.4, Autumn 1982, pp. 258–66.

10 For a detailed account see Michael Dwyer, '10 Days that Shook the Irish Film Industry', *In Dublin*, 8 April 1982, repr. *Film West*, 30, November 1997, pp. 24–8; and Kevin Rockett, 'History, Politics and Irish Cinema', *Cinema and Ireland*, by Kevin Rockett, Luke Gibbons, and John Hill (Syracuse: Syracuse University Press, 1988), p. 119.

11 See John Orr, 'The Art of Identity: Greenaway, Jarman, Jordan', *The Art and Politics of Film* (Edinburgh: Edinburgh University Press, 2000), p. 121.

12 Chris Menges had previously worked with Ken Loach and Stephen Frears. He

later did the cinematography for Jordan's *Michael Collins* (1996) and *The Good Thief* (dir. Neil Jordan, Century Fox, 2002).

13 Neil Jordan, 'Neil Jordan: *Angel*', interview with Stephen Lowenstein, Lowenstein (ed.), *My First Movie* (London: Faber & Faber, 2000), p. 166. *Angel*'s editor, Pat Duffner, later co-edited Jordan's *Michael Collins* (1996).

14 James Park, *Learning to Dream: The New British Cinema* (London: Faber & Faber, 1984), p. 47.

15 On 31 July 1975 the Ulster Volunteer Force (UVF) murdered three members of the Dublin-based Miami Showband near Newry in Co. Down. Two UVF members were also killed when the bomb they were planting went off prematurely. The UVF gang, which included members of the official Northern Ireland military reserve, the Ulster Defence Regiment (UDR) had set up a fake UDR roadblock as part of the ambush. In 1975 sectarian tit-for-tat killings were at an all-time high: 247 people died and 1,199 people were charged with terrorist offences. In January of that year the IRA had ended their three-week truce, partly in response to the upsurge in murders by loyalist 'death squads' – 'the greatest assassination campaign of innocent Catholics to date'. See Paul Bew and Gordon Gillespie, *Northern Ireland: A Chronology of the Troubles, 1968–1993* (Dublin: Gill & Macmillan, 1993), p. 103.

16 Jordan, interview with Lowenstein, p. 161.

17 Neil Jordan, 'Brute Music: First Treatment, June 1980', part of the uncatalogued Neil Jordan MS Collection held at the National Library Archive, Dublin. This treatment is contained in a large envelope entitled 'Brute Music Re: Angel'. The envelope also includes the final working screenplay of *Angel*; several draft versions of the script (under its original title); and two other early treatments (both undated).

18 Jordan, 'Brute Music', Neil Jordan MS Collection, undated and unpaginated.

19 Neil Jordan, '*Angel* Takes Wing', interview with Ray Comiskey, *Irish Times*, 11 May 1982, p. 8.

20 The Irish showbands of the 1960s and '70s were a fascinating – and hugely popular – phenomenon. Showbands emerged out of the big-band era, replete with full brass sections, but gradually began to incorporate rock 'n' roll numbers from Britain and America into their acts. This hybrid mimicry included the adoption of kitsch costumes and camp postures borrowed from the dominant rock culture. As one dedicated fan website nostalgically notes: 'The showbands were a showpiece of Seán Lemass's 1960s Ireland, as the State emerged from the dreary 1950s, and pseudo-plush ballrooms with exotic names like the Borderland, Limerick's Jetland and the Dreamland in Athy replaced the parish hall as a dance venue. For a time, there were hundreds of showbands, dressed in colourful suits, criss-crossing Ireland [North and South] to midweek and weekend venues.' See Ian Gallagher, 'The Showband Era' <www.iangallagher.com/rip1.htm>.

21 As an index of *Angel*'s uncertainty principle this scene is a good example of Jordan's oblique style. Critic Tim Pulleine, for instance, interpreted it as a 'chaste assignation', while Ray Comiskey noted how Danny and Annie 'have sex, neatly and delicately hinted at'. See Pulleine, 'Underworld N.I.: *Angel*', *Sight and Sound*, 51, 4, Autumn 1982, p. 303; and Comiskey, 'Violence in the North', review of *Angel*, *Irish Times*, 17 May 1982, p. 10.

22 As Brian McIlroy astutely notes: 'Interestingly, the clue of a clubfoot sets off Danny's search for revenge. A non-specific Irish saying to determine religion is to ask whether someone kicks with the "other" or "left" foot. In this instance, the culprit kicks with a malformed foot!' See McIlroy, 'The Repression of Communities: Visual Representations of Northern Ireland during the Thatcher Years', Lester Friedman (ed.), *British Cinema and Thatcherism* (London: UCL Press, 1993), p. 99.

23 Neil Jordan, *Angel* screenplay, with an introduction by John Boorman (London: Faber & Faber, 1989), p. 18.

24 *Angel* screenplay, with an introduction by John Boorman (London: Faber & Faber, 1989), p. 24.

25 Ibid., p. 26.

26 Ibid., p. 33.

27 Ibid., p. 36.

28 Ibid., p. 38.

29 Ibid., p. 41.

30 Ibid., p. 43.

31 Ibid., p. 50.

32 Derek Malcolm, 'Neil Jordan's *Angel*', *Guardian*, repr. *Film Directions*, 7, 26, Spring 1985, p. 27.

33 John Coleman, 'Poetic Licence', review of *Angel*, *New Statesman*, 104,2694, 5 November 1982, p. 32. Elsewhere, Jordan conceded the influence of the New German Cinema: 'I suppose it's most like the early films of Fassbinder and Wenders. It's a kind of anti-narrative in a way, and it's there for the purpose of getting certain themes and emotions on to the screen'. See Jordan, 'Neil Jordan', interview with Mario Falsetto, in Falsetto (ed.), *Personal Visions: Conversations with Independent Film-makers*, (London: Constable, 1999), p. 162.

34 Richard Cook, 'Angel of Death', review of *Angel*, *New Musical Express*, 13 November 1982, p. 27.

35 Pulleine, pp. 302–3. Paul Taylor also noted the influence of *Point Blank*: 'Jordan has found his own route to, and uses for, the concept of "point blank": from Annie's world of silence, through Danny's literal and metaphorical concussion, to the various oblivions sought or feared by the victims of his vendetta'. See Taylor, '*Angel*', *Monthly Film Bulletin*, 49, 586, November 1982, p. 258.

36 Nick Roddick, '*Angel*', *Films and Filming*, p. 337, Oct. 1982, p. 32.

37 Comiskey, 'Violence in the North', p. 10.

38 For a fuller discussion of this see my '"Cat-Calls from the Cheap Seats": The Third Meaning of Neil Jordan's *Michael Collins*', *The Irish Review*, 21 Autumn/Winter 1997, pp. 1–28.

39 Kevin Rockett, 'Jordan, Neil', *The Companion to British and Irish Cinema*, John Caughie with Kevin Rockett, (London: Cassell/BFI, 1996), p. 93. This argument is ultimately derived from John Hill's magisterial essay, 'Images of Violence', *Cinema and Ireland*, pp. 147–93.

40 Margo Harkin, *Irish Cinema: Ourselves Alone?*, dir. Donald Taylor Black (Ireland and GB: BFI TV and Centenary Productions in association with Poolbeg Productions, Radio Telefis Éireann and The Irish Film Board/Connoisseur Academy Video, 1995).

41   Maher, 'From Angel to Vampire', p. 17. As Jordan himself remarked: 'I wanted to remove the social and political context entirely from the story. [*Angel*] was not about people taking up arms because they exist in a post-colonial situation, but about the attraction of a weapon, and the attraction of the idea of killing'. See Jordan, interview with Lowenstein, p. 161.

42   Louisa Burns-Bisogno, *Censoring Irish Nationalism: The British, Irish and American Suppression of Republican Images in Film and Television, 1909–95* (London: McFarland, 1997), p. 126.

43   Hill, p. 150.

44   Hill, p. 149.

45   Hill, pp. 148–9.

46   Kevin Rockett, 'Aspects of the Los Angelesation of Ireland', *Irish Communications Review*, 1, 1991, p. 20.

47   Hill, pp. 151–2.

48   John Ford, dir, *The Quiet Man* (Republic Pictures, 1952).

49   John Ford, dir, *The Informer* (RKO Pictures, 1935).

50   Hill, p. 185. See also Patrick F. Sheeran, in Keith Hopper and Gráinne Humphreys (eds.), *The Informer*, Ireland into Film series (Cork University Press, 2002).

51   David Bordwell, *Narration in the Fiction Film* (London: Routledge, 1995), p. 73.

52   Joe Comerford, dir, *Traveller* (RTE, 1981).

53   Kevin Barry, 'Discarded Images: Narrative and the Cinema', *Crane Bag*, 6,1, 1982, p. 47.

54   Barry, p. 48.

55   Barry, p. 51.

56   Barry, p. 47. See also Kristin Thompson, 'The Concept of Cinematic Excess', in Philip Rosen (ed.), *Narrative, Apparatus, Ideology: A Film Theory Reader* (New York: Columbia University Press, 1986), pp. 130–42; and Stephen Heath, 'Narrative Space', *Questions of Cinema* (London: Macmillan, 1981), pp. 19–75.

57   Hill, p. 184.

58   Luke Gibbons, 'Romanticism, Realism and Irish Cinema', *Cinema and Ireland*, p. 195.

59   Gibbons, p. 194. As Terry Eagleton wryly points out, 'The exquisite clarity of the debate over realism is now such that we can speak of realist realism, non-realist realism, realist non-realism and non-realist non-realism. All of which suggests that we are less in need of an aesthetician than of a linguistic philosopher'. See Eagleton, 'Realism and Cinema', *Screen*, 21, 2, Summer 1980, p. 93.

60   Gibbons, p. 200.

61   Hill, p. 180.

62   Matthew Ryan, 'Ourselves Alone: Solipsism in Neil Jordan's Novels and Films', *Barcelona English Language and Literature Studies*, 11, 2000, p. 189. For further endorsement of this view, see Conor McCarthy, 'Film and Politics: Neil Jordan, Bob Quinn and Pat Murphy', *Modernisation, Crisis and Culture in Ireland, 1969–1992* (Dublin: Four Courts Press, 2000), pp. 165–196.

63   Jordan later suggested that this particular ending came about because he 'couldn't afford an army helicopter' and had to use a commercial helicopter whose markings could not be shown. (See Jordan, interview with Lowenstein, p. 165.) However, Nick Roddick compared it to the end of *Through a Glass*

Darkly (dir. Ingmar Bergman, 1962), where there is also the sound and wind of a helicopter landing; 'Once again, God has arrived too late. The game is played out.' See Roddick, '*Angel*', p. 33.

64 Richard Kearney, 'Nationalism and Irish Cinema', *Transitions: Narratives in Modern Irish Culture* (Manchester University Press, 1988), pp. 172–92. Kearney derives his reading from Roland Barthes's seminal essay 'The Third Meaning' (1970), which he discusses in an appendix to his own essay. See Barthes, 'The Third Meaning: Research Notes on Some Eisenstein Stills', in Susan Sontag (ed.), *A Roland Barthes Reader*, (London: Vintage, 1993), pp. 317–33.

65 Kearney, p. 174.

66 The scene was based on Jordan's own experience: 'I was playing in a band [and] they used to run a gig in Portlaoise, in the mental hospital there . . .. In the film Danny is playing to people into whose lives has entered a similar kind of distortion [and] I wanted [them] to function like ghosts from his past or his conscience.' See Jordan, '*Angel* Takes Wing', p. 8.

67 Kearney, 180–3. James Park notes Jordan's admiration for Andrei Tarkovsky – cf. *Solaris* (dir, Tarkovsky, 1972), *Mirror* (1975), *Stalker* (1979) – especially for his use of slow tracking shots to modify images: 'The moving camera is the whole magic really. The camera expresses the relationship between the actor and the background environment.' See Jordan, quoted in Park, p. 114.

68 Maria Pramaggiore, 'The Celtic Blue Note: Jazz in Neil Jordan's 'Night in Tunisia', *Angel* and *The Miracle*', *Screen*, 39, 3, Autumn 1998, p. 277. Pramaggiore notes that Stan Getz – a white jazz player – can be distinguished from Charlie Parker (the bebop guru who presides over Jordan's 'Night in Tunisia') by the fact that Getz, like Danny, was a popular rather than an esoteric performer.

69 Pramaggiore, p. 279.

70 Bernardo Bertolucci, dir, *The Conformist* (Paramount Italy, 1970).

71 David Thompson, 'As I Lay Dying: *Point Blank*', *Sight and Sound*, 8, 6, June 1998, p. 17.

72 Michael Open, 'A Language of Vision: The Films of John Boorman', *Film Directions*, 2,7, 1979, p. 5.

73 '[*Angel*] was a contrast between the world of music and the world of the downbeat, concrete-and-clay kind of thriller. So there were these contrasts, all this glitter and colours like gold, purple and pink . . .. In the end, it was about having this guy in this pink suit wandering through a rural landscape, being exposed like a peacock, being out of his place.' See Jordan, interview with Falsetto, 162.

74 Open, 'A Language of Vision', p. 5.

75 Thompson, 'As I Lay Dying', p. 17.

76 John Boorman, 'Introduction', *Angel*, viii. Elsewhere, Jordan himself noted: 'There's quite a lot of *Point Blank* in [*Angel*]. I wanted to take the bones of the thriller . . . and add certain kinds of metaphysical concerns and obsessions.' See Jordan, 'Face to Face with Evil', interview with Michael Open, *Film Directions*, 18.5, December 1982, p. 4.

77 Michelangelo Antonioni, dir, *Blow Up* (MGM, 1966).

78 Michelangelo Antonioni, dir, *The Passenger* (MGM, 1975).

79 Jordan, 'Face to Face with Evil', p. 30.

80 Michelangelo Antonioni, dir, *L'Avventura* (Cino del Duca, 1960).

81   *Angel* screenplay, pp. 20–1.

82   Pauline Kael, '*L'Avventura*', *Cinemania* (Washington: Microsoft CD-Rom, 1995).

83   Geoffrey Nowell-Smith, in Rob White (ed.), *L'Avventura, BFI Film Classics* series, (London: BFI, 1997), pp. 47–50.

84   Barthes, 'Dear Antonioni . . .', p. 67.

85   See, for example, my '"A Gallous Story and a Dirty Deed": Word and Image in Neil Jordan and Joe Comerford's *Traveller* (1981)', *Irish Studies Review* 9,2 (August 2001), pp. 179–91; and '"Hairy on the Inside": Re-visiting *The Company of Wolves*', special Cinema/Media issue of *The Canadian Journal of Irish Studies*, 29, 2, Autumn 2003, pp. 17–26.

86   As a poem, 'Strange Fruit' was inspired by a photograph of a double lynching in Indiana, which took place in 1930. Abel Meeropol, a New York communist and schoolteacher, first published it in 1937, under the pen-name 'Lewis Allan'. He later set it to music, and it was recorded by Billie Holiday in 1939. Since then, it has gained iconic status in the US, both as a jazz song and as a Civil Rights anthem. See David Margolick, 'Strange Fruit: The Story of a Song', *Guardian*, Friday Review section, 16 February 2001, pp. 2–4.

87   Jordan, '*Angel* Takes Wing', p. 8.

88   Seamus Heaney, 'Strange Fruit', *North* (London: Faber & Faber, 1975), p. 39.

89   Desmond Fennell, *Whatever You Say, Say Nothing: Why Seamus Heaney is No.1* (Dublin: ELO Publications, 1991), p. 16.

90   Seamus Heaney, 'Unhappy and at Home: Interview with Seamus Deane', *Crane Bag*, 1,1, 1977, repr. in Mark Patrick Hederman and Richard Kearney (eds.), *The Crane Bag Book of Irish Studies*, (Dublin: Blackwater, 1982), p. 67.

91   Jordan, 'Face to Face with Evil', p. 16.

92   Taylor, p. 258.

93   William Blake, 'To Nobodaddy' (1791–92), *The Complete Poems*, 2nd edn, (ed.) W.H. Stevenson (London and New York: Longman, 1989), 155. This archetype reappears in Blake's 'Let the Brothels of Paris be Opened' (1791–92): 'Then old Nobodaddy aloft/Farted and belched and coughed,/And said, I love hanging and drawing and quartering/Every bit as well as war and slaughtering', p. 168.

94   Richard Kearney, 'Myth and Martyrdom I', *Transitions*, p. 311 (endnote 25).

95   Allen Feldman, *Formations of Violence: The Narrative of the Body and Political Terror in Northern Ireland* (Chicago and London: University of Chicago Press, 1991), p. 1.

96   Ibid., p. 18.

97   Ibid., p. 81.

98   Ibid., p. 84.

99   Alexander Walker, *National Heroes: British Cinema in the Seventies and Eighties* (London: Harrap, 1985), p. 260.

100   Kearney, 'Nationalism and Irish Cinema', p. 183.

101   Hill, p. 180.

102   See Kearney, 'Nationalism and Irish Cinema', p. 179; and Brian McIlroy, *Shooting to Kill: Filmmaking and the "Troubles' in Northern Ireland* (Trowbridge: Flicks Books, 1998), pp. 56–7. Significantly, Danny was played by Stephen Rea, a founding member of the Field Day Theatre Company and a Belfast Protestant sympathetic to Irish nationalism.

103 McIlroy, 'The Repression of Communities', p. 99.

104 Neil Jordan, 'Debut of Style', interview with Monty Smith, *New Musical Express*, 13 November 1982, p. 27.

105 See, for example, Peter Taylor, *Stalker: The Search for Truth* (London: Faber Faber, 1987); John Stalker, *Stalker: Ireland, Shoot to Kill and the Affair* (Harmondsworth: Penguin, 1988); and Sean McPhilemy, *The Committee: Political Assassination in Northern Ireland*, 2nd edn (Boulder, Colorado: Roberts Rinehart, 1999).

106 Ken Livingstone, 'The Secret Conspiracy to Destroy Peace in Ireland', *Independent*, Friday Review section, 21 May 1999, p. 4. Nairac himself was abducted and killed by the IRA in May 1977 under mysterious circumstances; his body was never found.

107 Gilles Deleuze, 'The Language of Sade and Masoch', in Becky McLaughlin and Bob Coleman (eds.), *Everyday Theory: A Contemporary Reader* (New York: Longman, 2005), p. 518.

108 Seamus Heaney, 'Place and Displacement: Recent Poetry of Northern Ireland', The Pete Laver Memorial Lecture (1984), quoted in Fennell, *Whatever You Say, Say Nothing*, p. 16.

CIARAN CARSON: THE NEW URBAN POETICS

1 Thomas Kinsella, 'The Irish Writer', *Eire-Ireland*, 2, 2, 1967, pp. 8–15.

2 Edna Longley, *The Living Stream: Literature and Revisionism in Ireland* (Newcastle upon Tyne: Bloodaxe, 1994), p. 105.

3 Louis MacNeice, 'Snow', *Collected Poems* (London: Faber & Faber, 1979), p. 30.

4 Derek Mahon, *Collected Poems* (Loughcrew: Gallery Books, 1999), p. 13.

5 Longley, p. 106.

6 Louis MacNeice, 'Carrick Revisited', *Collected Poems*, p. 224.

7 Mahon, p. 231.

8 Seamus Heaney, 'The Strand at Lough Beg', *Field Work* (London, Faber, 1979), p. 17.

9 Seamus Heaney, 'Casualty', *Field Work* (London, Faber, 1979), p. 23

10 Michael Longley, 'Wounds', *Poems 1963–1983* (Harmondsworth: Penguin, 1985), p. 86.

11 Seamus Heaney, *Preoccupations: Selected Prose 1968–1978* (London: Faber & Faber, 1980), p. 149.

12 Raymond Williams, *The Politics of Modernism: Against the New Conformists*, (ed.) Tony Pinckney (London, Verso, 1989), pp. 44–5.

13 Eamonn Hughes, '"What itch of Contradiction?" Belfast in Poetry', in Nicholas Allen and Aaron Kelly (eds.) *The Cities of Belfast* (Dublin: Four Courts Press, 2003), pp. 101–16, 112.

14 Seamus Heaney, 'A Northern Hoard', *Wintering Out* (London: Faber & Faber, 1972), pp. 39–44.

15 Seamus Heaney, *North* (London: Faber & Faber, 1975).

16 Ciaran Carson, '"Escaped from the Massacre"?' in *The Honest Ulsterman*, 50, Winter 1975, pp. 183–6.

17 Neil Corcoran, '"One Step Forward, Two Steps Back": Ciaran Carson's 'The Irish for No', in Neil Corcoran (ed.), *The Chosen Ground: Essays on the Contemporary Poetry of Northern Ireland* (Bridgend: Seren Books, 1992), pp. 213–237, p. 215.

18 Ibid., p. 216.
19 Ciaran Carson, *The Ballad of HMS Belfast* (Loughcrew: Gallery Press, 1999), p. 23.
20 Ciaran Carson, *Belfast Confetti* (Loughcrew: Gallery Press, 1989), pp. 57–73.
21 Friedrich Nietzsche, *On the Genealogy of Morals*, quoted in R. J. Hollingdale (ed.), *A Nietzsche Reader* (Harmondsworth: Penguin, 1977), p. 109.
22 *Ballad of HMS*, p. 26.
23 *Belfast Confetti*, pp. 93–4.
24 *Ballad of HMS*, p. 73.
25 Ibid., p. 71.
26 Ibid., p. 70.
27 Ibid., p. 68.
28 Ibid., p. 72.
29 Peter Barry, *Contemporary British Poetry and the City* (Manchester: Manchester University Press, 2000), p. 228.
30 Seamus Heaney, 'The Toome Road', *Opened Ground*, p. 150.
31 *Ballad of HMS*, p. 26.
32 Ciaran Carson, 'Dresden', *The Irish For No* (Loughcrew: Gallery Press, 1987).
33 *Ballad of HMS*, p. 24.
34 Seamus Heaney, 'Clearances VIII', *Opened Ground*, p. 314.
35 *Ballad of HMS*, p. 28.
36 *Belfast Confetti*, p. 58.
37 *Ballad of HMS*, p. 25.
38 Ibid., p. 53.
39 Ibid., pp. 48–52.
40 Henry James, *The Art of the Novel* (New York: Scribners, 1934), p. 5.
41 *Ballad of HMS*, p. 13.
42 Ibid., p. 18.
43 Paul Muldoon, 'Something Else', *Poems 1968–1998* (London: Faber & Faber, 2001), p. 173.
44 *Ballad of HMS*, p. 17.
45 Ibid., p. 18.
46 Ibid., p. 58.
47 Wallace Stevens, 'The Snow Man', *The Collected Poems of Wallace Stevens* (New York: Knopf, 1954), pp. 9–10.
48 Seamus Heaney, 'A Sofa in the Forties', *Opened Ground*, p. 397.
49 Louis MacNeice, 'Snow', *Collected Poems*, p. 30.
50 Paul Muldoon, 'History', *Staying Alive: Real Poems for Unreal Times*, ed. Neil Astley (Tarset: Bloodaxe, 2002), p. 74.
51 Derek Mahon, 'In Carrowdore Churchyard', *Collected Poems* (Loughcrew: Gallery Books, 1999), p. 17.
52 Longley, p. 259.
53 *Ballad of HMS*, p. 56.
54 Ibid., p. 54.
55 Ibid., p. 54.
56 Ibid., p. 34.
57 'Queen's Gambit', *Ballad of HMS*, p. 69.
58 Ibid., p. 69.

59 'Second Language', *Ballad of HMS*, p. 98.
60 Ciaran Carson, 'Two to Tango', *First Language* (Loughcrew: Gallery Press, 1993), p. 18.
61 Ciaran Carson, *Opera Et Cetera* (Loughcrew: Gallery Press, 1996).
62 John Locke, *Essay Concerning Human Understanding*, ed. John W. Yolton, rev. edn (London: Everyman, 1964), bk. 3 , chap. 3, sect. 11.
63 Ciaran Carson, *Breaking News* (Loughcrew: Gallery Press, 2003), p. 16.
64 Ibid., p. 17.
65 'Gate', *Breaking News*, p. 45.
66 'Queen's Gambit', *Ballad of HMS*, p. 67.
67 William Carlos Williams, 'The Red Wheelbarrow', *The Collected Poems of William Carlos Williams* (New York: New Directions, 1986).
68 *Breaking News*, p. 11.
69 Seamus Heaney, 'The God in the Tree', *Preoccupations: Selected Prose 1968–1978* (London: Faber & Faber, 1980), p. 181.
70 Ibid.
71 *Breaking News*, p. 53.
72 Ezra Pound, 'Vorticism', in *Gaudier-Brzeska: A Memoir* (New York: New Directions, 1970), pp. 81–94, 90.
73 *Breaking News*, p. 39.
74 Ibid., p. 40.
75 Ibid., p. 23.
76 Ibid., p. 12.
77 Ibid., p. 37.
78 *Ballad of HMS*, p. 113.
79 *Breaking News*, p. 34.
80 Ibid., p. 41.
81 Lionel Trilling, 'Introduction', *Isaac Babel: Collected Stories* (London: Penguin, 1961), p. 10.
82 *Ballad of HMS*, p. 23.
83 *Breaking News*, p. 68.
84 Ibid., p. 72.
85 Martin Heidegger, 'The Age of the World Picture', in Martin Heidegger, *The Question Concerning Technology and Other Essays* (New York: Harper & Row, 1977), p. 154.
86 *Breaking News*, p. 54.
87 Ibid., p. 48.
88 Ibid., p. 33.

MEMORY, HISTORY, STORY: BETWEEN POETICS AND ETHICS

1 Paul Ricoeur, 'Reflections on a New Ethos for Europe' in Richard Kearney (ed.), *Paul Ricoeur: The Hermeneutics of Praxis* (London: Sage, 1996), pp. 3–14.
2 In Caroline Wiedmer's *The Claims of Memory: Representations of the Holocaust in Contemporary Germany and France* (Ithaca, New York: Cornell University Press, 1999), the problem of avoidance of mourning is made relevant as well as the difficulty in commemorating Jews separately or collectively. See also Tony Judt, *Postwar* (New York: Penguin, 2005) and the abridged version of his conclusion to this work, 'From the House of the Dead: On Modern European

Memory', *New York Review of Books*, October 2005, pp. 12–16.

3   Steven Spielberg, dir, *Schindler's List* (Universal Pictures, 1993).

4   Claude Lanzmann, dir, *Shoah* (Films Aleph, Historia Films, 1985).

5   Located in Yale University Manuscripts and Archives, Sterling Memorial Library.

6   I discuss questions of historical testimony and the filmic controversies around Spielberg and Lanzmann at length in *On Stories* (London and New York: Routledge, 2002), pp. 47–60. The conclusion I reach in that chapter is that the 'task of all representations of the Shoah is, it would seem, to sustain a delicate balance between (1) a historical fidelity to truth (respecting the distance of the past as it was in the past) and (2) an aesthetic fidelity to imaginative vivacity and credibility (presenting the past as if it were present). This implies a double or "split" narrative reference to the past "as it was" and "as it was not". . . . In sum, if the testimony of the horror is too immediate, we are blinded by the experience. But if it is too distant, we are untouched by it', p. 60. The difficult question of how to represent experiences of violence and trauma respecting the double need for poetical efficacy (the audience must be somehow moved and struck by the violence) and ethical sensitivity to the irreducible inhumanity and ineffability of the violence remains critical for all contemporary debates on the subject.

7   In *Symploke: A Journal for the Intermingling of Literary, Cultural and Theoretical Scholarship*, 10, 1–2 (2002), pp. 13–31.

8   I am very grateful to my Boston College colleague, Robin Lydenberg, for her illuminating and instructive essay on this work, 'From Icon to Index: Some Contemporary Visions of the Irish Stone Cottage' in *Eire/land*, (ed.) Vera Kreilkamp (Boston: McMullen Museum, 2003), pp. 127–33. Lyndenberg also kindly brought my attention to the following relevant and informative literature on the topic, Philip Nobel, 'Going Hungry' *Metropolis Magazine,* New York, November 2002; Margaret Kelleher, 'Hunger and History: Monuments to the Great Irish Famine' in *Textual Practice*, 16, 2 (Summer 2002), pp. 249–76; Yvonne Moran, 'Taking Mayo to Manhattan', *Irish Times*, 1 September, 2001; David Dunlap, 'Memorial to the Hunger', *The New York Times*, 15 March, 2001; Marita Sturken, 'The Wall, the Screen and the Image: The Vietnam Veterans Memorial', in *The Representations*, 35 (Summer 1991), pp. 118–142; Daniel Libeskind's 'Jewish Museum in Berlin: The Uncanny Arts of Memorial Architecture', in *Jewish Social Studies*, 6, 2, 2000; Vivian Patraka, 'Spectacular Suffering: Performing Presence, Absence and Witness at U.S. Holocaust Museums', in *Spectacular Suffering* (Bloomington, Indianapolis: Indiana University Press, 1999).

9   Paul Ricoeur, *La Mémoire, L'histoire, L'oubli* (Paris: Editions du Seuil, 2000), pp. 82f.

10 Act Two, Scene Three, Shakespeare, *Henry V*, edited by John Russell Brown. Signet Classics Series (New York: New American Library, 1965).

11 Declan Kiberd, *Inventing Ireland* (London: Vintage, 1996), R.F. Foster, *The Irish Story: Telling Tales and Making it up in Ireland* (see especially his critique of famine heritage parks and the cult of 'Faminism' for foreign export, pp. 23 f), (London: Allan Lane, 2001), and Luke Gibbons, *Transformations in Irish Culture* (Cork: Cork University Press, 1996).

12 It is worth noting here that discontinuous readings of the Irish Famine in terms of rupture and trauma are always dialectically linked to continuous readings of the Famine in terms of an unbroken historic past which is still somehow present, or at least representable. Whereas romantic interpretations tend to stress the latter approach and postmodern interpretations the former, most contemporary memorials (including Tolle's) signal some sort of balance or tension between the two.

13 Sigmund Freud, 'Mourning and Melancholy' (edited by Angela Richards) in *The Pelican Freud Library*, vol. 2, (London and New York: Penguin, 1984), pp. 251–68.

14 Robin Lydenberg, 'From Icon to Index', p. 131.

15 See 'The Fifth Province' in Richard Kearney, *Postnationalist Ireland* (London and New York: Routledge, 1997), pp. 99–100: ' Modern Ireland is made up of four provinces. And yet, the Irish word for a province is *coiced* which means fifth. This fivefold division is as old as Ireland itself, yet there is disagreement about the identity of the fifth. Some claim that all the provinces met at the Stone of Divisions on the Hill of Uisneach, believed to be the mid-point of Ireland. Others say that the fifth province was Meath *(mide)*, the 'middle'. Both traditions divide Ireland into four quarters and a 'middle', though they disagree about the location of this middle or 'fifth' province. Although Tara was the political centre of Ireland, this fifth province acted as a second centre, which if non-political, was just as important, acting as a necessary balance. The present unhappy state of our country would seem to indicate a need for this second centre of gravity. The obvious impotence of the various political attempts to unite the four geographical provinces would seem to warrant another kind of solution . . . one which would incorporate the 'fifth' province. This province, this place, this centre, is not a political or geographical position, it is more like a disposition.' For an illuminating application of this concept of the Fifth Province to contemporary Irish-British literature and politics, including the vexed question of Nationalist-Unionist violence, see Aidan O'Malley's doctoral dissertation *In Other Words: Coming to Terms with Irish Identities through Translation*, European University Institute at Florence, 2004, especially pp. 20–41.

16 Robin Lydenberg, 'From Icon to Index', p. 132.

17 Ibid., p. 131.

18 I am grateful to Joel Gereboff of Arizona State University for this notion of 'counter-text'.

19 Scorsese, dir, *Gangs of New York* (Miramax, 2002).

20 Derrida challenges the hermeneutic-psychoanalytic model of 'working through', 'mourning' and 'forgiveness' in a number of late texts such as *Spectres of Marx* (London and New York: Routledge, 1994) and *On Cosmopolitanism and Forgiveness* (London and New York: Routledge, 2001). See especially pp. 50–1 where Derrida argues for the need to 'distinguish between forgiveness and (the) process of reconciliation, the reconstitution of a health or a "normality", as necessary and desirable as it would appear through amnesties, the "work of mourning" etc. A "finalised" forgiveness is not forgiveness; it is only a political strategy or a psycho-therapeutic economy.' Derrida admits to being 'torn' between two irreducible but indissociable poles – 'between a "hyperbolic" ethical vision of forgiveness, pure forgiveness, and the reality of a society at

work in pragmatic processes of reconciliation', p. 51. For a contrasting view of the tension between the hermeneutic and deconstructive takes on forgiveness and violence see the final section of Paul Ricoeur's *Memory, History and Forgetting*, trans. David Pellauer (University of Chicago Press, 2005), entitled 'Difficult Pardon'.

21   Paul Ricoeur, 'Reflections on a New Ethos for Europe', p. 7. See our own argument along these lines in our *On Stories,* p. 140, particularly as it relates to the question of violence: 'If we possess narrative sympathy – enabling us to see the world from the other's point of view – we cannot kill. If we do not, we cannot love.'

22   Hans-Georg Gadamer, *Truth and Method* (London: Sheed and Ward, 1975).

23   Paul Ricoeur, 'Reflections on a New Ethos for Europe', p. 7.

24   Ibid., p. 8.

25   Ibid., p. 9.

26   Ibid., p. 8.

27   Ibid., p. 8.

28   Ibid., p. 9.

29   Ibid., p. 11.

Bibliography

The information included is designed to both reflect the particular works cited in the volume and also act as a resource for readers interested in doing broader reading in violence studies.

GOVERNMENT SOURCES

Berwick, Walter, 'Unpublished Letter from Walter Berwick to the Earl of Clarendon', 22 September 1849 (Public Record Office, London, HO 45/2603/58–81.

Brady, Maziere, 'Unpublished Letter from Maziere Brady to the Earl of Roden, Francis Beers and William Beers', 6 October 1849 (Public Records Office, London, HO 45/2603/88–91.

Clarendon, Earl of, 'Unpublished Letter from the Earl of Clarendon to Sir George Grey', 20 July 1849 (Public Record Office, London, HO 45/2603/54).

—, 'Unpublished Letter from the Earl of Clarendon to Lord Monteagle', 27 November 1849 (Monteagle Papers, National Library of Ireland, MS 13, 199).

Inquest and Depositions into the Deaths at Magheramayo, 14–18 July 1849 (National Archives of Ireland CSORP 8/322 and /357)

Letter Re: Ribbonism in County Down, 17 March 1849 (Public Record Office of Northern Ireland D.682/146).

Petition of County Down Magistrates 1849 (Public Record Office, HO 45/2603/180–182)

Report from the select committee to inquire into the nature, character, extent, and tendency of Orange lodges, associations, or societies in Ireland, with minutes of evidence and appendix, HC 1835(377) XV

Report of the Evidence Taken Before the Government Commissioner, Walter Berwick Esq., Q.C., at Court Held in Castlewellan from 30th July to 4th August, and by Adjournment on Tuesday 18th September1849.

Rutheven, Charles, 'Unpublished Letter from Charles Rutheven to T. N. Redington', 2 August 1849 (National Archives of Ireland, CSORP, Registered Papers 1849/8/363).

NEWSPAPERS AND PERIODICALS

America
American Spectator
Belfast Newsletter
Boston Daily Record
Boston Evening American
Boston Evening Transcript
Boston Globe
Boston Herald
Boston Post
Boston Record
Boston Traveler
Catholic World
Daily Mail
Daily Express
Downpatrick Reporter
Dublin Evening Press
Evening Herald
Evening News
Freeman's Journal
Harvard Crimson
Illustrated London News
Irish Independent
Irish Press
Irish Tatler and Sketch
Irish Times
Irish Weekly Independent
Kilkenny Moderator
The Leader
Nation
New Republic
New Statesman and Nation
New York Post
New York Herald Tribune
New York Times
New York World-Telegram
Northern Whig
The Protestant Watchman
Scotsman
Standard
Theatre Arts Monthly
The Times
The Warder

UNPUBLISHED COLLECTION

O'Casey file, Billy Rose Theater Collection, Lincoln Center for the Performing Arts Library, New York.

BOOKS, ARTICLES AND MANUSCRIPTS

Aijmer, Göran and Jon Abbink (eds.), *Meanings of Violence: A Cross-Cultural Perspective* (Oxford and New York: Berg, 2000).

Akenson, Donald Harman. *Small Differences: Irish Catholics and Irish Protestants, 1815–1922: An International Perspective* (Montréal: McGill-Queen's University Press, 1988).

Arendt, Hannah, 'A Special Supplement: Reflections on Violence', in *The New York Review of Books*, 12, 4, 27 Feb. 1969.

Armstrong, Nancy and Leonard Tennenhouse (eds.), *The Violence of Representation: Literature and the History of Violence* (London: Routledge, 1989).

Augustine, *The Confessions of St Augustine*, trans. Rex Warner (New York: New American Library, 1963).

Auty, Martin. 'But is it Cinema?', in Martin Auty and Nick Roddick (eds.), *British Cinema Now* (London: BFI, 1985).

Ayling, Ronald, *Sean O'Casey's Theatre of War* (Vernon, British Columbia: Kalamalka Press, 2004).

Backus, Margot, *Gothic Family Romance: Heterosexuality, Child Sacrifice and the Anglo-Irish Colonial Order* (Durham: Duke University Press, 1999).

Barry, Kevin, 'Discarded Images: Narrative and the Cinema', *Crane Bag* 6, 1 (1982).

Barry, Peter, *Contemporary British Poetry and the City* (Manchester: Manchester University Press, 2000).

Barry, Shane, review in *Film Ireland*, 48, August/September 1995.

Barry, Tom, *Guerrilla Days in Ireland* (Dublin: Irish Press, 1949).

Barthes, Roland 'Dear Antonioni . . .', *Cahiers du Cinéma*, 311, May 1980.

—, 'The Third Meaning: Research Notes on Some Eisenstein Stills', in Susan Sontag, (ed.), *A Roland Barthes Reader* (London: Vintage, 1993).

Barthorp, Michael, *Blood-Red Desert Sand: the British invasions of Egypt and the Sudan, 1882–1898* (London: Cassell and Co., 1984).

Bartlett, Thomas, David Dickson, Dáire Keogh and Kevin Whelan (eds.), *1798: A Bicentenary Perspective* (Dublin: Four Courts Press, 2003).

—, 'An End to Moral Economy: The Irish Militia Disturbances of 1793', *Past and Present*, 99, May 1983.

Bell, J. Bowyer, *On Revolt: Strategies of National Liberation* (Cambridge, Massachusetts: Harvard University Press, 1976).

Benjamin, Walter, 'Critique of Violence', in Peter Demetz, (ed.), *Reflections: Essays, Aphorisms, Autobiographical Writings* (New York: Harcourt Brace, 1978).

Bew, Paul and Gordon Gillespie, *Northern Ireland: A Chronology of the Troubles, 1968– 1993* (Dublin: Gill & Macmillan, 1993).

Blake, William, 'To Nobodaddy' (1791–92), *The Complete Poems*, 2nd edn, (ed.) W.H. Stevenson (London and New York: Longman, 1989).

—, 'Let the Brothels of Paris be Opened' (1791–92), *The Complete Poems*, 2nd edn, (ed.) W.H. Stevenson (London: Longman, 1989).

Bordwell, David, *Narration in the Fiction Film* (London: Routledge, 1995).

Boucher, Caroline, 'How We Met: Neil Jordan and Stephen Woolley', *Independent on Sunday*, 8 November 1992, magazine section.

Bourke, Angela, *The Burning of Bridget Cleary* (London, Pimlico, 1999; New York: Viking, 2000).

Bowman, Glenn, 'The Violence of Identity', in Bettina E. Schmidt, (ed.), *Anthropology of Violence and Conflict* (London: Routledge, 2001).

Boyd, Andrew, *Holy War in Belfast* (Tralee: Anvil Books, 1969).

Brass, Paul, (ed.), *Riots and Pogroms* (New York: Macmillan, 1996).

Brown, Terence, *Ireland, A Social and Cultural History 1922 to the Present* (London: Cornell University Press, 1985).

Brustein, Robert, *The Theater of Revolt, An Approach to Modern Drama* (Boston: Little Brown, 1964).

Bryan, Dominic, *Orange Parades: The Politics of Ritual, Tradition and Control* (London, 2000).

—, 'Interpreting the Twelfth', *History Ireland*, 2, 2, Summer 1994.

Burns-Bisogno, Louisa, *Censoring Irish Nationalism: The British, Irish and American Suppression of Republican Images in Film and Television, 1909–95* (London: McFarland, 1997).

Buck, David D., (ed.), *Recent Studies of the Boxer Movement: Chinese Studies in history*, xx: 3–4, Spring/Summer 1987.

Carson, Ciaran, *The Ballad of HMS Belfast* (Loughcrew: Gallery Press, 1999).

—, *Belfast Confetti* (Loughcrew: Gallery Press, 1989).

—, *Breaking News* (Loughcrew: Gallery Press, 2003).

—, '"Escaped from the Massacre"?', *The Honest Ulsterman*, 50, Winter 1975.

—, *First Language* (Loughcrew: Gallery Press, 1993).

—, *Opera Et Cetera* (Loughcrew: Gallery Press, 1996).

Cerulo, Karen A., *Deciphering Violence: the Cognitive Structure of Right and Wrong* (New York: Routledge, 1998).

Clark, Anna, *The Struggle for the Breeches: Gender and the Making of the British Working Class* (Berkeley: University of California Press, 1995).

Clark, Samuel and James S. Donnelly, Jr., *Irish Peasants: Violence and Political Unrest, 1780–1914* (Dublin: Gill & Macmillan, 1983).

Cleves, Rachel Hope, 'On Writing the History of Violence', *Journal of the Early Republic*, 24, 4, Winter 2004).

Clutterbuck, Richard, *The Media and Political Violence,* Foreword by Robin Day (London: MacMillan, 1981).

Coakley, John, 'The Election that Made the First Dáil', in Brian Farrell, (ed.), *The Creation of the Dáil* (Dublin: Blackwater Press, 1994).

Colley, Linda, *Britons: Forging the Nation, 1707–1837* (London: Yale University Press, 2003).

Cook, Richard, 'Angel of Death', review of *Angel, New Musical Express*, 13 November 1982.

Corcoran, Neil, "One Step Forward, Two Steps back": Ciaran Carson's *The Irish for No*, in Neil Corcoran, (ed.), *The Chosen Ground: Essays on the Contemporary Poetry of Northern Ireland* (Bridgend: Seren Books, 1992).

Crenshaw, Martha, (ed.), *Terrorism, Legitimacy, and Power: the Consequences of Political Violence* (Middletown, Connecticut: Wesleyan University Press, 1983).

Cronin, Michael, '"He's My Country": Liberalism, Nationalism, and Sexuality in Contemporary Irish Gay Fiction', *Éire-Ireland* 39, 3, Fall/Winter 2004.

—, *Romantic Ireland Revisited,* www.sussex.ac.uk/cssd/courses/michael's diss/pdf, p. 4.

Curtis, L. Perry, *Apes and Angels: the Irishman in Victorian Caricature* (London: Smithsonian Institute Press, 1997).

D'Cruze, Shani, (ed.), *Everyday Violence in Britain, 1850–1950: Gender and Class* (Harlow: Longman, 2000).

Daiches, David, *A Critical History of English Literature, Vol. IV* (London: Secker and Warburg, 1968).

Darby, John, *Conflict in Northern Ireland* (Dublin: Gill and Macmillan, 1976).

Darby, John and Nicholas Dodge (eds.), *Political Violence: Ireland in a Comparative Perspective* (Belfast: Appletree Press, 1990).

Das, Veena, *Mirrors of Violence: Communities, Rioters and Survivors in South Asia* (Dehli and New York: Oxford University Press, 1990).

Davis, Natalie Zemon. 'The Rites of Violence', in *Society and Culture in Early Modern France* (Stanford, CA: Stanford University Press, 1975).

de Nie, Michael, *The Eternal Paddy: Irish identity and the British press, 1798–1882* (Madison: University of Wisconsin Press, 2004).

Deleuze, Gilles, 'The Language of Sade and Masoch', in Becky McLaughlin and Bob Coleman (eds.), *Everyday Theory: A Contemporary Reader* (New York: Longman, 2005).

Derrida, Jacques, *On Cosmopolitanism and Forgiveness* (London: Routledge, 2001).

—, *Spectres of Marx* (London: Routledge, 1994).

Desan, Suzanne, 'Crowds, Community, and Ritual in the Work of E.P. Thompson and Natalie Davis', in Lynn Hunt, (ed.), *The New Cultural History* (Berkeley: University of California Press, 1989).

Dewar, M.W., *Orangeism: An Historical Appreciation* (Belfast: Grand Orange Lodge of Ireland, 1967).

Dillon, Martin, *The Shankill Butchers: A Case Study of Mass Murder* (London: Hutchinson, 1989).

Donnelly, James S., Jr. *Irish Agrarian Rebellion* (Dublin: Irish Academic Press, 1997).

—, 'Pastorini and Captain Rock: Millenarianism and Sectarianism in the Rockite Movement of 1821–24', in *Irish Peasants: Violence and Political Unrest, 1780–1914* (Dublin: Gill & Macmillan, 1983).

Doyle, Roddy, *A Star Called Henry* (London: Jonathan Cape, 1999).

Duytschaever, Joris and Geert Lernout (eds.), *History and Violence in Anglo-Irish Literature* (Amsterdam: Rodopi, 1988).

Dwyer, Michael, '10 Days that Shook the Irish Film Industry', *In Dublin,* (8 April 1982, repr. *Film West,* 30 November 1997).

Eagleton, Terry, 'Realism and Cinema', *Screen,* 21, 2, Summer 1980.

Elias, Norbert, *The Civilizing Process: State Formation and Civilization* (Oxford: Blackwell, 1978).

Elliott, Jane E., *Some did it for Civilization, Some did it for their Country: a Revised View of the Boxer War* (Hong Kong: The Chinese University of Hong Kong, 2002).

Engels, Friedrich, *Herrn Eugen Dührings Umwälzung der Wissenschaft* (1878, repr. London: Electric Books, 2001).

Farrell, Sean, *Rituals and Riots: Sectarian Violence and Political Culture in Ulster, 1784–1886* (Lexington: University of Kentucky Press, 2000).

Feldman, Allen, *Formations of Violence: The Narrative of the Body and Political Terror in Northern Ireland* (London: Chicago University Press, 1991).

Fennell, Desmond, *Whatever You Say, Say Nothing: Why Seamus Heaney is No.1* (Dublin: ELO Publications, 1991).

Finney, Angus, *The Egos Have Landed: The Rise and Fall of Palace Pictures* (London: Mandarin, 1997).

Fitzpatrick, David, *Politics and Irish Life: Provincial Experience of War and Revolution 1913–1921* (Dublin: Gill & Macmillan, 1977).

Fletcher, Jonathan, *Violence and Civilization: An Introduction to the Work of Norbert Elias* (Cambridge: Cambridge University Press, 1997).

Foster, David William, *Violence in Argentine Literature: Cultural Responses to Tyranny* (Columbia: University of Missouri Press, 1995).

Foster, R. F., *The Irish Story: Telling Tales and Making it up in Ireland* (London: Allan Lane, 2001).

Foucault, Michel, *Discipline and Punish: the Birth of the Prison*, trans. Alan Sheridan (Harmondsworth: Penguin, 1977; New York: Vintage, 1979).

—, *Surveiller et Punir: Naissance de la Prison* (Paris: Éditions Gallimard, 1975).

Freitag, Sandra B. *Collective Action and Community: Public Arenas and the Emergence of Communalism in North India* (Berkeley: University of California Press, 1989).

Freud, Sigmund, 'Mourning and Melancholy', (ed.), Angela Richards, in *The Pelican Freud Library*, vol. 2 (New York: Penguin, 1984).

Gadamer, Hans-Georg, *Truth and Method* (London: Sheed and Ward, 1975).

Gallagher, Ian, 'The Showband Era' <www.iangallagher.com/rip1.htm>.

Gibbons, Luke, 'Romanticism, Realism and Irish Cinema', *Cinema and Ireland*.

—, *Transformations in Irish Culture* (Cork: Cork University Press, 1996).

Girard, René, *Violence and the Sacred* (Baltimore: Johns Hopkins University Press, 1977).

Giroux, Henry A., 'Racism and the Aesthetic of Hyperreal Violence: *Pulp Fiction* and Other Visual Tragedies', *Social Identities*, 1, 2, 1995.

Glandon, Virginia, *Arthur Griffith and the Advanced Nationalist Press in Ireland, 1900–1922* (New York: P. Lang, 1985).

González, Aníbal, *Killer Books: Writing, Violence, and Ethics in Modern Spanish American Narrative* (Austin: University of Texas Press, 2001).

Gramsci, Antonio, *An Antonio Gramsci Reader: Selected Writings, 1916–1935*, (ed.), David Forgacs (New York: Schocken Books, 1988).

Grant, Patrick, *Literature, Rhetoric, and Violence in Northern Ireland, 1968–98: Hardened to Death* (Houndmills: Palgrave, 2001).

Greaves, Desmond, *The Life and Times of James Connolly* (London: Lawrence and Wishart, 1972).

—, *Sean O'Casey, Politics and Art* (London: Lawrence and Wishart, 1979).

Grein, J.T., 'The World of the Theatre', *Illustrated London News*, 3 March 1934.

Hall, Catherine, *Civilising Subjects: Metropole and Colony in the English Imagination 1830–1867* (Chicago and London: University of Chicago Press, 2002).

Hanssen, Beatrice, *Critique of Violence: Between Poststructuralism and Critical Theory* (New York: Routledge, 2000).

Harkin, Margo, *Irish Cinema: Ourselves Alone?* Dir. Donald Taylor Black (Ireland and GB: BFI TV and Centenary Productions in association with Poolbeg Productions, RTE and The Irish Film Board/ Connoisseur Academy Video, 1995).

Hart, Peter, Interview in *History Ireland*, 13.3, May/June 2005.

—, *The I.R.A. and its Enemies: Violence and Community in Cork, 1916–1923* (Oxford: Clarendon, 1998).

—, *The IRA at War 1916–1923* (Oxford: Oxford University Press, 2003).

—, *Mick: the Making of Michael Collins* (London: Macmillan, 2005).

Heaney, Seamus, *North* (London: Faber & Faber, 1975).

—, *Opened Ground: Poems 1966–1996* (London: Faber & Faber, 1998).

—, 'Place and Displacement: Recent Poetry of Northern Ireland', The Pete Laver Memorial Lecture (1984), quoted in Fennell, *Whatever You Say, Say Nothing: Why Seamus Heaney is No. 1* (Dublin: Elo Publications, 1991).

—, *Preoccupations: Selected Prose 1968–1978* (London: Faber & Faber, 1980).

—, 'Unhappy and at Home: Interview with Seamus Deane', *Crane Bag*, 1, 1, 1977, repr. *The Crane Bag Book of Irish Studies*,(ed.) Mark Patrick Hederman and Richard Kearney (Dublin: Blackwater, 1982).

—, *Wintering Out* (London: Faber & Faber, 1972).

Heath, Stephen, 'Narrative Space', *Questions of Cinema* (London: Macmillan, 1981).

Heidegger, Martin, 'The Age of the World Picture', in Martin Heidegger, *The Question Concerning Technology and Other Essays* (New York: Harper & Row, 1977).

Hepburn, A.C., *A Past Apart: Studies in the History of Catholic Belfast* (Belfast: Ulster Historical Foundation, 1996).

Hill, John, 'Images of Violence', *Cinema and Ireland*, by Kevin Rockett, Luke Gibbons, and John Hill (Syracuse, New York: Syracuse University Press, 1988).

Hirst, Catherine, *Religion, Politics and Violence in Nineteenth-Century Belfast: The Pound & Sandy Row* (Dublin: Four Courts Press, 2002).

Holmes, Michael and Denis Holmes, *Ireland and India: Connections, Comparisons, Contrasts* (Dublin: Four Courts Press, 1997).

Hopkinson, Michael, *The Irish War of Independence* (Montréal: McGill-Queen's University Press, 2002).

Hopper, Keith, '"Cat-Calls from the Cheap Seats": The Third Meaning of Neil Jordan's Michael Collins', *The Irish Review*, 21, Autumn/Winter 1997.

—, '"A Gallous Story and a Dirty Deed": Word and Image in Neil Jordan and Joe Comerford's *Traveller* (1981)', *Irish Studies Review*, 9, 2, August 2001.

—, '"Hairy on the Inside": Re-visiting *The Company of Wolves*', special Cinema/Media issue of *The Canadian Journal of Irish Studies*, 29, 2, Autumn 2003.

Horne, Alistair, *A Savage War of Peace: Algeria, 1954–1962* (New York: Penguin, 1977).

Howe, Stephen, *Ireland and Empire: Colonial Legacies in Irish History and Culture* (Oxford: Oxford University Press, 2000).

Hufstader, Jonathan, *Tongue of Water, Teeth of Stones: Northern Irish Poetry and Social Violence* (Lexington: University Press of Kentucky, 1999).

Hughes, Eammon, '"What itch of Contradiction?" Belfast in Poetry', in Nicholas Allen and Aaron Kelly (eds.), *The Cities of Belfast* (Dublin: Four Courts Press, 2003).

Jackson, Alvin, 'British Ireland: What if Home Rule Had Been Enacted in 1912?', in Niall Ferguson, (ed.), *Virtual History: Alternatives and Counterfactuals* (London: Papermac, 1998).

—, 'Ireland, the union and the Empire, 1800–1960', in Kevin Kenny, (ed.), *Ireland and the British empire* (Oxford and New York: Oxford University Press, 2004).

James, Henry, *The Art of the Novel* (New York: Scribners, 1934).

Jarman, Neil, *Material Conflicts: Parades and Visual Displays in Northern Ireland* (Oxford: Oxford University Press, 1997).

Jeffrey, Keith, (ed.) *An Irish empire? Aspects of Ireland and the British Empire* (Manchester: Manchester University Press, 1996).

Jolly, Rosemary Jane, *Colonization, Violence, and Narration in White South African Writing: Andre Brink, Breyten Breytenbach, and J.M. Coetzee* (Athens: Ohio University Press, 1996).

Jordan, John, 'Illusion and Actuality in the Later O'Casey', (ed.) Ronald Ayling, *Sean O'Casey, Modern Judgments* (London: Macmillan, 1969).

Jordan, Justine, 'Rebellions of the Heart', *The Guardian: Saturday Review*, 22 September 2001.

Jordan, Neil, wr./dir., *Angel* (Ireland and GB: Motion Picture Company of Ireland, 1982).

—, *Angel* screenplay, with an introduction by John Boorman (London: Faber & Faber, 1989).

—, '*Angel* Takes Wing', interview with Ray Comiskey, *Irish Times*, 11 May 1982.

—, 'Brute Music', Neil Jordan MS Collection, National Library Archive, Dublin, undated and unpaginated.

—, dir, 'Debut of Style', interview with Monty Smith, *New Musical Express*, 13 November 1982.

—, 'Face to Face with Evil', interview with Michael Open, *Film Directions* 18, 5, December 1982.

—, 'Neil Jordan: *Angel*', interview with Stephen Lowenstein, (ed.) Lowenstein, *My First Movie* (London: Faber & Faber, 2000).

—, 'Neil Jordan', interview with Mario Falsetto, (ed.) Falsetto, *Personal Visions: Conversations with Independent Film-Makers* (London: Constable, 1999).

Judt, Tony, 'From the House of the Dead: On Modern European Memory, *New York Review of Books*, 3 October 2005.

—, *Postwar* (New York: Penguin, 2005).

Kael, Pauline, '*L'Avventura*', *Cinemania* (Washington: Microsoft CD-Rom, 1995).

Kaplan, Cora, 'White, black, and green: racialising Irishness in Victorian England', in Peter Gray, (ed.), *Victoria's Ireland: Irishness and Britishness, 1837–1901*, (Dublin: Four Courts Press, 2004).

Kearney, Richard, 'The Fifth Province' in Richard Kearney, *Postnationalist Ireland: Politics, Culture, Philosophy* (London and New York: Routledge, 1997).

—, 'Myth and Martyrdom I', *Transitions: Narratives in Modern Irish Culture* (Manchester: Manchester University Press, 1988).

—, 'Nationalism and Irish Cinema', *Transitions: Narratives in Modern Irish Culture* (Manchester: Manchester University Press, 1988).

—, *On Stories* (London: Routledge, 2002).

Keegan, John, *The First World War* (London: Hutchinson, 1998).

Kelly, P.T., *TV Violence: A Guide to the Literature* (Commack, New York: Nova Science Publishers, 1996).

Kellcher, Margaret, 'Hunger and History: Monuments to the Great Irish Famine', *Textual Practice*, 16, 2, Summer 2002.

Kenny, Kevin, (ed.), *Ireland and the British empire* (Oxford: Oxford University Press, 2004).

—, *Making Sense of the Molly Maguires* (New York: Oxford University Press, 1998).

Kerr, Donal A. '*A Nation of Beggars'?*: *Priests, People, and Politics in Famine Ireland, 1846–1852.* (Oxford: Oxford University Press, 1994).

Kertzer, David, *Ritual, Politics and Power* (London: Yale University Press, 1988).

Kiberd, Declan, *Inventing Ireland* (London: Vintage, 1996).

Kinealy, Christine, 'A Right to March? The Conflict at Dolly's Brae', in D.G. Boyce and Roger Swift (eds.), *Problems and Perspectives in Irish History Since 1800* (Dublin: Four Courts Press, 2004).

Kinsella, Thomas, 'The Irish Writer', *Éire-Ireland*, 2, 2, 1967.

Kosok, Heinz, *O'Casey the Dramatist* (Gerards Cross Bucks, and Totowa, New Jersey: Colin Smythe and Barnes and Noble, 1985).

Krause, David and Robert Hogan, *The Experiments of Sean O'Casey* (New York: St Martin's Press, 1960).

—, *Sean O'Casey The Man and His Work* (1960, London and New York: Macmillan, 1975).

—, (ed.), *The Letters of Sean O'Casey 1955–58, Vol. III* (Washington DC: Catholic University Press, 1989).

Laffan, Michael, *The Resurrection of Ireland: The Sinn Féin Party, 1916–1923* (Cambridge: Cambridge University Press, 1999).

Lanters, Jose, 'Demythologizing/Remythologizing the Rising: Roddy Doyle's *A Star Called Henry*', *Hungarian Journal of English and American Studies*, 8, 1, 2002.

Lattimore, Richmond, trans and intro., *Aeschylus I: Oresteia* (Chicago and London: University of Chicago Press, 1953).

Legg, Mary Louise, *Newspapers and Nationalism: the Irish Provincial Press, 1850–1892* (Dublin: Four Courts Press, 1999).

Ledbetter, Mark, *Victims and the Postmodern Narrative, or, Doing Violence to the Body: an Ethic of Reading and Writing* (New York: St Martin's Press, 1996).

Lernout, Geert, (ed.), *The Crows behind the Plow: History and Violence in Anglo-Irish Poetry and Drama* (Amsterdam: Rodopi, 1991).

Lennon, Joseph, *Irish Orientalism: A Literary and Intellectual History* (Syracuse, NY: Syracuse University Press, 2004).

Lepore, Jill, *The Name of War: Philip's War and the Origins of American Identity* (New York: Knopf, 1998).

Libeskind, Daniel, 'Jewish Museum in Berlin: The Uncanny Arts of Memorial Architecture', *Jewish Social Studies*, 6, 2, Winter, 2002.

Locke, John, *Essay Concerning Human Understanding*, (ed.) John W. Yolton, rev. edn (London: Everyman, 1964).

Longley, Edna, *The Living Stream: Literature and Revisionism in Ireland* (Newcastle upon Tyne: Bloodaxe, 1994).

Longley, Michael, 'Wounds', *Poems 1963–1983* (Harmondsworth: Penguin, 1985).

Lowery, Robert, *A Whirlwind in Dublin, 'The Plough and the Stars' Riots* (London: Greenwood Press, 1984).

Lyndenberg, Robin, 'From Icon to Index: Some Contemporary Visions of the Irish Stone Cottage', *Eire/land*, (ed.) Vera Krielkamp (Boston: McMullen Museum, 2003).

MacNeice, Louis, *Collected Poems* (London: Faber & Faber, 1979).

Madden, Kyla, *Forkhill Protestants and Forkhill Catholics* (Montréal: McGill-Queen's University Press, 2005).

Maher, Kevin, 'From Angel to Vampire', *Film Ireland*, no. 45, February/March 1995.

Mahon, Derek, *Collected Poems* (Loughcrew: Gallery Books, 1999).

Malcolm, Derek, 'Neil Jordan's *Angel*', *Guardian*, repr. *Film Directions*, 7, 26 (Spring 1985).

Malkin, Jeannette R., *Verbal Violence in Contemporary Drama: from Handke to Shepard* (Cambridge: Cambridge University Press, 1992).

Martin, Barker and Julian Petley, (eds.), *Ill Effects: The Media/Violence Debate* (London: Routledge, 2001).

Martin, Declan, 'Migration within the Six Counties of Northern Ireland, with Special Reference to the City of Belfast 1911–37', MA thesis, Queens University of Belfast (1977).

Martin, W. J., *The Battle of Dolly's Brae, 12th July 1849* (Belfast: Grand Orange Lodge of Ireland, 1967).

Maume, Patrick, 'Standish James O'Grady: Between Imperial Romance and Irish Revival', *Éire-Ireland*, xxxix, 1–2, Spring–Summer 2004.

McCabe, Eugene, 'Victims', *Christ in the Fields* (London: Minerva, 1993).

McCarthy, Conor, 'Film and Politics: Neil Jordan, Bob Quinn and Pat Murphy', *Modernisation, Crisis and Culture in Ireland, 1969–1992* (Dublin: Four Courts Press, 2000).

McCarthy, Dermot, *Roddy Doyle: Raining on the Parade* (Dublin: Liffey Press, 2003).

McCourt, Frank, *'Tis* (New York: Scribner, 1999).

McCullogh, Jock, 'Empire and Violence, 1900–1939', in Phillippa Levine, (ed.), *Gender and Empire: Oxford History the British Empire – Companion Series* (Oxford: Oxford University Press, 2004).

McDonald, Peter, *Mistaken Identities: Poetry and Northern Ireland* (Oxford: Clarendon Press, 1997).

McIlroy, Brian, 'The Repression of Communities: Visual Representations of Northern Ireland during the Thatcher Years', in Lester Friedman, (ed.), *British Cinema and Thatcherism* (London: UCL Press, 1993).

—, *Shooting to Kill: Filmmaking and the 'Troubles' in Northern Ireland* (Trowbridge: Flicks Books, 1998).

McMullen, Kim, 'New Ireland/Hidden Ireland', *The Kenyon Review*, 26, 2, Spring 2004.

McPhilemy, Sean, *The Committee: Political Assassination in Northern Ireland*, 2nd edn (Boulder, Colorado: Roberts Rinehart, 1999).

McSwiney, Seamus, 'Taking the Gun Out of Irish Politics: An Interview with Neil Jordan', *Cineaste*, May 1997.

Miller, David W. 'The Armagh Troubles', in Samuel Clark and James S. Donnelly, Jr., (ed.), *Irish Peasants: Violence and Unrest, 1784–1914* (Dublin: Gill & Macmillan, 1983).

—, *Peep O'Day Boys and Defenders: Selected Documents on the County Armagh Disturbances, 1784–96* (Belfast: PRONI Publications, 1990).

—, *Queen's Rebels: Ulster Loyalism in Historical Perspective* (Dublin: Gill & Macmillan, 1978).

Mitchell, Jack, *The Essential O'Casey, A Study of the Twelve Major Plays of Sean O'Casey* (New York: International Publishers, 1980).

Moore-Harrell, Alice, *Gordon and the Sudan: Prologue to the Mahdiyya* (London: Frank Cass, 2001).

Mornin, Daniel, *All Our Fault* (London: Hutchinson, 1991).

Moses, Antoinette, 'British Film Production 1981: Survey', *Sight and Sound*, 51, 4, Autumn 1982.

Moulden, John, *12 Songs of the Twelfth: Dolly's Brae 1849* (Portrush and Ennistymon: The Library, 1999).

Muldoon, Paul, 'Something Else', *Poems 1968–1998* (London: Faber & Faber, 2001).

Murray, Christopher, *Sean O'Casey Writer at Work* (Dublin: Gill & Macmillan, 2004).

Musgrave, Sir Richard, *Memoirs of the Different Rebellions in Ireland* (Dublin: J. Milliken and J. Stockdale, 1801).

Nairn, Tom, *The Break-Up of Britain: Crisis and Neo-Nationalism* (London: Verso, 1981).

Neillands, Robin, *The Dervish Wars: Gordon and Kitchener in the Sudan, 1880–1898* (London: John Murray, 1996).

Neillands, Robin and Edward M. Spiers, (ed.), *Sudan: the Reconquest Reconsidered* (London: Frank Cass, 1998).

Nicoll, Fergus, *The Sword of the Prophet: The Mahdi of Sudan and the Death of General Gordon* (Gloucestershire: Sutton Publishing, 2004).

Nietzsche, Friedrich, *On the Genealogy of Morals*, quoted in R.J. Hollingdale, (ed.), *A Nietzsche Reader* (Harmondsworth: Penguin, 1977).

Nowell-Smith, Geoffrey, *L'Avventura, BFI Film Classics* series, (ed.) Rob White (London: BFI, 1997).

O'Casey, Sean, 'Bonfire Under a Black Sun', *The Green Crow* (New York: George Braziller, 1956).

—, 'Drums Under the Windows', *Autobiographies I* (London: Macmillan, 1963).

—, *The Flying Wasp* (London: Macmillan, 1937).

—, 'From Within the Gates', *New York Times*, 21 October 1934, section 9.

—, *The Green Crow* (New York: George Braziller, 1956).

—, 'I Knock at the Door', *Autobiographies I* (London: Macmillan, 1963).

—, 'Letter', *Times* 19 February 1926.

—, 'Letter to the Editor', *Irish Independent*, 20 February 1926.

—, 'Letter to the Editor', *Irish Times*, 19 February 1926.

—, 'Pictures in the Hallway', *Autobiographies I* (London: Macmillan, 1963).

—, 'The Plough and the Stars', *Collected Plays, Vol. I* (London: Macmillan, 1963).

—, 'Purple Dust', *Complete Plays, Vol. 3* (London: Macmillan, 1984).

—, 'The Silver Tassie', *Collected Plays, Vol. II* (London: Macmillan, 1964).

—, *The Story of the Irish Citizen Army* (1919, Dublin: Talbot Press, 1971).

—, 'Tender Tears for Poor O'Casey', *The Green Crow* (New York: George Braziller, 1956).

—, 'Unpublished Letter from Sean O'Casey to Dr Edward Barsky', *Abraham Lincoln Brigade Archives 125*, Joint Anti-Fascist Refugee Committee Correspondence, Box 1, Folder 20, Tamiment Library/Robert Wagner Labor Archives, Elmer Bobst Library, New York University Libraries.

—, 'Unpublished Letter from Sean O'Casey to the Veterans of the Abraham Lincoln Brigade', *Canadian Journal of Irish Studies*, 25, 1/2, 1999.

—, 'Within the Gates', *Complete Plays of Sean O'Casey, Vol. 2* (London: Macmillan, 1984).

O'Faolain, Seán, Introduction to Neil Jordan, *Night in Tunisia* (1976; Dublin: Irish Writers' Co-operative, Kerry: Brandon, 1982).

O'Flaherty, Liam, *Insurrection* (1950, Dublin: Wolfhound Press, 1993).

O'Malley, Aidan, in 'Other Words: Coming to Terms with Irish Identities through Translation', diss., European University Institute at Florence, 2004.

O'Neill, Jamie, *At Swim, Two Boys* (London: Scribner, 2001).

—–, 'Paperback Writer', *The Guardian*, 3 August 2002.

Open, Michael, 'A Language of Vision: The Films of John Boorman', *Film Directions*, 2,7, 1979.

Orr, John, 'The Art of Identity: Greenaway, Jarman, Jordan', *The Art and Politics of Film* (Edinburgh University Press, 2000).

Pandey, Gyanendra, *Memory, History, and the Question of Violence: Reflections on the Reconstruction of Partition* (Cambridge: Cambridge University Press, 2001).

—, *Remembering Partition: Violence, Nationalism and History in India* (Cambridge: Cambridge University Press, 2001).

Park, James, *Learning to Dream: The New British Cinema* (London: Faber & Faber, 1984).

Parkinson, Alan, *Belfast's Unholy War: The Troubles of the 1920s* (Dublin: Four Courts Press, 2004).

Patraka, Vivian, 'Spectacular Suffering: Performing Presence, Absence and Witness at U.S. Holocaust Museums', *Spectacular Suffering* (Bloomington, Indiana: Indiana University Press, 1999).

Potter, W. James, *The 11 Myths of Media Violence* (Thousand Oaks, California: Sage Publications, 2003).

Pound, Ezra, 'Vorticism', in *Gaudier-Brzeska: A Memoir* (New York: New Directions, 1970).

Pramaggiore, Maria, 'The Celtic Blue Note: Jazz in Neil Jordan's "Night in Tunisia", *Angel* and *The Miracle*', *Screen*, 39,3, Autumn 1998.

Pulleine, Tim, 'Underworld N.I.: *Angel*, *Sight and Sound* 51.4, Autumn 1982).

Redmond, James, (ed.), *Violence in Drama* (Cambridge: Cambridge University Press, 1991).

Ricoeur, Paul, 'Reflections on a New Ethos for Europe', in *Paul Ricoeur: The Hermeneutics of Praxis* (London: Sage, 1996).

—, *La Mémoire, L'histoire, L'oubli* (*Memory, History and Forgetting*), trans. David Pellauer (University of Chicago Press 2005) (Paris: Editions du Seuil, 2000).

Robson, Brian, *Fuzzy-Wuzzy: the Campaigns in the Eastern Sudan, 1884–85* (Tunbridge Wells: Spellmount Ltd, 1993).

Rockett, Kevin, 'Aspects of the Los Angelisation of Ireland', *Irish Communications Review*, 1, 1991.

—, 'History, Politics and Irish Cinema', in Kevin Rockett, Luke Gibbons, and John Hill, *Cinema and Ireland* (Syracuse, New York: Syracuse University Press, 1988).

—, 'Jordan, Neil', in John Caughie with Kevin Rockett, *The Companion to British and Irish Cinema* (London: Cassell/BFI, 1996).

Roddick, Nick, '*Angel*, *Films and Filming*, 337, Oct. 1982.

—, 'New Audiences, New Films.' in Martin Auty and Nick Roddick, (ed.), *British Cinema Now* (London: BFI, 1985).

Rudé, George. *The Crowd in History: A Study of Popular Disturbances in England and France, 1730–1848* (New York: Wiley, 1964).

Ryan, Matthew, 'Ourselves Alone: Solipsism in Neil Jordan's Novels and Films', *Barcelona English Language and Literature Studies*, 11, 2000.

Said, Edward, *Orientalism* (New York: Pantheon Books, 1978).

Scheper-Hughes, Nancy, *Death Without Weeping: The Violence of Everyday Life in Brazil* (Berkeley: University of California Press, 1992).

—, and Phillippe Bourgois, (eds.), *Violence in War and Peace: An Anthology* (London: Blackwell, 2003).

Schrank, Bernice, 'A Portrait of the Artist as an Irish Socialist, Ideology and Identity in the Autobiographical Writings of Sean O'Casey', *Works and Days, Essays in the Socio-Historical Dimensions of Literature and the Arts*, Fall, 1993.

—, *Sean O'Casey A Research and Production Sourcebook* (London: Greenwood Press, 1996).

—, 'Studies of the Self, Irish Autobiographical Writing and the Discourses of Colonialism and Independence', *a/b, Auto/Biography Studies*, Fall, 1994.

Schrecker, Ellen W., *No Ivory Tower, McCarthyism and the Universities* (Oxford: Oxford University Press, 1986).

Scott, James C., *Domination and the Arts of Resistance: Hidden Transcripts* (London: Yale University Press, 1990).

—, *Weapons of the Weak: Everyday Forms of Peasant Resistance* (London: Yale University Press, 1985).

Sheeran, Patrick, F., Keith Hopper and Gráinne Humphreys (eds.), *The Informer, Ireland Into Film* series (Cork: Cork University Press, 2002).

Sheridan, Michael, 'Father Ned's Drums Hollow at the Abbey', *Irish Press*, 10 May 1985.

Sibbett, R.M., *Orangeism in Ireland and Throughout the Empire*, 2 vols. (London: Thynne and Co., 1938).

Smith, Bobby L., *O'Casey's Satiric Vision* (Kent, OH: Kent State University Press, 1978).

Spiers, Edward M., (ed.), *Sudan: the Reconquest Reconsidered* (London: Frank Cass, 1998).

Stalker, John, *Stalker: Ireland, Shoot to Kill and the Affair* (Harmondsworth: Penguin, 1988).

Steger, Manfred B. and Nancy C. Lind, *Violence and its Alternatives* (New York: St Martin's Press, 1999).

Stewart, A.T.Q., *The Narrow Ground: The Roots of Conflict in Ulster* (London: Faber & Faber, 1977).

Stewart, Pamela J. and Andrew Strathern, *Violence: Theory and Ethnography* (London: Continuum, 2002).

Strachey, Lytton, *Eminent Victorians*, (ed.), John Sutherland (Oxford: Oxford University Press, 2003).

Sturken, Marita, 'The Wall, the Screen and the Image: The Vietnam Veterans Memorial', *Representations*, 35, Summer, 1991.

Sunstein, Cass R., 'Is Violent Speech a Right?', *American Prospect*, 22, Summer 1995.

Tan, Chester C., *The Boxer Catastrophe* (New York: Columbia University Press, 1955).

Taussig, Michael, 'Culture of Terror – Space of Death. Roger Casement's Putamayo Report and the Explanation of Torture', *Comparative Studies in Society and History*, 26, July, 1984.

Taylor, Paul, '*Angel*', *Monthly Film Bulletin*, 49, 586, November 1982.

Taylor, Peter, *Stalker: The Search for Truth* (London: Faber & Faber, 1987).

Temple, Sir John, *History of the Irish Rebellion* (London: R. White, 1646).

Thompson, David, 'As I Lay Dying: *Point Blank*', *Sight and Sound*, 8, 6, June 1998.

Thompson, E.P., 'The Moral Economy of the English Crowd in the Eighteenth Century', *Past and Present*, 50, February 1971.

Thompson, Kristin, 'The Concept of Cinematic Excess', in Philip Rosen (ed.), *Narrative, Apparatus, Ideology: A Film Theory Reader* (New York: Columbia University Press, 1986).

Townend, Paul A., 'Between Two Worlds: Irish Nationalists and Imperial Crisis, 1878– 1880', *Past and Present*, 194, 1, February 2007.

Townshend, Charles, *Political Violence in Ireland: Government and Resistance since 1848.* (Oxford: Clarendon Press, 1983).

—, *Easter 1916: the Irish Rebellion* (London: Penguin, 2006).

—, 'The Irish Railway Strike of 1920: Industrial Action and Civil Resistance in the Struggle for Independence', *Irish Historical Studies*, 21, 83, 1979.

Trilling, Lionel, 'Introduction', *Isaac Babel: Collected Stories* (London: Penguin, 1961).

Valente, Joseph, 'Race/Sex/Shame: The Queer Nationalism of *At Swim, Two Boys*', *Éire-Ireland*, 40, 3&4 (Fall/Winter 2005).

van der Veer, Peter, *Religious Nationalism: Hindus and Muslims in India* (Berkeley: University of California Press, 1994).

von Clausewitz, Carl, *On War*, ed. and trans. Michael Howard (Princeton, New Jersey: Princeton University Press, 1976).

Walker, Alexander, *National Heroes: British Cinema in the Seventies and Eighties* (London: Harrap, 1985).

Walker, Brian M., *Dancing to History's Tune: History, Myth and Politics in Ireland* (Belfast: Institute of Irish Studies, Queen's University of Belfast, 1996).

Wesseker, Carol, (ed.), *Violence in the Media* (San Diego: Greenhaven Press, 1995).

Wheatley, Michael, *Nationalism and the Irish Party: Provincial Ireland 1910–1916* (Oxford: Oxford University Press, 2005).

Whitman, Walt, *Walt Whitman: Leaves of Grass*, (ed.), Scully Bradley (New York: W. W. Norton & Company, 1973).

Whyte, John, *Interpreting Northern Ireland* (Oxford: Clarendon Press, 1990).

Wiedmer, Caroline, *The Claims of Memory: Representations of the Holocaust in Contemporary Germany and France* (Ithaca, New York: Cornell University Press, 1999).

Wiener, Philip P. and John Fisther, (eds.), *Violence and Aggression in the History of Ideas* (New Brunswick, New Jersey: Rutgers University Press, 1974).

Willentz, Sean, (ed.), *Rites of Power* (Philadelphia, PA: University of Philadelphia Press, 1985).

Williams, Raymond, *The Politics of Modernism: Against the New Conformists*, (ed.), Tony Pinckney (London and New York: Verso, 1989).

Wilson, Kathleen, *The Island Race: Englishness, Empire and Gender in the Eighteenth Century* (London: Routledge, 2002).

Wright, Frank, *Two Lands on One Soil: Ulster Politics Before Home Rule* (New York: St Martin's Press, 1996).

Xiang, Lanxin, *The Origins of the Boxer War: a Multinational Study* (London: Routledge Curzon, 2003).

Zimmerman, Georges Denis, *Songs of Irish Rebellion: Political Street Ballads and Rebel Songs* (Dublin: Allen Figgis, 1967).

FILMS

Angel (dir. Neil Jordan, Miramax, 1982)

Ascendancy (dir. Edward Bennett, BFI, 1982)

Bloody Sunday (dir. Paul Greengrass, Hell's Kitchen International, 2002)

Blow Up (dir. Michelangelo Antonioni, MGM, 1966)

December Bride (dir. Thaddeus O'Sullivan, British Screen and Film Four Productions 1990)

Divorcing Jack (dir. David Caffrey, Scala Productions, 1998)

Fools of Fortune (dir. Pat O'Connor, Channel Four Films, 1990)

Four Days in July (dir. Mike Leigh, BBC, 1984)

Gangs of New York (dir. Martin Scorsese, Miramax, 2002)

In the Name of the Father (dir. Jim Sheridan, Universal, 1993)

L'Avventura (dir. Michelangelo Antonioni, Cino del Duca, 1960)

Michael Collins (dir. Neil Jordan, Geffen Pictures, 1996)

Mirror (dir. Andrei Tarkovsky 1975)

Missing (dir. Costas-Gavras 1982)

No Surrender (dir. Peter Smith, Channel Four Films, 1985)

Nothing Personal (dir. Thaddeus O'Sullivan, Channel Four Films, 1995)

Omagh (dir. Pete Travis, Hell's Kitchen International, 2004)

Platoon (dir. Oliver Stone, Orion Pictures, 1987)

Point Blank (dir. John Boorman 1967)

Resurrection Man (dir. Marc Evans, Revolution Films, 1998)

Schindler's List (dir. Stephen Spielberg, Universal Pictures, 1993)

Shoah (dir. Claude Lanzmann, Films Aleph, Historia Films, 1985)

Solaris (dir. Andrei Tarkovsky 1972)

Some Mother's Son (dir. Terry George, Columbia, 1996)

Stalker (dir. Andrei Tarkovsky 1979)

The Boxer (dir. Jim Sheridan, Universal, 1997)

The Company of Wolves (dir. Neil Jordan, Cannon Film, 1984)

The Conformist (dir. Bernardo Bertolucci, Paramount Italy, 1970)

The Crying Game (dir. Neil Jordan, Miramax, 1992)

The General (dir. John Boorman, Sony Brothers, 1998)

The Good Thief (dir. Neil Jordan, Century Fox, 2002)

The Informer (dir. John Ford, RKO Pictures, 1935)

The Passenger (dir. Michelangelo Antonioni, MGM, 1975)

The Quiet Man (dir. John Ford, Republic Pictures, 1952)
The Wind that Shakes the Barley (dir. Ken Loach, Pathé International, 2006)
This is the Sea (dir. Mary McGuckian, Paramount, 1997)
Titanic Town (dir. Roger Mitchell, BBC/Alliance, 1998)
Through a Glass Darkly (dir. Ingmar Bergman 1962)
Traveller (dir. Joe Comerford, RTE, 1981)
Unforgiven (dir. Clint Eastwood, Warner Brothers, 1992)
Yol (dir. Yilmiz Gurney and Serif Goren, Triumph Films, 1982)

Index